Golfing Breaks

THE COMPLETE GUIDE TO
HOTELS WITH COURSES
IN GREAT BRITAIN & IRELAND

Foreword

by Nigel Mansell OBE

First published in Great Britain 1999 by
BEACON BOOKS
Koinonia House, High Street, Cranbrook, Kent TN17 3EJ.

ISBN 1 901839 13 3

© Finley Brand Communications Ltd. 1999

The moral right of the publisher has been asserted.

Distributed by The Globe Pequot Press, 6 Business Park Road, PO Box 833
Old Saybrook, Connecticut 06475.

Cover design by Roland Davies.

Regional introduction by Alastair Tait.

Typesetting & Repro by Typecast, Tonbridge Kent.

Printed and bound in Italy.

Corporate editions and personal subscriptions of any of the Beacon Book guides are available.
Call for details – tel: 0044 1580 720222.

Also published in the series: **Golfing Gems of Scotland**
                                 Golfing Gems of Ireland
                                 Golfing Gems of England & Wales

Golf Monthly is published on the last Thursday of every month by IPC Magazines
Limited, King's Reach Tower, Stamford Street , London SE1 9LS. For subscription
enquiries call: 01444 445555 (fax no: 01444 445599) or write to: Quadrant Subscription
Services, FREEPOST CY1061, Haywards Heath, West Sussex RH16 3ZA.

Contents

Acknowledgements

As with any book there have been many people who have contributed enormously and without whose help this book would never have been possible. We thank them all but in particular wish to express our sincerest appreciation to the following: To Christine for keeping us organised, to Mike for his stylish subbing, to Nicola for keeping our spirits up and to Daisy for keeping us on our toes. But finally to you, for deeming our effort worthy of your hard-earned cash. Many thanks.

Andrew Finley   *Robert Brand*

Acknowledgements

We offer our sincere thanks to the following for supplying photographs:

The Heart of England Tourist Board
Southern Tourist Board, photographed by Peter Titmus
The Scottish Tourist Board
The Northern Ireland Tourist Board
The West Country Tourist Board
The Bord Failte – Irish Tourist Board
The Isle of Man Tourism & Leisure
The State of Guernsey Tourist Board
East of England Tourist Board Collection
The Wales Tourist Board Photo Library
The North West Tourist Board
The South East England Tourist Board

Foreword

*O*ne of the benefits of being a racing driver is that travelling throughout the world I have had the good fortune to play golf on some of the finest courses mainland Europe, America, Asia and Australia have to offer. Whilst these experiences have been a privilege and a pleasure, to my mind no other region can match Britain and Ireland for the beauty, diversity and challenge of their golf courses. From windswept links and heather-clad heath to rolling parkland, the kaleidoscope of golf in all its guises lies here.

A single reference guidebook dedicated to the golf resorts of Britain and Ireland is long overdue. I am delighted that at last the touring golfer can find information on every facility in one handy book. Packed with stunning photographs and presented in a clear and user-friendly way, I am sure that you will keep this book with you at all times using it both for holiday breaks and astute business travel.

I wish you sunny days and straight driving!

Nigel Mansell OBE

Welcome

*W*elcome to Golf Monthly Golfing Breaks, the definitive guide to the golf resorts of Britain and Ireland. Our aim has been to provide you with a comprehensive book which will lead you to every hotel which has a golf facility – be it a full-blown championship layout or pitch and putt course.

No charge was made to the hotels for an entry in the guide, however, some opted for an extended double-page feature for which they paid a nominal fee.

Whether your choice is a short weekend break or an extended stay, this book will provide you with a wealth of potential destinations backed with details of the golf facilities on offer and knowledgeable recommendations for classic courses to play in the area. For those non-golfers in the party, local places of interest are included and many hotels provide a host of other activities to keep the golf widow(er) amused!

Other books in the series feature the Golfing Gems of England & Wales, Scotland and Ireland. More are in production ensuring that with a Beacon Guide, the travelling golfer will never be far from a little piece of golfing heaven.

Happy Golfing!

International Dialling Codes

From UK to Eire	00353	(delete first 0 of local number)
From Eire to Northern Ireland	0044	(delete first 0 of local number)
From USA to UK	01144	(delete first 0 of local number)
From USA to Eire	011353	(delete first 0 of local number)

Introduction

Research indicates that as many as 89,000 Golf Monthly readers took a golfing break at some time or another during 1997 and that number seems to be increasing on an annual basis. Golf plays an important part in the lives of Golf Monthly readers and it is a pastime which large numbers of them are willing to spend a great deal on.

Golf Monthly readers are no different from most other British golfers in as much as many will cite such destinations as the Bahamas, Mauritius and the States at the top of their shopping lists. But for the great majority, the choice is closer to home - and that is not necessarily just a matter of cost.

Britain and Ireland are blessed with an enormous number of great golf courses and we are fortunate because those courses have an abundance of good hotels to serve them. It doesn't matter whether it's Aberdovey or Aberdeen, the Cotswolds or the Home Counties where you want to play your golf, because there is always an ample choice of excellent hotels to serve a golfer's needs. Some, like those in this book, have their own courses to offer.

In Golf Monthly Golfing Breaks we have put together a comprehensive guide to all the hotels available, providing a wide choice for the discerning golfer. There's something for everyone here and packages to suit all pockets.

Here at Golf Monthly we are serious about our golf and we know that our readers are too. That's why we have taken a great deal of care putting this edition together and why we have no hesitation in recommending the facilities contained herein. We are sure you will enjoy your golf and the rest of your stay.

Colin Callander

Kent & The South Coast

Dunorlan Park, Tunbridge Wells

Kent & The South Coast

N o less than 13 Open Championships have been held on the Kent coastline. In fact, this coastline was the first area of England to see an Open Championship. The Open was first held in England at Sandwich (now Royal St George's) in 1894 after 33 consecutive years in Scotland.

It was fitting then that an Englishman, John H Taylor, won The Open that year, the first of Taylor's five Open wins.

This part of England was meant for golf. Royal St George's, Prince's, Royal Cinque Ports, the trio make for a fantastic stretch of traditional links golf at its very best. Prince's held the Open back in 1932, when Gene Sarazen triumphed, while Royal Cinque Ports has had that honour twice, in 1909 and 1920.

Strong winds are the main defences of these south-coast courses, because very seldom will you find them on a calm day.

The same can be said of Littlestone and Rye just along the coast. The former is an Open Qualifying course that is currently undergoing renovations to defend it against the onslaught of modern technology. The latter is actually in Sussex and is quite difficult to play unless you are accompanied by a member. So if you know anyone remotely connected with a member of Rye, do your best to nurture the relationship for Rye is the equal of any of the good Kent links.

There's no problem getting onto some of the inland courses in this area, some of which offer excellent golf. For example, courses at Chart Hills and Hever Castle in Kent, and East Sussex National are relative newcomers to the area, but are built to championship standard and conditioning. Nick Faldo is the man responsible for the design of Chart Hills, and a fine job he's done, too. While East Sussex National's two courses – the East and the West – are creations of Robert Cupp, a one time assistant to Jack Nicklaus. East Sussex National's East course was considered good enough to play host for a couple of years to the European Tour's European Open.

To the north of East Sussex National you will find gems in Crowborough Beacon, Royal Ashdown Forest and Mannings Heath. Crowborough Beacon, for example, is a fine example of traditional heathland golf, with good views over the surrounding countryside.

Heading back to the coast you should pay a visit to West Sussex at Pulborough, one of the loveliest courses in the south of England, before heading due south to Littlehampton and its fine links like course.

Further to the west along this coast you will find great golf in Hampshire and Wiltshire. For example, inland from the coast in Hampshire you will be hard pressed to find a better trio of golf courses than Liphook, North Hants and Blackmoor, three that will gladden a purist's heart. In this neck of the woods, or heather perhaps, you will also find Old Thorns and the Army golf club, the former a longish heathland course, the latter a Peter Alliss/Dave Thomas creation in fine wooded countryside.

Towards Southampton you will find good courses in the New Forest in the shape of Bramshaw and Brokenhurst Manor. And if you like golf of the clifftop variety, then pay a visit to Barton-on-Sea. The course isn't too long but the views to the Isle of Wight are worthy of the green fee.

Dorset isn't exactly short of good golf either. While the county has some 30 courses, four are definitely worth highlighting. In Ferndown, Broadstone, Isle of Purbeck and Parkstone, the county has four prime assets. Ferndown has two courses and they are kept in fine condition throughout the year. The golf is heathland in style, so expect heather if you miss a fairway.

The Isle of Purbeck dates back to 1892 and was once owned by Enid Blyton and her husband. The course isn't too long or taxing, but its biggest selling point is the views it offers of this coastline.

Broadstone and Parkstone are courses that fall into the heathland category, with lots of heather and gorse to catch the errant shot. They are a must for anyone visiting this part of the South Coast.

Kent & The South Coast

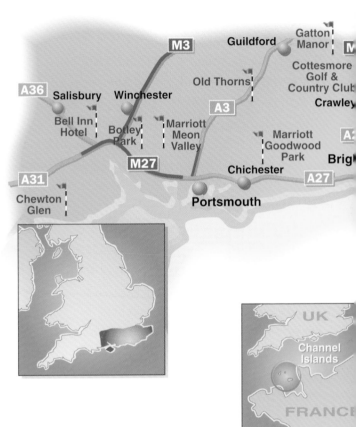

Page

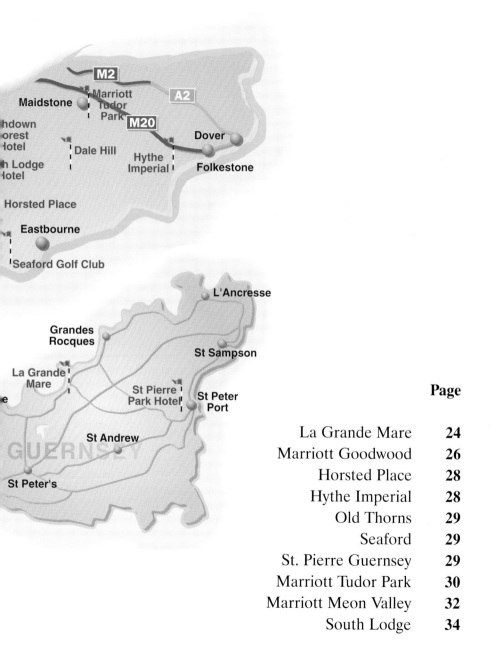

Page

Ashdown Forest Golf Hotel

*T*he Hotel is idyllically set in Ashdown Forest in the heart of the Sussex countryside and away from main traffic thoroughfares. Each of the 19 bedrooms has ensuite facilities with satellite television, tea and coffee making facilities. The West 19 restaurant is a particular feature, with imaginative dishes and

vegetarian choices always available. The W.B. Yeats bar, named after the renowned Irish poet who spent his honeymoon at the Hotel, is open for pre-dinner or quiet evening drinks.

Managed exclusively by the Hotel, the Royal Ashdown Forest West Course is adjacent to the hotel complex. Golfers can play the West Course on a daily basis or as part of a golfing break, golf society meeting or event. Constructed in the 1890s and added to in the 1920s, the course was chosen as the venue for the 1932 British Ladies Open. The West Course is not long by modern standards but is a strong test for golfers of all abilities. Tree-lined fairways with small, fast greens will test one's shotmaking. The course has no sand bunkers but the natural terrain is more than ample defence of its par 68, SSS67.

There are numerous other notable courses nearby which we can incorporate into your stay, with reserved Tee Times.

LOCAL ATTRACTIONS

The Hotel is well located for visits to many famous gardens, historic locations and other attractions. Brighton, the South Coast and Gatwick are all nearby and London is only 40 minutes by train.

GOLF INFORMATION

18 hole, 5606 yard heathland/woodland course Par 68

Golf Professional: Martyn Landsborough
Tel: 01342 824866

Practice facilities: Outdoor driving range.

Instructions: Groups and individuals catered for.

Hire: Clubs

Green fees by arrangement.

CARD OF THE COURSE

1	386	Par 4	10	450	Par 4
2	153	Par 3	11	311	Par 3
3	352	Par 4	12	122	Par 4
4	270	Par 4	13	357	Par 4
5	156	Par 3	14	435	Par 3
6	328	Par 4	15	388	Par 4
7	240	Par 3	16	196	Par 4
8	312	Par 4	17	502	Par 4
9	353	Par 4	18	295	Par 4
Out	2550	Par 33	In	3056	Par 35

HOTEL INFORMATION

Ashdown Forest Golf Hotel
Chapel Lane
Forest Row
East Sussex RH18 5BB
Tel: 01342 824866
Fax: 01342 824869

Rating: Member American Society of Travel Agents and South East England Tourist Board. Great Golf Hotel Guide Member.
Rooms: 19.
Restaurants: English Food + Vegetarian Options.
Other Sporting Facilities: Riding, Fishing, Tennis and Forest Walks all nearby.
Other Leisure Activities: Arranged on an occasional basis.

TARIFF

B&B from £65.00 (Single) £80.00 (Double/Twin).
Dinner + B&B from £81.50 (Single) £113.00 (Double/Twin).
No Weekend supplements.

Special Golf Packages:
B&B including 18 holes £80.00 + £42/£52 based on two people sharing room.

Other Special Golf Packages:
Available on request.

DIRECTIONS

Take the A22 south from East Grinstead towards Eastbourne. Turn left in Forest Row onto the B2110 towards Tunbridge Wells. Chapel Lane is the fourth on the right. Bear right at the top of the lane and the Hotel is on the right.

The Bell Inn

*T*he Bell Inn has been owned by the same local family for 200 years and offers a relaxed and welcoming atmosphere in the heart of the New Forest. The original building dates from 1782 and has many period features, notably in the Bar with its inglenook fireplace, and in the beamed bedrooms in the old part of the Inn.

LOCAL ATTRACTIONS

There is much to see and do in and around the New Forest, and some of the country's finest historic buildings are close at hand: Wilton and Breamore Houses near Salisbury, Beaulieu Abbey with its famous National Motor Museum, and Broadlands at Romsey. For those with a love of the sea and our naval heritage there are the extensive museums at Portsmouth, including HMS Victory and the Mary Rose. For the simple love of peaceful countryside there is, of course, the 100 square miles of the New Forest itself.

All golfing guests can experience our three unique contrasting 18 hole courses, all of which are under the same ownership as the Hotel – the first tee is only a wedge away from the front door! The Manor and Dunwood Courses were both built in 1970, and set out over landscaped parkland amidst mature specimen trees and manicured fairways. The Forest Course is the oldest in Hampshire, and is situated on The New Forest itself providing a complete contrast to the other two courses with its open aspect and rolling heathland. The ever changing scenery of humps, hollows and meandering streams will test golfing skills and judgement.

Luxury self-catering accommodation is also available, and is perfectly situated adjacent to the Clubhouse on the Dunwood Course. Guests can choose from either the completely refurbished and converted Dunwood Farmhouse, which sleeps up to eight, or one of the three brand new purpose built Golf Lodges, each sleeping up to six. All the bedrooms have en-suite bathrooms, and all accommodation is fully furnished and equipped.

Guests are assured of reserved tee times and temporary membership of the Club during their stay.

GOLF INFORMATION

54 holes: Manor 6298 yard; Forest 5552 yard; Dunwood 5506 yard.
Three contrasting 18 hole courses, two parkland, one links/heathland
Par: Manor 72; Forest 69; Dunwood 69
Golf Professional: Clive Bonner
Tel: 01703 813434
Practice facilities: Covered driving range and separate practice ground.
Instructions: Groups and individuals catered for.
Hire: Clubs and buggies.

CARDS OF THE COURSES

Manor Course		Forest Course		Dunwood Course	
1	356 Par 4	1	286 Par 4	1	262 Par 4
2	528 Par 5	2	284 Par 4	2	486 Par 5
3	364 Par 4	3	457 Par 5	3	147 Par 3
4	145 Par 3	4	337 Par 4	4	274 Par 4
5	492 Par 5	5	199 Par 3	5	161 Par 3
6	405 Par 4	6	332 Par 4	6	382 Par 4
7	265 Par 3/4	7	483 Par 5	7	401 Par 4
8	393 Par 4	8	164 Par 3	8	329 Par 4
9	187 Par 3	9	275 Par 4	9	431 Par 4
Out	3135 Par 36	Out	2817 Par 36	Out	2893 Par 35
10	308 Par 4	10	414 Par 4	10	201 Par 3
11	400 Par 4	11	416 Par 4	11	309 Par 4
12	257 Par 4	12	132 Par 3	12	402 Par 4
13	196 Par 3	13	332 Par 4	13	338 Par 4
14	324 Par 4	14	385 Par 4	14	431 Par 5
15	538 Par 5	15	205 Par 3	15	348 Par 4
16	385 Par 4	16	323 Par 4	16	172 Par 3
17	422 Par 4	17	193 Par 3	17	244 Par 4
18	333 Par 4	18	335 Par 4	18	168 Par 3
In	3163 Par 36	In	2735 Par 33	In	2613 Par 34

HOTEL INFORMATION

The Bell Inn
Brook
Lyndhurst
Hampshire SO43 7HE
Tel: 01703 812214
Fax: 01703 813958
Email: bell@bramshaw.co.uk
Website: www.bramshaw.co.uk
Rating: AA 3 Star, Red Rosette
Rooms: 25.
Restaurants: English and French.
Childcare: Baby minding; high chairs; childrens cutlery; childrens play area and garden.
Other Sporting Activities: Extensive horse riding facilities locally available through reception

TARIFF

Winter Weekend Breaks from £49
Summer Weekend Breaks from £78
both breaks based on per person, per night including full English breakfast, 4 course dinner, and all golf.

Self Catering Summer Rate £230

Self Catering Winter Rate £155
Per person per week including golf.

DIRECTIONS

The Bell Inn is situated in the hamlet of Brook which is signposted 2 miles directly off Junction One of the M27, on the B3079.

BOTLEY PARK HOTEL, GOLF & COUNTRY CLUB

Winchester Road, Boorley Green, Botley, Southampton, SO32 2UA.
Tel: 01489 780888 Fax: 01489 789242

18 HOLES PAR 70 6341 YARDS
TYPE OF GOLF COURSE: Parkland
RATING: 4 Star
GOLF PROFESSIONAL: Tim Barter
TEL: 01489 789771
B&B + 18 HOLES: £60.00
OTHER SPECIAL GOLF PACKAGES:
Dinner, B&B + Golf –
Weekdays £75.00, Weekends £90.00.
Sunday Night £60.00

Your first impression of the Botley Park Hotel, Golf & Country Club is likely to be one of space. Surrounded by the rolling hills of Hampshire, the estate stretches across 176 acres of landscaped parkland containing an 18 hole par 70 golf course. Walk through the door to find one of the most extensive leisure complexes in the region, also an award winning restaurant. You will enjoy the service and accommodation expected of a four star hotel.

CHEWTON GLEN

Christchurch Road, New Milton, Hants BH25 6QS. Tel: 01425 275341 Fax: 01425 272310

9 HOLES PAR 3 826 YARDS
TYPE OF GOLF COURSE: Parkland
HOTEL RATING: 5 Red Stars, Blue Ribbon Award
B&B + 18 HOLES: From £220 room only, £340 Half Board – for two people.

Set on the edge of the New Forest, Chewton Glen is an ideal base to discover the south coasts' wonderful courses such as Ferndown, Parkstone, Isle of Purbeck and Barton-on-Sea. A beautiful country house hotel recently voted as the best hotel in Europe by Conde Nast Traveler Magazine.

COTTESMORE GOLF & COUNTRY CLUB

Buchan Hill, Pease Pottage, Crawley, West Sussex RH11 9AT. Tel: 01293 528256 Fax: 01293 522819

18/18 HOLES PAR 71/69 6248/5514 YARDS
TYPE OF GOLF COURSE: Parkland
GOLF PROFESSIONAL: Andrew Prior
TEL: 01293 535399
OTHER SPECIAL GOLF PACKAGES:
B&B + EM + 36 Holes (min 2 nights)
£78.50 Midweek – £83.50 Weekend per person, per night.

Cottesmore is a privately owned country club set in 247 acres of unspoilt countryside. The Club was originally a French style farmhouse and has been thoughtfully developed over the years; now offering all the essentials for either a business meeting or a leisure break. Cottesmore features two 18 hole golf courses, a luxurious health club, ensuite accommodation and two spacious function rooms. The Club is within easy reach of the major towns of Horsham and Crawley, whilst Gatwick Airport is only four miles away.

DALE HILL
Ticehurst, Wadhurst, East Sussex TN5 7DQ. Tel: 01580 200112 Fax: 01580 201249

Home to the new Woosnam course, Dale Hill is a modern and elegant 4 star hotel with extensive leisure facilities situated high on the Kentish Weald. Many rooms have superb views across the 18th and the surrounding Wealden countryside. Close to the A21, Dale Hill is well situated for London, the coast and ferryports.

36 **HOLES PAR** DHC 69/IWC 71 DHC 5856/IWC 6512 **YARDS**
TYPE OF GOLF COURSE: Dale Hill Course: 25 year old parkland course
Ian Woosnam Course: New USGA standard parkland.
RATING: AA 4 Star
GOLF PROFESSIONAL: Andrew Good
TEL: 01580 201 090
B&B + 18 HOLES: £104.00 per person
OTHER SPECIAL GOLF PACKAGES:
Please enquire, usually available throughout the year

Scotney Castle, Kent

Gatton Manor Hotel

Set within its own golf course Gatton Manor Hotel, Golf and Country Club is situated between the towns of Dorking and Horsham in an area of outstanding beauty. The local beauty spot of Leith Hill provides a scenic backdrop to the old Manor House that was constructed in 1729 and was originally the Dower House of the Abinger Estate.

In 1968 when the 18 hole, 6,629 yard, par 72 Championship length golf course was constructed good use was made of the many water obstacles, ponds, small lakes and streams. The result is that water hazards come into play on 14 of the 18 holes. The whole course has character but if one hole was to be highlighted it would be the 18th, arguably one of the best finishing holes in the south.

Gatton Manor is one of the most popular and comprehensive venues in the South of England and offers and an entertainment package that is unique in Surrey. The superior Gallery Restaurant offers an extensive à la carte menu and is renowned for its Continental and English cuisine. All hotel rooms are en-suite and have been refurbished to a high standard, retaining many of the features of the 18th century Manor house. The bar, which is open to members and non-members throughout the year, stocks a fine selection of ales, wines and spirits.

The lovely surroundings and the olde world ambience make it an ideal venue to get away and enjoy your golf.

18 hole, 6629 yard parkland course
Par 72

Golf Professional: Rae Sargent
Tel: 01306 627557

Practice facilities: Outdoor driving range.

Instructions: Groups and individuals catered for.

Hire: Clubs and buggies

Green Fees: Week day – Per round £21.00, per day £36.00. Weekends – Per round £28.00.

CARD OF THE COURSE

1	435	Par 4	10	178	Par 3
2	144	Par 3	11	271	Par 4
3	413	Par 4	12	377	Par 4
4	174	Par 3	13	501	Par 4½
5	479	Par 5	14	176	Par 3
6	369	Par 4	15	553	Par 5
7	187	Par 3	16	432	Par 4
8	510	Par 5	17	585	Par 5
9	443	Par 4	18	402	Par 4
Out	3154	Par 35	In	3475	Par 37

SURREY

Gatton Manor Hotel,
Golf & Country Club
Standon Lane
Ockley, Dorking
Surrey RH5 5PQ
Tel: 01306 627555
Fax: 01306 627713
Rating: AA & RAC – 3 Star, ETB – 3 Crowns commended
Rooms: 16.
Restaurants: Gallery and Lake Restaurants – English and French cuisine.
Childcare: Childcare can be provided by arrangement.
Hair and Beauty: Aromatheraphy, make-up, body treatments, waxing, manicure, pedicure, massage etc...
Fitness Facilities: Gymnasium and health club includes jacuzzi, saunas and sun bed.
Other Sporting Facilities: Tennis, Bowls, Coarse fishing.
Other Leisure Activities: Assault course (team building events).

B&B twin/double
p.p. £45.00
Single £60.00

B&B+ Dinner
twin/double p.p. £63.00
Single £78.00

B&B+ Dinner + 36 Holes
from £86 to £110

Special Golf Packages:
B&B including 18 holes from £73.00 to £88.00

From M25, exit at junction 9 – Leatherhead – and take the A24 (signposted Dorking). Stay on the A24 to the end of the dual carriageway, at the large roundabout turn right onto the A29 (signposted Ockley, Bognor Regis). Continue through Ockley (3 miles) and at the far end of Ockley village on the right hand side is a pub called 'The Old School House'; 200 yards past this turn right into Cat Hill Lane and follow the signs. Main entrance is on the right – approximately 2 miles.

La Grande Mare Hotel

*L*a Grande Mare Hotel & Country Club is adjacent to a beautiful sandy bay and has private grounds of just over 100 acres incorporating an 18 hole golf course.

The Hotel is open throughout the year and guests can enjoy golf, coarse fishing, swimming in the hotel's heated pool, croquet or just a short stroll across to the bay,

LOCAL ATTRACTIONS

St Peter Port, just 10 minutes away by car, offers an array of chic trendy outlets mixed into the old harbour front town, all offering VAT free shopping.
Guernsey Pearl – a palace of pearls and jewellery being created by craftspeople on site.
Bruce Russel Silversmith – set in a 16th century building, the craft of a silversmith.
Oatlands Craft Centre – a unique craft centre offering pottery, glass, hand-made cheese and chocolate.
Longchamps indoor tennis centre – enjoy tennis whatever the weather – four indoor and four outdoor courts available.
Guernsey Bowl – tenpin bowling in a brand new facility.

jogging, windsurfing or sailing.

Fred Hawtree designed a course in keeping with the natural landscape of the area, but also to create a true test of skill. Though not long, it is deceptive and challenging. Christened "The Thinking Man's Course" on the island, you need to be accurate in order to safely negotiate the hazards. The large greens with their true surfaces ensure that all aspects of your game will be put to the test!

The Golf Shop stocks a full range of clothing together with a fine array of clubs by all the leading manufacturers – all at VAT free prices. The golf professionals are on hand to give PGA advice not just on equipment but also refine your swing and analyse it in our modern indoor teaching room equipped with video recording facility.

There is a choice of rooms all with en-suite bathrooms. A new conservatory area serves light snacks for lunch or dinner, alternatively dine in our award-winning La Grande Mare restaurant.

The luxurious new health suite offers a gymnasium, indoor pool, steam room, spa and sauna rooms.

18 hole, 5112 yard parkland style coastal course

Par 67

Golf Professional: Matthew Groves

Tel: 01481 56532

Practice facilities: Covered driving range, with video.

Instructions: Groups and individuals catered for.

Hire: Clubs and trollies

CARD OF THE COURSE

1	323	Par 4	10	187	Par 3
2	144	Par 3	11	174	Par 3
3	175	Par 3	12	319	Par 4
4	480	Par 5	13	421	Par 4
5	133	Par 3	14	387	Par 4
6	468	Par 5	15	323	Par 4
7	121	Par 3	16	148	Par 3
8	270	Par 4	17	226	Par 3
9	344	Par 4	18	469	Par 5
Out	2458	Par 34	In	2654	Par 33

GUERNSEY

La Grande Mare Hotel,
Golf & Country Club
Vazon Bay, Castel, GY5 7LL
Tel: 01481 56576
Fax: 01481 56532
Website: www.lgm.guernsey.net
Rating: Five Crown Deluxe Hotel, Two AA
Rosette Rest. Les Routiers, Gold Key.
Rooms: 27 hotel suites, 10 self catering units.
Restaurants: Award winning cuisine, French style,
Lobsters, Dover soles & Flambe.
Childcare Facilities: Baby Listening all rooms
Hair and Beauty: Nearby (5mins) The World famous
salon "Ann Ayres".
Fitness Facilities: Gymnasium, sauna, steam, spa,
indoor and outdoor pool, outdoor spa, health suite.
Other Sporting Facilities: Windsurfing, tennis & clay
pigeon are all nearby.
Other Leisure Activities: Romantic breaks.

Hotel: Prices per person per night based on 2 persons sharing including B&B. Dinner supplement £16. Single occupancy supplement £10.
Double Twin Bedroom: from £40.00
Double Deluxe Studio: from £45.00
Luxury Suite: from £65.00

Self Contained Apartments: Sleeping 4-6 person, prices are per unit per week including of weekly valet, electric and water. Meals are not included.
One Bed Unit: from £612.00
Two Bed Unit: from £628.00

Special Golf Packages:
B&B including 18 holes from £40.00 + £12.50 based on 2 sharing.

Other Special Golf Packages:
3 day golf breaks available, from £132.50 including car hire Oct-Mar.

From airport, turn right & keep driving until you come to the coast road at L'Erée (5mins). Turn right again and take the coast road all the way to Vazon. The course and Hotel are right at the middle of the bay. From the harbour, drive up past the Old School, take the road to Castel Church, drive straight on until you reach Vazon (10mins).

Marriott Goodwood Park Hotel & Country Club

Goodwood Park Hotel has been sympathetically created in the grounds of Goodwood House, stately home to the Dukes of Richmond for nearly 300 years.

The 94 bedrooms are beautifully decorated and include a suite, a 4 poster and 10 Executive Rooms, each offering the very highest standard of comfort and all the facilities anticipated in such a venue. Good food is very much a feature of Goodwood Park Hotel and in the award-winning restaurant you will encounter a wide selection of modern English dishes, all using fresh, local ingredients. For more informal dining, visit the Goodwood Sports café bar.

At Goodwood Park leisure facilities are superb, the elegant indoor pool is ozone treated so a dip is doubly invigorating! Alternate lazy lengths of the pool with sorties to the spa bath, solarium, sauna or steam room. Alternatively, treat yourself with a visit to the Health and Beauty Salon, or try a workout in the state-of-the-art gym, or perhaps play some tennis or squash.

The grounds of the Estate make a wonderful backdrop for the Hotel's challenging, yet forgiving, 18 hole golf course. The course itself is fairly generous over the opening holes and gets progressively harder as you reach the turn. A word of warning though, beware the 475 yard 11th – the deer leap provides a testing obstacle for any golfer foolhardy enough to stray into the ditch with its flint wall. The par 4 17th is aptly named "Ha! Ha!", but whether it's you or the course that gets the last laugh remains to be seen.

LOCAL ATTRACTIONS

Goodwood House boasts a celebrated collection of paintings by Van Dyke, Stubbs and Canaletto, as well as Goodwood Race Course, Aerodrome and Motor Racing Circuit. Chichester, the Norman walled Cathedral City is just three miles away. Other attractions include Arundel Castle, Bosham Harbour and Saxon Church, beaches and nature reserves.

18 hole, 6579 yard heathland/woodland

Par 72

Practice facilities: Covered driving range, Tuition & Video facilities

Instructions: Groups and individuals catered for.

Hire: Trolley, buggy & club hire

CARD OF THE COURSE

1	352	Par 4	10	434	Par 4
2	196	Par 3	11	493	Par 5
3	382	Par 4	12	344	Par 4
4	348	Par 4	13	202	Par 3
5	488	Par 5	14	421	Par 4
6	299	Par 4	15	464	Par 4
7	352	Par 4	16	319	Par 4
8	159	Par 3	17	390	Par 4
9	368	Par 4	18	565	Par 5
Out	2944	Par 35	In	3632	Par 37

SUSSEX

Marriott Goodwood Park Hotel & Country Club
Goodwood, Chichester,
West Sussex PO18 0QB

Tel: 01243 775537

Fax: 01243 520120

Rooms: 94

Restaurants: Award winning Restaurant, Goodwood Sports Café Bar, Cocktail Bar, Spike Bar.

Hair and Beauty: Health and Beauty Salon.

Other Sporting Facilities: Indoor heated swimming pool, spa bath, sauna, steam room, extensive fitness gymnasium and Aerobic studio.

Other Leisure Activities: Tennis courts.

DINNER, BED & BREAKFAST
(Mon-Sun)

Prices start from **£72** per person, per night, including a round of golf. Based on two sharing.

Just off the A285, three miles north-east of Chichester look out for signs to Goodwood and once within the area of the Goodwood Estate you will see signs to Goodwood Park Hotel Golf and Country Club. Gatwick Airport 50 miles, Southampton/Eastleigh Airport 35 miles.

HORSTED PLACE HOTEL

Little Horsted, Nr Uckfield, East Sussex TN22 5TS. Tel: 01825 750581 Fax: 01825 750459

2x18 HOLES   PAR 72/72   7000 YARDS
RATING: AA 3 Star
GOLF PROFESSIONAL: Phil Lewin
TEL: 01825 880088
B&B + 18 HOLES: From £135.00

Rated as one of the best hotels in the British Isles, Horsted Place is a delightful example of an English Manor. In 1986 after acquisition by the present owners and extensive restoration Horsted Place opened as a country house hotel. It now has 20 bedrooms and suites, a magnificent Victorian drawing room, morning room, library and dining room, as well as a tennis court and swimming pool. It sits in its own 1100 acre estate which contains the renowned East Sussex National Golf Club, 2 courses, both over 7000 yards, which have established themselves as amongst the finest in the country. Venue for the 1993 & 1994 European Open.

St. Peter Port, Guernsey

THE HYTHE IMPERIAL

Prince's Parade, Hythe, Kent CT21 6AE. Tel: 01303 267441 Fax: 01303 264610

9/(18 tee) HOLES   PAR 68   5421 YARDS
TYPE OF GOLF COURSE: Links
RATING: 4 Star AA/RAC
GOLF PROFESSIONAL: Gordon Ritchie
TEL: Via Hotel 01303 267441
B&B + 18 HOLES: £79.50 pppn based on 2 people sharing twin/double for 2 nights – unlimited golf

The Hythe Imperial overlooking the seafront is set within its own 50 acre estate with splendid sea, golf course and garden views. The hotel offers 100 individually designed bedrooms including four poster or jacuzzi suites as well as doubles, twins family or single rooms. The leisure centre incorporates the Terrace Bistro and bar providing guests with an informal alternative to the hotel's award winning restaurant. First class leisure facilities include indoor swimming pool, luxurious spa bath with steam and sauna, gymnasium, snooker, squash, all weather and grass tennis courts, putting, croquet and bowls.

OLD THORNS HOTEL & GOLF COURSE
Griggs Green, Liphook, Hampshire GU30 7PE. Tel: 01428 724555 Fax: 01428 725036

Set in 400 acres of countryside this haven of relaxation is situated just off the A3 London to Portsmouth route. As well as the hotel and championship golf course we provide a leisure club, swimming pool, fitness centre, sauna, solarium, tennis and beauty treatments, driving range and practice putting green.

There are both European and Nippon Kan Japanese restaurants and conference facilities for up to 80 delegates.

18 HOLES	PAR 72	6130 YARDS

TYPE OF GOLF COURSE: Parkland

RATING: AA 3 Star

GOLF PROFESSIONAL: Philip Loxley

B&B + 18 HOLES: £90.00 sharing twin

OTHER SPECIAL GOLF PACKAGES:
Golfing breaks from £85.00

SEAFORD GOLF CLUB
Firle Road, Seaford, East Sussex BN25 2JD. Tel: 01323 892442 Fax: 01323 894113

Dormy House offering twin room facilities for twenty guests. Thirty six holes of golf, room and breakfast, plus excellent five course dinner. One of the finest courses in Sussex, with easy walking despite being situated on the glorious South Downs.

18 HOLES	PAR 71	6651 YARDS

TYPE OF GOLF COURSE: Downland

GOLF PROFESSIONAL: David Mills
TEL: 01323 894160

B&B + 18 HOLES: Full package
£70–£95 per person per night.

ST PIERRE PARK HOTEL, GUERNSEY
Rohais, St Peter Port, Guernsey, Channel Islands GY1 1FD. Tel: 01481 728282 Fax: 01481 712041

Set in 45 acres of parkland and lakes, the St Pierre Park boasts two award winning restaurants, a 9-hole Tony Jacklin designed golf course, 3 tennis courts, snooker room and a superb health suite with heated indoor swimming pool, spa bath, saunas, steam rooms, fitness room and a wide range of beauty treatments.

All 132 en-suite rooms are luxuriously appointed with trouser press, hairdryer, colour television with satellite channels, 24 hour room service and tea/coffee making facilities.

9 HOLES	PAR 3	2610 YARDS

TYPE OF GOLF COURSE: Parkland & Lakes
HOTEL RATING: 4 Star RAC & AA, 2 AA Rosettes, 5 Crown Deluxe Guernsey Tourism
GOLF PROFESSIONAL: Roy Corbett
TEL: 01481 728282
B&B + 18 HOLES: From £98.50 (sharing twin/double)
OTHER SPECIAL GOLF PACKAGES:
Golfing break – 2 nts – B&B, 2 rounds of 18 holes, 10% discount in golf shop, pack of 3 golf balls, golf gift and use of Le Mirage Health Suite. £195.00

Marriott Tudor Park Hotel & Country Clu

Situated in the heart of the Garden of England the Marriott Tudor Park Hotel & Country Club is merely an hour's drive from London and easily accessible from the motorway network.

Most of the hotel's 118 bedrooms look out either onto the tranquil central courtyard garden or across the beautiful old trees and rolling landscape of the golf course, and all have TV, free Sky channels, radio, hair dryer, direct dial telephone, mini-bar, tea and coffee making facilities, trouser press. The Fairviews Restaurant offers an enjoyable selection of fine dishes, or the Long Weekend Bar and Restaurant presents a more informal dining setting.

Leisure facilities available at Tudor Park include an indoor pool, sauna, spa bath, steam room, solarium, Tidro circuit gym, aerobics, tennis and health and beauty treatments.

Donald Steel designed a particularly challenging course for Tudor Park. He has cleverly used the natural features of the old undulating Milgate Deer Park, including its many magnificent stands of Scots pines. The par 70 course is 6041 yards long and has a number of interesting holes to test your handicap. The 520 yard 14th for example, is a par 5 and is tree lined on both sides with a slight dog leg to the left. A covered practice ground and putting green are also available.

LOCAL ATTRACTIONS

Besides the countryside with its hop gardens and white-cowled oast houses, a short drive from Tudor Park will take you to such historic castles as Leeds, Hever and Dover, Canterbury with its Cathedral and Canterbury Tales Exhibition, Royal Tunbridge Wells and the historic Pantiles, the famous Brands Hatch motor racing circuit, The Hop Farm Country Park and numerous beautiful gardens open to the public, such as Sissinghurst.

Milgate Course, 6041 yards, par 70, 18-holes.

Practice facilities: Covered practice ground and putting green.

Instructions: Tuition and video facilities.

Hire: Trolley, buggy and club hire.

CARD OF THE COURSE

1	371	Par 4	10	177	Par 3
2	394	Par 4	11	359	Par 4
3	365	Par 4	12	372	Par 4
4	181	Par 3	13	308	Par 4
5	353	Par 4	14	521	Par 5
6	333	Par 4	15	337	Par 4
7	117	Par 3	16	442	Par 4
8	494	Par 5	17	193	Par 3
9	392	Par 4	18	332	Par 4
Out	3000	Par 35	In	3041	Par 35

KENT

Marriott Tudor Park Hotel
& Country Club
Ashford Road, Bearsted,
Maidstone, Kent ME14 4NQ
Tel: 01622 734334
Fax: 01622 735360
Rooms: 118.
Restaurants: Fairviews Restaurant, Long Weekend Bar & Restaurant, Leisure Bar, Piano Bar
Hair and Beauty: Health & Beauty Salon, Hairdressing Salon.
Other Fitness Facilities: Indoor heated swimming pool, spa bath, sauna, steam room, 2 gyms, Tidro circuit gym.
Other Sporting Facilities: Tennis courts, solarium and aerobics studio.

DINNER, BED & BREAKFAST
(Mon-Sun)

Prices start from **£74** per person, per night, including a round of golf. Based on two sharing.

Leave the M20 at Junction 8 and take the Lenham exit at the first roundabout. At second roundabout take right-hand exit signposted Bearsted and Maidstone. Tudor Park can be found approximately 1½ miles on the left.

Marriott Meon Valley Hotel & Country Club

The Marriott Meon Valley Hotel & Country Club is surrounded by the Shedfield House Estate, amidst 225 acres of the picturesque Meon Valley in Hampshire.

Following extensive refurbishment the hotel has 113 bedrooms designed to suit all business and leisure needs with facilities such as mini-bar, trouser press, hairdryer, voice mail, fax/modem link and free Sky channels. The Treetops Restaurant has an unrestricted view of the 17th hole of the golf course, which actually has a section of the old Roman road running through it, and both this restaurant and the Long Weekend Café Bar offer a comprehensive selection of carefully prepared dishes.

As with all Marriott hotels, leisure facilities are well provided for and Meon Valley offers, along with the golf and tennis, a heated indoor pool, sauna, spa bath, solaria, dance studio and steam room as well as the fully equipped weights gym and cardiovascular theatre, and a Health and Beauty Salon.

The 2nd and 12th holes on the par 71 Meon Course are a test of anyone's golfing ability, whilst the Valley Course (built around the remains of a Roman village) offers a mature nine holes which present a pleasant challenge for all golfers. Meon Valley has a Junior Academy, where young and old, men and women alike can benefit from popular tuition packages offered by the hotel's male and female golf professionals, complemented with club and equipment hire.

LOCAL ATTRACTIONS

The Hotel makes an excellent base for some fascinating sightseeing. Apart from the naval attractions of nearby Portsmouth – the Mary Rose, Nelson's Victory and HMS Warrior, there are numerous other historical points of interest such as the old Capital City of England, Winchester. Those with literary and outside interests can visit Jane Austen's house, enjoy the delights of Marwell Zoo, the beauty of the New Forest, Beaulieu National Motor Car Museum or the Watercress Steam Railway Line.

GOLF INFORMATION

Meon Course, 6520 yards, par 71, 18-hole. Valley Course, 5770 yards, par 70 (9-hole played twice).

Practice facilities: Practice ground with 7 covered bays and putting green.

Instructions: Tuition and video facilities.

Hire: Trolley, buggy and club hire.

CARD OF THE COURSE			
Meon Course			
1	496 Par 5	10	544 Par 5
2	448 Par 4	11	362 Par 4
3	412 Par 4	12	153 Par 3
4	167 Par 3	13	331 Par 4
5	446 Par 4	14	236 Par 3
6	366 Par 4	15	313 Par 4
7	157 Par 3	16	467 Par 4
8	550 Par 5	17	386 Par 4
9	392 Par 4	18	294 Par 4
Out	3434 Par 36	In	3086 Par 35

HOTEL INFORMATION

Marriott Meon Valley
& Country Club
Sandy Lane, Shedfield,
Near Southampton
Tel: 01329 833455
Fax: 01329 834411

Rooms: 113.

Restaurants: The Treetops Restaurant, The Long Weekend Café Bar, Golf Bar, Cocktail Bar.

Hair and Beauty: Health & Beauty Salon

Other Fitness Facilities: Indoor heated swimming pool, sauna, steam room, spa bath, solaria, , free weights gym, aerobics studio, cardiovascular theatre

Other Sporting Facilities: 3 Tennis Courts.

TARIFF

DINNER, BED & BREAKFAST
(Mon-Sun)

Prices start from **£70** per person per night, including a round of golf. Based on two sharing.

DIRECTIONS

From the west, leave the M27 at Junction 7. Take the A334 to Botley. Drive through the village of Botley and continue on the A334 to Wickham. Pass Wickham Vineyard. Sandy Lane is half a mile on your left. From the east, leave the M27 at Junction 10 and take the A32 towards Alton. At Wickham take the A334 towards Botley. Sandy Lane is on the right two miles from Wickham. Southampton Eastleigh Airport is eight miles away.

South Lodge Hotel

*S*outh Lodge and Camellia Restaurant, a magnificent Victorian country house renowned for its hospitality was built as a family home in 1883 by Frederick Ducane Godman, a noted explorer and botanist.

South Lodge became a hotel in 1985 and since then it has been honoured with

LOCAL ATTRACTIONS

Situated 6 miles from Horsham, South Lodge is only 12 miles from Gatwick Airport and within easy reach of both central London and Heathrow. The county of Sussex is well known for the beauty of its countryside and the many gardens, stately homes, castles and scenic coastal areas provide a number of interesting places to visit.

numerous prestigious accolades, including AA Courtesy and Care Award, the RAC Blue Ribbon for excellence and Three Red Rosettes for outstanding cuisine and service in the restaurant. The award-winning chef takes the greatest care in selecting fine, fresh local produce to create superb traditionally English cuisine enhanced by Mediterranean influences. Herbs, soft fruits and vegetables are carefully chosen from the hotel's own walled garden. The extensive wine cellar, selected from the greatest wine regions of the world, provides the perfect accompaniment.

There are 39 individually-designed bedrooms to cater for every taste, ranging from a romantic mahogany four poster, a bubbling jacuzzi, rain bar shower or our renowned glorious views.

Leisure activities include tennis, croquet, archery, clay pigeon shooting, motorised sports or maybe some horse riding nearby.

GOLF INFORMATION

2 x 18 holes, Kingfisher 6217 yard, Waterfall 6378 downland course.

Par 70 and 73

Golf Professional: Mr Clive Tucker

Tel: 01403 210228

Practice facilities: Outdoor driving range.

Instructions: Groups and individuals catered for.

Hire: Clubs and buggies.

CARD OF THE COURSE

Kingfisher			Waterfall		
1	376	Par 4	1	325	Par 4
2	150	Par 3	2	289	Par 4
3	331	Par 4	3	399	Par 4
4	336	Par 4	4	372	Par 4
5	155	Par 3	5	184	Par 3
6	427	Par 4	6	377	Par 4
7	363	Par 4	7	425	Par 4
8	398	Par 4	8	499	Par 5
9	546	Par 5	9	376	Par 4
Out	3082	Par 35	Out	3246	Par 36
10	398	Par 4	1	141	Par 3
11	519	Par 5	2	368	Par 4
12	187	Par 3	3	368	Par 4
13	438	Par 4	4	486	Par 5
14	375	Par 4	5	153	Par 3
15	317	Par 4	6	247	Par 4
16	174	Par 3	7	466	Par 5
17	340	Par 4	8	487	Par 5
18	387	Par 4	9	416	Par 4
In	3135	Par 35	Out	3132	Par 37

HOTEL INFORMATION

South Lodge Hotel and Camellia Restaurant Lower Beeding, Nr. Horsham, West Sussex RH13 6PS
Tel: 01403 891711
Fax: 01403 891766
Rating: AA 4 Red Stars – 3 Red Rosettes. RAC – Blue Ribbon
Rooms: 39.
Restaurants: Camellia Restaurant – English with Mediterranean influences.
Other Sporting Facilities: Clay pigeon shooting, tennis, croquet, archery, (horse riding near by).

TARIFF

	Jan to Dec
Premier Suites:	£315.00
Suites:	£285.00
Superior Rooms:	£205.00
Deluxe Rooms:	£185.00
Executive Rooms:	£165.00

Other Special Golf Packages:
2 nights, dinner one evening to the value of £35 in The Camellia Restaurant, full English breakfast and two rounds of golf at Mannings Heath Golf Club
Jan to Dec £110.00 per person per night.

DIRECTIONS

From Guildford follow the A281 out of Monks Gate and South Lodge Hotel is on the right.
From Crawley follow the A23 to junction 12, then follow the B2110 to the end, join the A281 and South Lodge Hotel is on the right.
From Brighton follow the A23 to junction 23, then follow the A272 to A281, turn right then follow until South Lodge Hotel appears on the right.

The West Country

The West Country

*C*lotted Cream, good local ales, long sandy beaches – where are we? The first clue was a dead give away, but then if you've been to Cornwall and the West Country then the latter two may have given you the answer anyway.

There's good golf to be found west of Bristol, down towards Land's End. Links golf, parkland layouts, championship stuff, all located in a place where the rest of the non-golfing family will quite happily let you indulge your passion. The sane ones won't care less how many rounds you play – they'll be too busy lying on the beach or soaking up the charms of the West Country.

All the way back in 1890, a course called Burnham & Berrow was created about one mile north of Burnham-on-Sea, Somerset. Little did they know it, but the man the members chose as their first professional would go on to win five Open Championships. John Henry Taylor was given the job, and it was on the links of Burnham & Berrow that J.H. Taylor found the perfect place to develop the mashie (5-iron) play that was to win him the Open four years later at Sandwich. Quite simply, Burnham & Berrow is one of the finest links courses in the south of England.

Not so far away are to be found two other good links courses, albeit not quite up to the standard of Burnham. Minehead and Weston-Super-Mare are the links in question. Minehead is fairly flat for a links and can get quite busy in the summer. The same goes for Weston-Super-Mare. In other words, don't expect to show up at the height of summer and get a game – phone first.

Mendip is the exact opposite of the two aforementioned links. We go from sea level to a course set up on the Mendip Hills about 1,000 feet above sea level. Good views are the order of the day on this delightful 6,300 yard layout.

Devon is fortunate to have two stretches of coastline, yet the golf on either coast couldn't be more different. Golf on the south coast of Devon tends to be of the clifftop variety, as in the panoramic views from East Devon and Sidmouth, with the latter being quite a bit shorter than the former, by about 1,000 yards. Indeed the only links course on the south coast is to be found at Dawlish Warren on the other side of the Exe Estuary. Here you will find a delightful little links, under 6,000 yards, called the Warren.

If the south coast disappoints in the shortage of links golf, then the north coast more than makes up for it.

The Royal North Devon Golf Club, or Westward Ho! as its commonly called, is the oldest links in England. It also boasts the oldest ladies golf club in the world. As you would expect, this is a truly natural links – so natural that the land is also used by many four-legged creatures. Curious? Well, for years the locals have grazed their sheep on the links of Westward Ho!. Still do. Don't worry, they are well versed in the etiquette of the game, and indeed add a certain charm to your round.

Natural is the way you would describe Saunton, although you won't have to share the fairways with Baa Baa Black Sheep.

Saunton is blessed in more ways than one. It not only has some of the most natural duneland you are ever likely to find, it also has room for two courses, both of them fine links. The East and the West courses are the names given to the two layouts, and of the two the East is the better, measuring nearly 350 yards longer.

Many major amateur events have been played over Saunton's East links. This is a layout to test the very best, and it pays to be long off the tee – eight of Saunton's par-4s measure in excess of 400 yards.

It's not too long a drive from Saunton and Westward Ho! to Cornwall, where you will find another collection of fine courses.

The Duchy also has its own share of good links layouts. West Cornwall, Perranporth, Newquay, St. Enedoc and Trevose are natural links courses that you will want to return to, particularly St. Enedoc, Trevose and West Cornwall.

St. Enedoc's Church course is the older of the two layouts here, dating back to 1890. It's a links that will test every part of your game, a links that's as natural as they come. Trevose is slightly longer than St. Enedoc, although its dunes aren't as large. West Cornwall may be the shorter of the three at just under 5,900, yet its a lovely old fashioned links that you won't tire of playing.

Of course no trip to Cornwall would be complete without a crack at Jack's masterpiece – St. Mellion. For six years the Nicklaus course at St. Mellion was home to the Benson & Hedges International Open. Europe's top professionals didn't exactly find it a pushover, and neither will you. Played over lovely parkland, with several rises in elevation, this is a true championship course in every sense of the word.

Nearby you will find Looe Golf Club, with it's course on high ground where the wind plays an important part in how well you score.

The West Country

Burnham
&
Berrow

Willingcott Valley

Barnstable

Bridgwa

Highbullen Hotel

Taunto

Bideford

A361

A39

A3

Manor House Hotel, Exeter

Ashbury Golf Club (Manor House)

Exeter

Roserrow

Launceston

A30

Woodbury Park

Trevose

Lostwithiel

St Mellion

A38

Lanhydrock

Welbeck Manor

Palace Hotel

Tregenna Castle

Carlyon Bay

Elfordleigh Hotel

Torquay

Newquay

Dartmouth Go & Country Clu

Cape Cornwall

A30

St.Austell

Whitsand Bay

Plymouth

Budock Vean Hotel

Penzance

Falmouth

Page

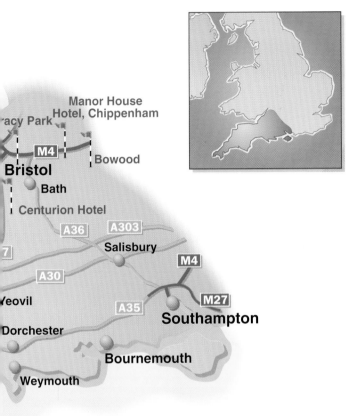

Page

Carlyon Bay Hotel

S tunning sea views from its clifftop position overlooking the beautiful St. Austell Bay await you at Carlyon Bay Hotel.

As a hotel resident, you are entitled to one free round of golf per night of your stay. The 6,500 yard course enjoys breathtaking views where the first nine holes run along the cliff

top before turning inland through beautiful countryside. In addition, set in the hotel's grounds is a 9 hole approach course and a putting green, also free to hotel guests.

The Club House extends a warm welcome to golfers and non-golfers alike. The Club has the benefit of two golf shops, the Pro Shop, open every day for golf equipment, tuition and equipment hire and the Ladies Shop catering exclusively for the lady golfer.

The hotel's Bay View Restaurant offers the best of modern and traditional cuisine. Afterwards, in the comfortable surroundings of the lounge, a variety of entertainment is provided.

In addition to the superb facilities of the hotel we are able to organise a number of outdoor activities including deep sea fishing, horse riding, fly fishing, clay pigeon shooting, yachting and watersports.

The hotel also offers a comprehensive school holiday entertainment programme to cater for all ages along with a playroom to keep the children amused.

LOCAL ATTRACTIONS

One of the prettiest shopping centres in the West Country is Truro. This cathedral city boasts a wealth of history in it's old cobbled streets and is home to some of the regions best shops. If you love gardens you can visit the Lost Gardens of Heligan (10 miles away) Glendurgan, Trebah, Lanhydrock House and Gardens and many more. The pretty fishing ports of Charlestown and Fowey are just minutes away, full of history and well worth a visit.

GOLF INFORMATION

18 hole, 6578 yard Cliff Top/ Parkland course

Par 72

Golf Professional: Mark Rowe
Tel: 01726 814228

Instructions: Groups and individuals catered for.

Hire: Clubs and buggies

CARD OF THE COURSE

1	385	Par 4	10	514	Par 5
2	467	Par 4	11	151	Par 3
3	192	Par 3	12	350	Par 4
4	516	Par 5	13	516	Par 5
5	191	Par 3	14	336	Par 4
6	368	Par 4	15	531	Par 5
7	364	Par 4	16	400	Par 4
8	372	Par 4	17	387	Par 4
9	350	Par 4	18	188	Par 3
Out	3205	Par 35	In	3373	Par 37

HOTEL INFORMATION

Carlyon Bay Hotel
Sea Road, St Austell
Cornwall PL25 3RD
Tel: 01726 812304
Fax: 01726 814938
Rating: 4 Star AA & RAC 5 Crowns ETB.
Rooms: 73.
Restaurants: Bayview Restaurant – style modern English.
Childcare: Playroom facilities and Entertainment Programme during school hols.
Hair and Beauty: Health & Beauty room specialising in Aromatherapy massage using Epsa Range.
Other Sporting Facilities: Tennis courts, 9 hole course, table tennis, snooker rooms, swimming pools, golf practice ground, Croquet Lawn.
Other Leisure Activities: Golf Tuition holidays, golf lesson break, Pretty as a Peach Break.

TARIFF

2 Night Break, Dinner Bed & Breakfast from £142 per person to £162 per person. For an inland facing room including golf.

Special Golf Packages:
Inland – Low Season £69.00 per person.

Other Special Golf Packages:
5 Day golf tuition from £335.00 per person.

DIRECTIONS

At M5 J29, turn left onto M5 for 6.6km, at A38(T) J31, turn right onto A30 for 100.9km, turn left onto A38 for 0.5km, turn right onto Local roads for 2.4km, bear left onto B3268 for 2.1km, go onto B3269 for 2.9km, turn right onto A390 for 7.7km, turn left onto A3082 for 0.5km, turn right onto Local roads for 1.3km, arrive Carlyon Bay, Cornwall.

MANOR HOUSE & ASHBURY HOTELS

Fowley Cross, Okehampton, Devon EX20 4NA.
Tel: 01837 53053/01837 55453 Fax: 01837 550207/01837 55468

Ashbury 18/Oakwood 18 HOLES
PAR 69/68   5803/5207 YARDS
TYPE OF GOLF COURSE: Rolling countryside
GOLF PROFESSIONAL: Reg Cade
TEL: 01837 55453
B&B + 18 HOLES: 3 nights £124/£147 – £159/£169. Approx prices Nov'98 – July'99
OTHER SPECIAL GOLF PACKAGES: Party Discounts/Bargain Breaks

Two country house hotels offering superb views, service and food. Two 18-hole + one 9-hole courses. Free golf on 3 night stays. Driving range, buggies, golf tuition. Unique craft centre – full daily tuition, pottery, candles, glass engraving, enamelling, painting and sketching. Heated indoor pools, sauna, squash, badminton, snooker, archery, laser clays, bowls, tennis, all indoors and free. Outdoor bowls, tennis, guided moor walks – all free. Evening entertainment includes line dancing, skittles, live music, 'casino' and quiz.

BOWOOD GOLF & COUNTRY CLUB

Derry Hill, Calne, Wiltshire SN11 9PQ. Tel: 01249 822228 Fax: 01249 822218

18 HOLES   PAR 72   7317 & 6890 YARDS
TYPE OF GOLF COURSE: Parkland
GOLF PROFESSIONAL: Nigel Blenkarne
TEL: 01249 822228
B&B + 18 HOLES: £32.00 + Queenwood Golf Lodge corporate + Society Packages available.

18 hole championship course designed by Dave Thomas and set in Capability Brown's 2,000 acre Great Park. Queenwood Golf Lodge provides accommodation for up to 8 guests, prices are per night and include unlimited golf, dinner, bed and breakfast. Practice facilities include 2 putting greens, academy course and floodlit driving range.

BUDOCK VEAN GOLF & COUNTRY HOUSE HOTEL

Helford River, Mannan Smith, Falmouth, Cornwall TR11 5LG.
Tel: 01326 250 288 Fax: 01326 250892

9/(18 tee) HOLES PAR 34/(68)
2657/(5153) YARDS
TYPE OF GOLF COURSE: Parkland
RATING: 3 Star, 2 Rosette
B&B + 18 HOLES: £59 – £89 per person
OTHER SPECIAL GOLF PACKAGES: Golf Schools

Set in 65 acres of sub-tropical gardens and parkland in a designated area of outstanding natural beauty on the banks of the Helford River, the Budock Vean Hotel enjoys and enviable reputation for service and cuisine, with local seafood a speciality.

Complete with its own golf course originally designed by James Braid, tennis courts indoor swimming pool and natural health spa, the hotel is an ideal base from which to enjoy a myriad of magnificent country and coastal walks and for visiting the great Cornish gardens. Enquire about residential golf schools, competition weeks, summer coaching and winter workshops.

BURNHAM & BERROW GOLF CLUB

St. Christopher's Way, Burnham-on-Sea, Somerset TA8 2PE.
Tel: 01278 785760 Fax: 01278 795440

Dormy House has 4 twin rooms en-suite with tea and coffee making facilities.

9/18 HOLES PAR 71/72 6606/6332 YARDS

TYPE OF GOLF COURSE:
Championship Links.

GOLF PROFESSIONAL:
Mark Crowther Smith
TEL: 01278 784545

B&B + 18 HOLES: From £61.00

CAPE CORNWALL GOLF & COUNTRY CLUB LTD

Cape Cornwall, St Just. Penzance, Cornwall, England TR19 7NL.
Tel: 01736 788611 Fax: 01736 788611

18 hole golf course with views over the only Cape in England the first and last. Selfcatering accommodation sleeping five to fourteen in all inclusive prices available.

18 HOLES   PAR 70   5462 YARDS

TYPE OF GOLF COURSE:
Clifftop Parkland

GOLF PROFESSIONAL: Paul Atherton

B&B + 18 HOLES: From £30.00

OTHER SPECIAL GOLF PACKAGES:
Self catering from March 1999.

CENTURION HOTEL

Charlton Lane, Midsomer Norton, Bath BA3 4BD. Tel: 01761 417711 Fax: 01761 418357

3 Star Hotel situated midway between Bath and Wells. All rooms are ensuite with TV, direct dial phone, courtesy tray and hairdryer. Restaurant, bars, indoor pool, squash courts and large car park. Many rooms have a view over the gardens and golf course.

9 HOLES   PAR 4   2139 YARDS

TYPE OF GOLF COURSE: Parkland

HOTEL RATING: 3 Star AA/RAC – 5
Crown commended ETB.

B&B + 18 HOLES: From £59.50 B&B +
£9 or £11 for golf.

Dartmouth Golf & Country Club

Dartmouth Golf & Country Club is set amid 225 acres of wonderful rolling countryside in the heart of South Devon. A golfers paradise with views over Torbay and the surrounding South Hams.

The 7200 yard Par 72 Championship Course has hosted the Western Region PGA Matchplay Championship for the past four years and was voted by the Professionals as one of the best courses in the South West. Designed to challenge these most proficient golfers, the careful positioning of the tees also ensures that it can be enjoyed by golfers of all abilities.

The 2600 yard Par 33 Club Course is an easier test. Nevertheless, the holes have been built to the same exacting technical standards as its larger counterpart. With slightly smaller greens, subtle borrows and less punishing hazards, it will delight even the most experienced golfer.

The club house provides first class changing facilities, restaurant, professional shop, leisure club/bar and a function suite. A driving range and putting green are also available.

Accommodation is available in a range of delightful cottages which can sleep from 4 to 12 people. Built in a traditional Devon stone each of the 9 cottages has been furnished to the highest standard.

LOCAL ATTRACTIONS

Dartmouth is only 5 miles from the golf club, a must for any visitor as it is steeped in maritime history with Britannia Royal Naval College being one of many attractions in this picturesque town. Only a 9 iron from the golf club is Woodlands Leisure Park – non stop fun: non stop value and ideal for kids. It has a toboggan run, bumper boats, indoor venture zones, falconry centre and many attractions. Locally we are blessed with a wonderful coast line and fantastic views.

18 hole Championship & 9 hole Club, 6663/5166 yard parkland courses

Par 72/65

Golf Professional: Jason Fullard

Tel: 01803 712650

Practice facilities: Covered driving range, + chipping and putting green.

Instructions: Groups and individuals catered for.

Hire: Clubs and buggies.

CARD OF THE COURSE

	Championship			Club	
1	404	Par 4	1	171	Par 3
2	329	Par 4	2	379	Par 4
3	163	Par 3	3	340	Par 4
4	491	Par 5	4	511	Par 5
5	145	Par 3	5	137	Par 3
6	366	Par 4	6	173	Par 3
7	209	Par 3	7	515	Par 5
8	524	Par 5	8	183	Par 3
9	495	Par 5	9	174	Par 3
Out	3126	Par 36	Out	2583	Par 33
10	384	Par 4	1	171	Par 3
11	445	Par 4	2	379	Par 4
12	378	Par 4	3	340	Par 4
13	336	Par 4	4	511	Par 5
14	422	Par 4	5	137	Par 3
15	425	Par 4	6	173	Par 3
16	539	Par 5	7	515	Par 5
17	394	Par 4	8	183	Par 3
18	214	Par 3	9	174	Par 3
In	3537	Par 36	Out	2583	Par 33

Dartmouth Golf & Country Club
Blackawton, Totnes
Devon TQ9 7DE
Tel: 01803 712650
Fax: 01803 712628

Rooms: 9 Cottages; sleep 4-12

Restaurants: Fully licenced bar & restaurant (food available all day)

Hair and Beauty: Beautition available + masseur.

Fitness Facilities: Fully equipped gym, swimming pool, sauna, jaccuzi, steam room + small childrens pool.

Other Sporting Facilities: Driving Range.

Championship Course:
Week day
£27.00 p/round – £32 p/day
Weekend
£37.00 p/round – £42 p/day

Club Course:
Week day: £10.00 9 holes
Weekend: £13.00 9 holes

Special Golf Packages:
B&B including 18 holes £49.95 inc use of leisure area.

Other Special Golf Packages:
Stay & Play breaks

5 miles west of Dartmouth on the A3122

47

Shaftesbury (N. Dorset)

ELFORDLEIGH GOLF CLUB
Colebrook, Plymouth, Plymouth PL7 5EB. Tel: 01752 336428 Fax: 01752 344581

9/(18 tees) HOLES   PAR 68   5210 YARDS
TYPE OF GOLF COURSE: Parkland
RATING: AA 3 star – RAC 3 star
GOLF PROFESSIONAL: Chris Rendell
TEL: 01752 336428
B&B + 18 HOLES: From £49.50 per person
OTHER SPECIAL GOLF PACKAGES: Various Society Packages

Set in tranquil surroundings of South Farm countryside, only 7 miles from the centre of Plymouth. The undulating parkland course with 6 par 3's and 2 par 5's, challenging to the experienced golfer and yet comfortable to the novice. Experienced European Golf Teachers Federation professional, Chris Rendell is always on hand to give advice. Full bar and catering facilities available, along with 18 bedroom hotel, two restaurants, outdoor pool and gymnasium. Handicap certificates are required. Societies always welcome.

HIGHBULLEN HOTEL
Chittlehamholt, Umberleigh, North Devon EX37 9HD. Tel: 01769 540561 Fax: 01769 540492

Highbullen is a splendid Victorian Gothic mansion. The hotel stands on high ground between the Mole and Taw Valleys in wooded seclusion, yet with fine views over surrounding country. A spectacular 18 hole golf course is set in the surrounding parkland.

Life at Highbullen is informal and relaxed. All 37 bedrooms have their own private bathrooms. The restaurant has appeared in all the reputable guides for over 30 years.

18 HOLES	PAR 68	5755 YARDS

TYPE OF GOLF COURSE: Parkland
GOLF PROFESSIONAL: Paul Weston
B&B + 3 COURSE DINNER:
Mid-week £57.50 to £85.00
Fri-Sun £62.50 to £90.00
OTHER SPECIAL GOLF PACKAGES:
3 nights or more:
Single rooms £65.00 to £80.00

LANHYDROCK GOLFING LODGE
Lostwithiel Road, Bodmin, Cornwall PL30 5AQ. Tel: 01208 73600 Fax: 01208 77325

Lanhydrock Golfing Lodge is located only 100 yards from the main clubhouse where all meals are taken. Featured in our sister publication "Golfing Gems" the course is a beautiful parkland design with lakes, trees and wide bunkers to test all standards. The lodge sleeps up to 9 people and will accept a minimum of 4.

18 HOLES	PAR 70	6100 YARDS

TYPE OF GOLF COURSE: Parkland

GOLF PROFESSIONAL: Jason Broadway
TEL: 01208 73600

OTHER SPECIAL GOLF PACKAGES:
D.B.B + unlimited golf from £64

MANOR HOUSE HOTEL
Castle Combe, Chippenham, Wiltshire SN14 7HR. Tel: 01249 782206 Fax: 01249 782159

15th century manor house nestling in wooded valley on the southern edge of the Cotswolds. Exceptional standard of comfort and hospitality; award-winning food. Spectacular and challenging championship golf course designed by Peter Alliss and rated one of the finest inland courses in the country.

18 HOLES	PAR 73	6340 YARDS

TYPE OF GOLF COURSE: Parkland
RATING: 4 Red Stars AA – RAC Blue Ribbon.
GOLF PROFESSIONAL: Chris Smith
TEL: 01249 783101
B&B + 18 HOLES: £221 x 2 people
OTHER SPECIAL GOLF PACKAGES:
£150 per person per night – 2 nights minimum.

Lostwithiel Hotel Golf & Country Club

*L*ostwithiel Hotel is unique, a hotel and country club of great charm and character. Lostwithiel offers outstanding comfort and service - idyllicly set amongst 150 acres of rolling wooden hills which look down onto the beautiful and tranquil valley of the River Fowey.

The spacious and individually designed bedrooms have been created from old Cornish buildings with their mellowed stone and beamed ceilings. The mood of rural tranquillity is reflected in the country pine furniture. Each room has colour TV, direct dial telephone, tea and coffee making facilities and bathroom.

Dine in style in the Black Prince restaurant where imaginative menus put the emphasis on fresh local produce supported by a carefully selected wine list.

As part of the Leisure Club facilities, the hotel has two all weather tennis courts, a gym and an indoor swimming pool. Activities can include golf, fishing, swimming, tennis and snooker in the sports bar. Excellent salmon and trout fishing can be enjoyed on the River Fowey, bordering the hotel grounds. The 18 hole golf course is one of the most interesting and varied in the county. Designed to take full advantage of the natural features of the landscape, it combines two very distinctive areas of hillside and valley. The challenging front nine rewards you with magnificent views of the surrounding countryside, while the picturesque back nine runs through leafy parkland, flanked by the waters of the Fowey.

LOCAL ATTRACTIONS

The hotel is the perfect base for discovering beautiful coastlines, quiet inland villages, ancient towns and historic houses. Explore the haunting landscape of Bodmin Moor, Llanhydrock House in its fascinating Edwardian timewarp or the Lost Gardens of Heligan.

GOLF INFORMATION

18 hole, 5781 yard parkland course Par 72

Golf Professional: Tony Nash
Tel: 01208 873822

Practice facilities: Covered driving range. Floodlit driving range with undercover and grass bays, putting greens and practice bunkers.

Instructions: Groups and individuals catered for + 4 day tuition breaks available.

Hire: Clubs and buggies.

Green Fee (Daily): Low Season £12.00
High Season £20.00.

CARD OF THE COURSE					
1	331	Par 4	10	169	Par 3
2	503	Par 5	11	307	Par 4
3	413	Par 4	12	258	Par 4
4	356	Par 4	13	448	Par 5
5	142	Par 3	14	365	Par 4
6	476	Par 5	15	176	Par 3
7	522	Par 5	16	270	Par 4
8	144	Par 3	17	120	Par 3
9	432	Par 5	18	349	Par 4
Out	3319	Par 38	In	2462	Par 34

HOTEL INFORMATION

Lostwithiel Hotel Golf & Country Club
Lower Polscoe, Lostwithiel
Cornwall PL22 0HQ
Tel: 01208 873550
Fax: 01208 873479
Rating: AA/RAC 2 Star. ETB 4 Crowns commended.
Rooms: 18.
Restaurants: Black Prince restaurant – English/French. Sports bar – Traditional pub style.
Childcare Facilities: Baby listening & sitting by arrangement.
Fitness Facilities: Gym, swimming pool (indoor) of 2 all weather tennis courts.
Other Sporting Facilities: Riding and Fishing available nearby.

TARIFF

B&B + Dinner 1/4 to 31/10 from **£47.00** p.p, per night.
Winter from **£37.50.**

Special Golf Packages:
DB&B including 18 holes from £52 Summer or £38 Winter.

Other Special Golf Packages:
Inclusive half board breaks. **Tuition breaks.**

DIRECTIONS

From A30 take A390. The hotel is _ mile off the A390 on the eastern outskirts of Lostwithiel, marked by brown tourist signs.

Roserrow Golf & Country Club

The Roserrow Golf and Country Club is set in 400 acres restling among the gentle hills and valleys of North Cornwall, close by a coastline of breathtaking cliffs and sandy beaches. The 18-hole, par 72 golf course, has been designed to appeal to golfers of all abilities combining relatively gentle holes with more demanding challenges. The course is automatically irrigated to ensure optimum playing conditions throughout the year and encompasses woodland, water and gently undulating hills and valleys.

There is a nine-hole putting green and driving range with swing analysis studio.

Accommodation consists of a number of individual self-catering houses adjacent to the golf course, built and finished to a very high standard, sleeping between two and twelve people. They are beautifully sited in the North Cornwall countryside, tucked behind the famous watersporting havens of Rock and Daymor Bay, surrounded by the golf course. Here is quality leisure time for all with sailing, windsurfing, water-skiing, surfing, tennis, spectacular coastal walks and country footpaths. The famous windy course of St. Enodoc is within a few miles. The leisure centre has a heated swimming pool, gymnasium, sauna and spa bath. Dine out in the brasserie with panoramic views of Polzeath and for a 'taste of the sea' visit the famous Rick Stein seafood restaurant at Padstow.

LOCAL ATTRACTIONS

The area is famous for its watersports and offers the beautiful beaches of Daymer Bay and Polzeath and many spectacular coastal walks through North Cornwall's scenery.

Padstow is a picturesque harbour town famous for its Seafood Restaurants and the "Obby Oss" May Day celebrations. The harbour is a thriving fishing port and offers many amenities just a short ferry ride across the Camel Estuary from Rock.

The quaint fishing port of Port Issac has a charm of its own with the narrow streets, charming cottages and many seafood restaurants. It is a very pretty village with a harbour on the North Cornish coast, in an area of outstanding beauty with both rocky and sandy beaches.

18 hole, 6651 yard sheltered woodland course

Par 72

Practice facilities: Covered 15 bay driving range, short game practice area, practice hole and putting green.

Golf Tuition:
PGA professional Andrew Cullen.
Individual and group tuition.
Video/computer swing analysis studio.

Hire: Clubs and buggies

CARD OF THE COURSE			
1	430 Par 4	10	373 Par 4
2	379 Par 4	11	428 Par 4
3	386 Par 4	12	183 Par 3
4	534 Par 5	13	296 Par 4
5	153 Par 3	14	389 Par 4
6	554 Par 5	15	529 Par 5
7	184 Par 3	16	110 Par 3
8	314 Par 4	17	486 Par 5
9	461 Par 4	18	362 Par 4
Out 3395 Par 36		In 3156 Par 36	

CORNWALL

SELF-CATERING INFORMATION

Roserrow Golf & Country Club
St Minver, Wadebridge,
Cornwall PH27 6QT
Tel: 01208 862424
Fax: 01208 862218
Rating: 5 Keys English Tourist Board
Rooms: Houses sleeping 2-12.

Restaurants: Brasserie open all day providing excellent food.
Childcare Facilities: Baby sitting can be arranged.
Hair and Beauty: Reflections beauty spa for beauty treatments.
Fitness Facilities: A state of the art fitness facility incorporating a swimming pool, steam room, beauty therapy room, sauna and spa.
Other Sporting Facilities: Tennis, bowling green, shuttle board and croquet lawn.
Other Leisure Activities: Superb sports and leisure shop selling designer leisure clothes.

TARIFF

ON APPLICATION – PLEASE SEND FOR A BROCHURE.

1st April '99 – 30th October '99
Individual £24, Groups (8 plus) £16,
Temp. resident £16.

1st Nov '99 – 31st March '00
Individual £16, Groups (8 plus) £10,
Temp. resident £10.

DIRECTIONS

From Exeter and the M5
Just past Exeter take the A30 sign to Launceston. Some 50 miles past Exeter is the sign to Launceston. Stay on the A30 for a few miles beyond Launceston and there is a sign to the right at Kennards House which says A395 to Camelford, Wadebridge and North Cornwall (A39) Take this turn to the right and follow it until T junction with the A39 which is approximately 12 miles from the A30. Take the left hand turn on the A39 towards Wadebridge. Approximately 2-3 miles along the A39 take the right hand turn which is signposted to Delabole, Tintagel and Port Isaac, the B3314. After a further 2-3 miles there is another cross roads, go straight across staying on the B3314 still signposted to Wadebridge. Take the right hand turn towards Port Quinn and Polzeath,follow the tourist sign to the Bee Centre. This is approximately 7 miles from Delabole. After one mile there is a further junction take the right hand turn towards the Bee Centre. Do not take the very sharp hand turn here to Port Quinn as it is a minor lane only. Continue down this road taking the left hand fork to Polzeath. Do not take the right hand turn to New Polzeath. Another half a mile down this road is the Roserrow sign post along with Trelewin on the left hand side.

MANOR HOUSE HOTEL & GOLF COURSE, MORETONHAMPSTEAD

Moretonhampstead, Devon TQ13 8RE. Tel: 01647 440355 Fax: 01647 440961

18 Holes   Par 69   6016 Yards
Type of Golf Course: Park and Moorland
Hotel Rating: AA 4 Star – RAC 4 Star – ETB 5 Crowns
Golf Professional: Richard Lewis **Tel:** 01647 440998
B&B + 18 Holes: From £72.50 p.p.p.n.
Other Special Golf Packages: Half Board inc golf from £75.00 p.p.p.n.

The Manor House Hotel is an imposing Jacobean style mansion set in 270 acres on the edge of Dartmoor. It's 90 bedrooms are complimented by lounges, bars and The Hambleden Restaurant. Also on site are tennis, croquet, fishing and snooker. Golf breaks for couples, groups and societies available throughout the year.

Bowemans Nose, Dartmoor

PALACE HOTEL

Babbacombe Road, Torquay TQ1 3TG. Tel: 01803 200700 Fax: 01803 299899

The Palace Hotel offers for your enjoyment a superb 9 hole championship golf course, set within mature wooded grounds offering challenging features including ponds and streams. The Palace Hotel is an independent four-star hotel which in addition to the golf course offers indoor and outdoor tennis courts and swimming pools, squash courts, snooker rooms and croquet lawn.

9 HOLES	PAR 3	710 YARDS

TYPE OF GOLF COURSE:
Short Championship Course

RATING: 4 Star RAC/AA 5 Crown commended

GOLF PROFESSIONAL: Bob Bradbury

B&B + 18 HOLES: £67.00

Tracy Park

*T*racy Park is one of the most beautiful and historic country estates in the Bristol and Bath area. The park, mentioned in the Domesday Book extends to about 221 acres and encompasses two outstanding Championship courses. With 18 en-suite bedrooms built in the old stables which adjoin the mansion house, staying at

Tracy Park will give you the feel of an elegant bygone era but with all the luxuries of modern living. With three restaurants on-site our historic Cavaliers Kitchen will make it a meal to remember. Dine either à la carte with an extensive selection of traditional and modern cuisine using only the freshest ingredients or in our historic kitchen where you can watch our chef create your meal.

Tracy Park Golf & Country Club, selected to host the 1999 County Championships, is a delightful blend of old and new with a traditional country mansion surrounded by modern golf courses constructed on parkland some 400 years old. The 36 holes present a challenge to all levels of player with water playing a part on a number of occasions. From the high holes there are magnificent views of the surrounding countryside.

Tuition and practice is never a problem with a 13 bay driving range and our resident professionals on hand with the right advice. Tony Jacklin was the original tournament professional attached to Tracy Park.

LOCAL ATTRACTIONS

The City of Bath only 4 miles away is the UK's most visited City outside of London. There are great shops and lots of historical interests. Dating back to Roman Times, including the world famous Natural Spring Baths and Pump Rooms. The City will appeal to people of all ages with an abundance of Architectural delights. A City not to be missed.

GOLF INFORMATION

36 hole, 6423 & 6222 yard parkland courses

Par 70 and 70

Golf Professional: Richard Berry

Tel: 0117 937 3521

Practice facilities: 13 bay driving range + chipping and bunker areas.

Instructions: Groups and individuals catered for.

Hire: Clubs and buggies

CARD OF THE COURSE				
Cromwell Course			**Crown Course**	
1	523	Par 5	1	562	Par 5
2	210	Par 3	2	428	Par 4
3	355	Par 4	3	440	Par 4
4	406	Par 4	4	165	Par 3
5	178	Par 3	5	390	Par 4
6	390	Par 4	6	135	Par 3
7	295	Par 4	7	389	Par 4
8	430	Par 4	8	422	Par 4
9	490	Par 5	9	401	Par 4
Out	3277	Par 36	Out	3332	Par 35
10	180	Par 3	10	419	Par 4
11	370	Par 4	11	530	Par 5
12	145	Par 3	12	360	Par 4
13	515	Par 5	13	160	Par 3
14	440	Par 4	14	359	Par 4
15	266	Par 4	15	405	Par 4
16	214	Par 3	16	142	Par 3
17	409	Par 4	17	319	Par 4
18	406	Par 4	18	397	Par 4
In	2945	Par 34	In	3091	Par 35

HOTEL INFORMATION

Tracy Park Golf and Country Club
Bath Road, Wick,
Bristol BS30 5RN

Tel: 0117 937 2251
Fax: 0117 937 4288

Rating: Highly Recommended. Provisional 3 Star – Rating applied for.

Rooms: 18.

Restaurants: A la carte with an extensive selection of traditional and modern cuisine.

TARIFF

B&B: Single £45, Single Suite £65, Double £65 and Double Suite £85.

Golf: Weekday £15, Weekend £20. These are reduced rates for hotel guests.

DIRECTIONS

The Tracy Park Golf & Country Club is easily accessible from all parts of the South West. From Junction 18 on the M4 it lies 4 miles from Bath, 8 miles from Bristol and 12 miles from Chippenham. The entrance to the course is off the A420, just to the east of the village of Wick. From Bath take the Lansdown Road towards Wick. From Bristol take the A420 east towards Chippenham. From the M4 take Junction 18 then A46 and A420.

Tregenna Castle Hotel

*I*magine a magnificent estate, with an 18 hole golf course, quiet wooded walks and tropical gardens set above the romantic Atlantic coast line with breathtaking views. This is the Tregenna Castle Hotel. Tregenna offers a range of accommodation from en-suite rooms, some with sea views to self catering apartments graded from 3-5 keys ET.

LOCAL ATTRACTIONS

St. Ives has long been the haunt of many artists, and the Tate Gallery now brings another dimension to the year round attractions in easy access of this unique resort. Among these are family theme parks such as Flambards, Lands End, Poldark Mine with its tin mining industry history and The St. Michaels Mount, imprisoned for two thirds of its life by water, with a history of sea battles and giants. There are also numerous Cornish gardens, castles and stately homes. These combine with a choice of magnificent beaches.

Leisure facilities include indoor and outdoor swimming pool, sauna, solarium, billiard room, squash, badminton and tennis courts, fully fitted gymnasium and children's play area. The Trelawney restaurant, offers a range of carvery and a-la-carte dishes, prepared to the highest standards, mostly from local produce. The Italian Fairways Restaurant is a more informal yet stylish alternative.

Tregenna Castle Golf Course is set in the beautiful grounds of the Tregenna Castle with some of the most picturesque views in the world. Being a par sixty Golf Course, which is made up of six par fours and twelve par threes it is a challenge to even the low handicap golfer, with its narrow fairways and small greens. The outward nine holes, which have a yardage of 1959 par thirty-one are situated to the rear of the Hotel. This is set in a woodland which has varied wildlife living in its boundaries. The inward nine holes which have a par of 29 and a yardage of 1519 yards have been said to have some of the best views ever seen on a Golf Course. It starts with an elevated tee which overlooks St Ives and the Bay.

GOLF INFORMATION

18 hole, 3478 yard parkland course

Par 60

Hire: Clubs

CARD OF THE COURSE			
1	150 Par 3	10	139 Par 3
2	159 Par 3	11	126 Par 3
3	347 Par 4	12	265 Par 4
4	313 Par 4	13	142 Par 3
5	143 Par 3	14	172 Par 3
6	216 Par 3	15	149 Par 3
7	230 Par 4	16	161 Par 3
8	240 Par 4	17	129 Par 3
9	161 Par 3	18	236 Par 4
Out 1959 Par 31		In 1519 Par 29	

HOTEL INFORMATION

Tregenna Castle Hotel
St Ives,
Cornwall TR26 2DE
Tel: 01736 795254
Fax: 01736 796066
Rooms: 80.
Restaurants: Trelawney-Carvery – Fairways Italian.
Childcare Facilities: Baby Listening & nursery within grounds.
Hair and Beauty: Hairdressing – all treatments. Various beauty treatments.
Fitness Facilities: Gym, sauna, solarium, steam room, squash, badminton, tennis, snooker room, indoor and outdoor pools.
Other Sporting Facilities: Golf.
Other Leisure Activities: Christmas & New year house parties.

TARIFF

B&B from £35.00 per night per person

Special Golf Packages:
B&B including 18 holes from £45 per person per night.

DIRECTIONS

A30 from Exeter to Levant just west of Hayle take A3074 to St. Ives.Immediately after Carbis Bay watch for directional signs to Tregenna Castle. The main entrance will be clearly seen.

Trevose Golf & Country Club

revose golf and Country Club is situated on one of the most beautiful stretches of the North Cornwall coast. It offers an ideal self-catering holiday for the real golf enthusiast or for others who may wish to mix their golf with the other amenities available on the complex or nearby.

LOCAL ATTRACTIONS

3 hard tennis courts, heated swimming pool open from mid May to mid September. Social club membership available. 7 glorious sandy bays within about a mile of the club house, with pools, open sea and surf bathing. Lovely coastline for walking. Convenient for shops.

There are three golf courses. The 18-hole championship course was laid out by Harry Colt who designed, among others, Muirfield, Lytham, Pine Valley, Wentworth and Sunningdale. The 9-hole New Course was opened in 1993 by Peter Alliss who had nothing but praise for its environmentally friendly layout. Measuring over 3000 yards with a par of 35 it is a real test. The Short Course is excellent for beginners, juniors not quite ready for the full course or seasoned golfers who want to brush up their iron shots.

The Clubhouse has an excellent bar & restaurant. There is a snooker room, three all-weather tennis courts and a heated outdoor pool open from mid-May to mid-September. Within a mile of the club are seven sandy bays with bathing, surfing and magnificent coastline for walking.

Accommodation is in 7 chalets sleeping five. 6 bungalows also to sleep five; 13 suites and the Club Flat with three double bedrooms and two bathrooms.

The complex is open all year. Mid-week bookings are encouraged and daily rates are available.

GOLF INFORMATION

18 hole + 2 x 9, 6608 yard Links course
Par 71
Golf Professional: Gary Alliss
Tel: 01841 520261
Instructions: Groups and individuals catered for.
Tennis coaching in July and August.
Hire: Clubs and buggies.
Temporary Membership Fees:
Nov – 21 Dec/4th Jan – 21Mar: Daily £22, 1 Week £80,
2 Weeks £100, 3 Weeks £125.
22 Dec-3 Jan/22 Mar-30 Jun/4 Sep-31 Oct: Daily
£32, 1 Week £125, 2 Weeks £170, 3 Weeks £180.
1 July-4 Sep: Daily £35, 1 Week £150, 2 Weeks £220,
3 Weeks £230

CARD OF THE COURSE

1	443	Par 4	10	467	Par 4
2	386	Par 4	11	199	Par 3
3	166	Par 3	12	448	Par 4
4	500	Par 5	13	507	Par 5
5	461	Par 4	14	317	Par 4
6	323	Par 4	15	327	Par 4
7	428	Par 4	16	225	Par 3
8	156	Par 3	17	388	Par 4
9	451	Par 5	18	416	Par 4
Out	3314	Par 36	In	3294	Par 35

HOTEL INFORMATION

Trevose Golf Club
Constantine Bay, Padstow,
Cornwall PL28 8JB
Tel: 01841 520208
Fax: 01841 521057
Rating: English Tourist Board.
Units: 35.
Restaurants: Licensed restaurant with
high standard English Food.
Childcare Facilities: Babysitting can be
arranged.
Hair and Beauty: In the area.
Other Sporting Facilities: Tennis,
snooker and swimming (in Summer).

TARIFF

**Double Dormy Suites
(2 beds):** from £30 per
night

**10% reduction on
accommodation rates for any
stay of 10 days or more
(excluding July/August).**

DIRECTIONS

8 miles from Civil Airport. Daily flight to and from London Gatwick.
From London: M4 to Bristol. M5 to Exeter then exit M5 to A30 then bypass Okehampton,Launceston and Bodmin. 4 miles after bypassing Bodmin roundabout at top of hill continue on A30 (signposted Truro,Newquay,Redruth) for about 3.5 miles to a right turn signposted to Padstow (B3274) DO NOT TAKE THIS ROAD but continue for another mile and exit to the right signposted RAF St. Mawgan. After 3.5 miles exit right to Wadebridge on A39. Next roundabout turn left to Padstow B3274. After 3 miles turn left to St. Merryn. After 3 miles you will come to St. Merryn crossroads. Turn left and after 600 yards turn right to Trevose Golf Club and Constantine Bay 1.5 miles.

Bath

ST. MELLION HOTEL GOLF & COUNTRY CLUB

St Mellion, Nr Saltash, Cornwall PL12 6SD. Tel: 01579 351351 Fax: 01579 350537

24 bedroom hotel and 32 luxury lodges. Leisure facilities - 25m swimming pool leisure pool, sauna, team room, spa pool, fitness suite, tennis, badminton, squash, golf driving range, swing analyser room.

36 HOLES PAR 72/68 6651/5782 YARDS	

TYPE OF GOLF COURSE: Both Parkland
RATING: AA 3 Star – Two AA Rosettes for cuisine
GOLF PROFESSIONAL: David Moon
TEL: 01579 352006
B&B + 18 HOLES: From £51.00 (old course) £55.00 (Nicklaus).
OTHER SPECIAL GOLF PACKAGES: Society Packages/Corporate packages

---

WELBECK MANOR HOTEL and SPARKWELL GOLF COURSE

Blacklands, Sparkwell, Devon. Tel & Fax: 01752 837374 E-mail: Welbeck Man@aol.com

Situated in the beautiful Forest of Dean in the heart of the M4, M5, M50 triangle, Bells Hotel is adjacent to the 1st Tee of it's own 18 hole course. Established in 1971 it has 32 en-suite bedrooms, conference and banqueting facilities for up to 160, bar and restaurant open all day, live music at weekends. Golf cars are for hire, practice and putting area, golf shop on site with extensive range of equipment and clothing.

9 HOLES   PAR: 1 Par 5 and 5 Par 4.

2749 YARDS

TYPE OF GOLF COURSE: Parkland

B&B: £55 per night per room.

OTHER SPECIAL GOLF PACKAGES:
More than 3 nights £45 B&B

WILLINGCOTT VALLEY GOLF & LEISURE COMPLEX

Willingcott, Woolacombe, North Devon EX34 7HN. Tel: 01271 870173 Fax: 01271 870800

Cottage accommodation in delightful grounds, clubhouse, bar and restaurant in beautifully converted 16th century farmhouse. Restaurant serves bar food all day and there is an a-la-carte facility in the evening. Outdoor swimming pool and sauna/solarium.

9/(18 tee) HOLES   PAR 69   6012 YARDS

TYPE OF GOLF COURSE: Parkland/Valley course

GOLF PROFESSIONAL: Jimmy McGhee
TEL: c/o 01271 870173

OTHER SPECIAL GOLF PACKAGES:
Tailor made golf packages.

Whitsand Bay Hotel Golf & Country Club

A magnificent country manor hotel overlooking the ocean and on the edge of a charming and picturesque Cornish fishing village.

The immaculately maintained 18 hole golf course probably commands the best views in the West Country, particularly from the par 3 3rd and 5th which are spectacular indeed.

LOCAL ATTRACTIONS

There are many other amenities locally which include pony trekking, squash, tennis, sea fishing and coarse angling, and 5 other golf courses within a 10 mile radius.

Laid in 1905 by "Fernie of Troon", this is a traditional cliff-top links in the Scottish style. The small greens and undulating fairways with the usual bumps and hollows provide a challenge to both low and high handicapper alike. The lack of trees and exposure to the wind from the sea ensures that all areas of your game will be tested to the full.

The Hotel just 100 yards from the beach, is an impressive mansion with oak panelled Bars, Restaurants and Public Rooms. Bedrooms are comfortably furnished with all the facilities you would expect from a quality hotel. The restaurants are renowned for the quality of their food, created by one of the finest chefs in the region.

The Leisure Centre has an indoor heated swimming pool, toddlers pool, steam room, sauna, solarium and games room. We are able to provide an extensive range of health and beauty treatments. The hotel has its own hairdressing salon, beautician and masseur.

Families are welcome and the general atmosphere is very relaxed and informal. Prices are very reasonable for what is an exceptional hotel.

GOLF INFORMATION

18 hole, 5950 yard clifftop course Par 69

Golf Professional: Steve Poole
Tel: 01503 230778

Instructions: Groups and individuals catered for.

Hire: Clubs and buggies.

CARD OF THE COURSE

1	420	Par 4	10	137	Par 3
2	300	Par 4	11	523	Par 5
3	190	Par 3	12	170	Par 3
4	322	Par 4	13	270	Par 4
5	353	Par 4	14	410	Par 4
6	176	Par 3	15	210	Par 3
7	425	Par 4	16	376	Par 4
8	490	Par 5	17	353	Par 4
9	476	Par 5	18	215	Par 3
Out	3152	Par 36	In	2664	Par 33

CORNWALL

HOTEL INFORMATION

Whitsand Bay Hotel Golf & Country Club
Whitsand Bay
Portwrinkle
Torpoint, Cornwall
Tel: 01503 230276
Fax: 01503 230329

Rooms: 40+.
Restaurants: 2 Restaurants serving English & Continental cuisine.
Childcare Facilities: Family sized room with baby listening.
Hair and beauty: Hairdressing salon, beautician & masseur.
Fitness Facilities: Gymnasium
Other Sporting Facilities: Clay pigeon shooting.
Other Leisure Activities: Various special weekends.

TARIFF

From £40 includes
5 course dinner &
Full English Breakfast.
Minimum stay 2 nights.

Special Golf Packages:
DB&B – 2 nights approx **£110**

DIRECTIONS

From the Tamar Bridge take the A38 approximately 5 miles to Trerulefoot roundabout, take the first exit A374 to Torpoint. Follow road for approximately 4 miles and turn right to Portwrinkle and Whitsand Bay Hotel at signpost.

Woodbury Park Golf & Country Club

*F*ive Swiss style holiday lodges each capable of accommodating up to 8 people sharing. A 55 bedroom hotel is currently under construction, due to open in May 1999.

Nestled in the woods on the edge of the golf course are the holiday lodges, one has been

adapted for the disabled and each lodge is fully fitted with all modern conveniences. Although the lodges are self catering, light snacks and refreshments can be purchased throughout the day and evening in the Clubhouse. Also available is our Restaurant, although booking is necessary. Included in the Lodge tariff is use of the non-chargeable facilities in the Leisure Club.

The Oaks is an 18 hole par 72, 6870 yard course, The Acorns a 9 hole par 33, 2350 yard course. The Oaks is a challenging parkland course with some outstanding holes. The European specification greens are renowned for their quality. The Acorns course is primarily aimed for the higher handicapped player or beginner. The specification and quality of greens is to the same standard as The Oaks.

Pro clinic, video swing analysis and a tour of Nigel Mansell's Trophy room are all available to our guests.

LOCAL ATTRACTIONS

Killerton – 18th century house featuring displays of clothing and set in beautiful grounds.

Castle Drogo – Lutyens-designed granite castle with elegant rooms and colourful gardens.

Tuckers Maltings – Take a guided tour of England's only working malthouse open to the public.

Kents Caverns Showcaves – Explore the underground world of these spectacular 2 million years old caves.

River Dart Country Park – Country fun for everyone in 90 acres of playgrounds, lakes trails and pony riding.

Lydford Gorge – Enchanting riverside walks leading to spectacular 90ft waterfall and Devil's Cauldron.

GOLF INFORMATION

27 hole (18 & 9), 6870 & 3204 yard parkland course
Par 72 & 33

Golf Professional: Alan Richards
Tel: 01395 233382

Practice facilities: Covered driving range.

Instructions: Groups and individuals catered for. Computerised video teaching aids. Residential golf schools. Extensive chipping facilities.

Hire: Clubs and buggies.

NB: Handicap certificates required for The Oaks course.

CARDS OF THE COURSES

The Oaks			The Acorns		
1	464	Par 4	1	291	Par 4
2	579	Par 5	2	191	Par 3
3	185	Par 3	3	437	Par 4
4	429	Par 4	4	175	Par 3
5	152	Par 3	5	289	Par 4
6	348	Par 4	6	301	Par 4
7	335	Par 4	7	134	Par 3
8	441	Par 4	8	340	Par 4
9	538	Par 5	9	139	Par 3
Out	3471	Par 36	Out	2297	Par 32
10	377	Par 4	1	308	Par 4
11	455	Par 4	2	208	Par 3
12	423	Par 4	3	486	Par 5
13	412	Par 4	4	163	Par 3
14	469	Par 5	5	280	Par 4
15	243	Par 3	6	292	Par 4
16	486	Par 5	7	125	Par 3
17	366	Par 4	8	295	Par 4
18	168	Par 3	9	128	Par 3
In	3399	Par 36	In	2285	Par 33

HOTEL INFORMATION

Woodbury Park Golf & Country Club
Woodbury Castle
Woodbury, Exeter EX5 1JJ
Tel: 01395 233382
Fax: 01395 233384

Rooms: 75.
Restaurants: A la carte & Bistro style restaurants.
Beauty: Resident beautician
Fitness Facilities: Indoor swimming pool, fully equipped gym with jacuzzi and sauna.
Other Sporting Facilities: Football pitch.

TARIFF

April '99 – October '99
All prices are per person on two people sharing Standard, Double or Twin. Minimum 4 people in party.

Golf & Leisure Rates
Dinner, Bed & Breakfast and 18 holes.

Weekday (Sun-Thurs)	**£99.00**
Weekends (Fri-Sat)	**£109.00**

Non Golfers in Party
Dinner, Bed & Breakfast and free use of Leisure club.

Weekday	**£80.00**
Weekends	**£85.00**

DIRECTIONS

Woodbury Park Golf & Country Club is fully signposted by AA road signs and is easy to find. Leave M5 at Junction 30 and follow A376 to Sidmouth/Exmouth. Then A3052 to Sidmouth until you reach the Halfway House Inn on your left. Turn right on the B3180 to Budleigh Salterton and continue onto Woodbury Common. Woodbury Park Golf Course is signposted clearly on your right hand side.

The Midlands

Longborough, Gloucestershire

The Midlands

*T*he heart of England is fine proof that you don't have to go to the sea to find great golf courses. In England's green and pleasant land you will find enough parkland courses to make you want to return year after year. Where better to start than in Lincolnshire? It is in this county that you will find perhaps the greatest inland course in all of England, perhaps in the whole of the British Isles.

A few years ago the American magazine Golf Digest compiled its top 100 courses in the world. Pine Valley in New Jersey came out top, and many fine links courses featured high up the list. Top British inland course was Woodhall Spa, an excellent accolade considering it was up against the likes of Gleneagles, Ganton and Sunningdale.

Harry Vardon originally laid out this course in 1905, but alterations were later made by Harry Colt of Wentworth fame, and by Colonel Hotchkin. What they created was a classic heathland course, one with lots of heather, trees and fairways sitting on lovely sandy subsoil. This classic course measures just short of 7,000 yards and what you will probably remember most about it are the huge gaping bunkers. A course not to be missed.

Golf of the heathland variety can also be found over in Nottinghamshire. Notts Golf Club, or Hollinwell as its also known, Coxmoor and Sherwood Forest provide a trio of heathland/moorland courses the county can be proud of.

Derbyshire isn't known for its great golf courses, but there are some little gems to be found. Buxton and High Peak and Cavendish certainly fall into that category. Both are to be found in the town of Buxton in some of the loveliest countryside in England. Other good courses in Derbyshire include Kedelston Park and Breadsall Priory near Derby. The former is a located in a beautiful setting while the latter is a golf and country club established in 1976.

Like Derbyshire, Leicestershire is not known for its great golf courses but it does contain one classic heathland gem, in the shape of Luffenham Heath. While not in the same league as, say, Woodhall Spa, Luffenham is a joy to play. Another joy can be found at Longcliffe, a heavily wooded course that requires you to hit the ball straight.

Of course the Midlands is the scene of one of the most famous golf events ever. It was at The Belfry, near Birmingham, in 1985 that Europe finally wrested the Ryder Cup from the Americans after years of losing. That event, and subsequent matches in 1989 and 1993 put The Belfry on the map. Everyone wants to play the courses two signature holes, the 10th and the 18th. Just don't expect to play them well.

Little Aston is another course associated with Birmingham. It's one known for its greens and its superb conditioning. One you should play if you get the chance. Other courses near Birmingham that have to be played include Fulford Heath, Kings Norton and Copt Heath, all to the south of the city.

A good addition to Midlands golf in recent years has been the Forest of Arden. Now owned by the Marriott hotel group, this course is now a regular venue on the PGA European Tour.

Just south of the Forest of Arden and Coventry, at Warwickshire, is to be found a new American style 36-hole complex called The Warwickshire. Comprising four separate nines, the holes have been built to a very high standard and provide a strong challenge.

Nearby in Stratford upon Avon are to be found two good courses at Stratford and the Welcombe Hotel. Both offer a pleasant day's golf, and the latter recently hosted an event on the European Seniors Tour.

In the extreme west Midlands, in Shropshire, you will find a collection of good courses that can provide several days of good golf. This little county beside the Welsh border has produced a number of fine golfers over the years – Ian Woosnam, Sandy Lyle and Peter Baker to name but three. Lyle learned his golf at Hawkstone Park, while Woosnam played as a lad at Llanymynech, a course where one hole, the 4th, calls for a tee shot to be played in Wales to a green that lies in England. Good golf is also to be found at Hill Valley.

To the north of Shropshire lies the county of Cheshire and the golf there is nothing to be sneezed at either. Mere, Delamere Forest, Sandiway, Mottram Hall, Carden Park and Portal are all worthy of a visit, especially Portal. This championship course near Tarporley lies in lovely parkland and offers a strong challenge to even the lowest of handicaps.

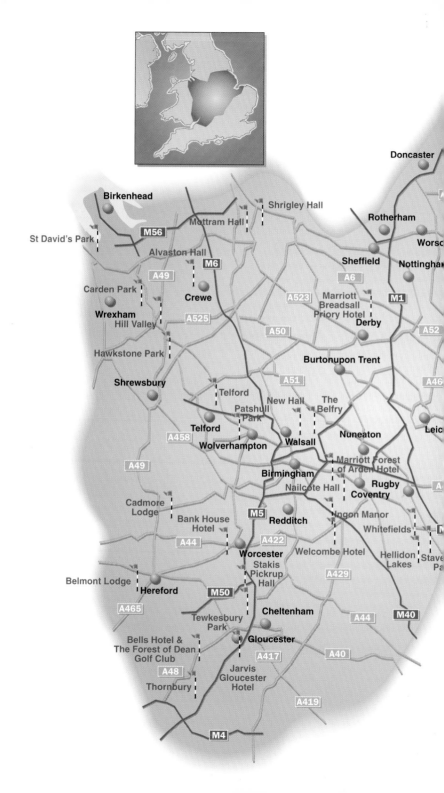

Doncaster

Birkenhead

Shrigley Hall

Rotherham

St David's Park

M56

Mottram Hall

Worsc

Alvaston Hall

Sheffield

Nottingha

M6

A49

A6

Carden Park

Crewe

A523

Marriott
Breadsall
Priory Hotel

M1

Wrexham
Hill Valley

A525

Derby

A52

A50

Hawkstone Park

Burtonupon Trent

Shrewsbury

A51

A46

Telford

New Hall

The
Belfry

Patshull
Park

Telford

Nuneaton

Leic

A458

Wolverhampton

Walsall

A49

Marriott Forest
of Arden Hotel

Birmingham

Rugby

Nailcote Hall

Coventry

A

Cadmore
Lodge

Ingon Manor

M5

Redditch

Whitefields

Bank House
Hotel

A44

A422

Welcombe Hotel

Hellidon
Lakes

Stave
Pa

Worcester

Belmont Lodge

Stakis
Pickrup
Hall

A429

Hereford

M50

A465

Cheltenham

A44

M40

Tewkesbury
Park

Bells Hotel &
The Forest of Dean
Golf Club

Gloucester

A48

A417

A40

Jarvis
Gloucester
Hotel

Thornbury

A419

M4

Midlands & Cotswolds

Page

Page

Belton Woods Hotel

Set in 475 acres of tranquil Lincolnshire countryside, Belton Woods has an extensive selection of health & leisure facilities, including three challenging golf courses, the Championship Lakes, the Woodside and the Par 3 Spitfire course. The courses feature 12 lakes, 275 bunkers and one of Europe's longest holes at 615 yards. Non-golfers are equally catered for. Indoors there is a well equipped gym with swimming pool, sunbeds, sauna and Hair & Beauty Salon. In the grounds, regular activities include tennis, archery and jogging.

There are a choice of two restaurants. You can experience the French cuisine of the Rosette winning Manor restaurant or enjoy a more relaxed atmosphere in the Plus Fours restaurant.

The extensive facilities include a wide choice of accommodation, 136 bedrooms, complemented by four deluxe suites and executive rooms with their breathtaking views. All bedrooms are en-suite and are fully equipped with tea and coffee making facilities, trouser press, TV with Satellite channels available.

Belton Woods is easily accessible to all major road links, the A1 being only 5 minutes away with East Midlands Airport less than 45 minutes drive and London's Kings Cross being 60 minutes by rail, 90 minutes drive from Birmingham and 60 minutes drive away from Leeds and Sheffield.

LOCAL ATTRACTIONS

Those who feel the need to venture beyond Belton Woods' own rural setting will discover that Lincolnshire is a lovely county of gently rolling countryside, rich in period architecture. The mellow stone of Lincoln itself displays all the influences of the centuries, dominated by the third largest cathedral in England. Belvoir Castle has a fascinating if rather bloody history while, in gentler vein, Belton House is a fine example of Christopher Wren's work. Belton village and nearby Manthorpe are two of the county's showpiece villages.

GOLF INFORMATION

36 hole, Lakes 6781 yard; Woodside 6605 yard parkland courses.
Par 72 Lakes; 73 Woodside
Golf Professional: Tony Roberts
Tel: 01476 514332

Practice facilities: Covered driving range.

Instructions: Groups and individuals catered for. Video playback tuition available + chipping green, on course playing, putting green.

Hire: Clubs and buggies

Green fees £27 per person per round

CARD OF THE COURSE

Lakes Course			Woodside Course		
1	505	Par 5	1	428	Par 4
2	167	Par 3	2	371	Par 4
3	439	Par 4	3	397	Par 4
4	402	Par 4	4	163	Par 3
5	183	Par 3	5	493	Par 5
6	421	Par 4	6	376	Par 4
7	402	Par 4	7	482	Par 5
8	330	Par 4	8	180	Par 3
9	606	Par 5	9	357	Par 4
Out	3455	Par 36	Out	3247	Par 36
10	361	Par 4	10	401	Par 4
11	187	Par 3	11	201	Par 3
12	504	Par 5	12	330	Par 4
13	421	Par 4	13	378	Par 4
14	420	Par 4	14	543	Par 5
15	320	Par 4	15	176	Par 3
16	410	Par 4	16	503	Par 5
17	218	Par 3	17	351	Par 4
18	485	Par 5	18	475	Par 5
In	3326	Par 36	In	3358	Par 37

HOTEL INFORMATION

Belton Woods Hotel
Belton
Grantham
Lincolnshire NG32 2LN
Tel: 01476 593200
Fax: 01476 574547
Rating: AA 4 Star.
Rooms: 136.
Restaurants: Plus Fours Restaurant – Carvery Restaurant and Manor Restaurant – Fine Dining French à la Carte.
Childcare: Creche; Splash times Pool; High teas; Babysitters.
Hair and Beauty: Hair & Beauty Salon.
Fitness Facilities: Gym, swimming pool, steam room, sauna.
Other Sporting Facilities: Tennis, Squash, Snooker, Archery.
Other Leisure Activities: Murder Mystery.

TARIFF

From £78.00 p.p.p.n. – Double + B&B + Three Course Dinner in the Plus Fours Restaurant.
From £125.00 p.p.p.n. – Double + B&B + Three Course Dinner in the Plus Fours Restaurant and unlimited golf.
From £25.00 Single Supplement per night.
From £125.00 p.r.p.n – Double + B&B
From £115.00 p.p.p.n – Single + B&B

Special Golf Packages: are available.

Golf School Packages: also available. Please telephone for further information and the best rates.

DIRECTIONS

Follow the A1 to Gonerby Moor Services South. Turn left on B1174 towards Great Gonerby. At top of hill turn left towards Manthorpe/Belton. At 'T' junction turn left on A607, hotel is ¼ mile on the left. (Alternatively follow signs for Belton House - opposite Belton Woods Hotel).

Marriott Breadsall Priory Hotel & Country Club

Just outside the pretty Derbyshire village of Breadsall, only four miles from the centre of Derby, stands the beautiful Grade 2 listed building which forms part of the Marriott Breadsall Priory Hotel & Country Club.

All 112 bedrooms have been decorated in a traditional style, with a number of carefully restored rooms in the old Priory itself, offering guests a particularly high standard of comfort. Many rooms offer panoramic views over the old Priory Course, as well as the formal gardens and ornamental lake.

In the Priory Restaurant, created out of the Priory's old wine cellar, you'll find an array of contemporary and traditional dishes produced from fresh, local ingredients. For more informal dining, the Long Weekend Bar and Restaurant offers a wide selection of tempting dishes.

Breadsall Priory has two 18 hole golf courses, each of which offers its own particular challenges to golfers of all standards. The Priory Course is the older and, with its mature trees and gently rolling hillsides, is both highly English in character, and suitably challenging. The Moorland Course is set deep in the heart of a typical Derbyshire landscape with its open fairways threading between old stone walls.

The superbly equipped Leisure Club offers you tennis and aerobics, cardio, free weights and resistance gymnasiums. Or you can opt for an hour of indulgence in the Health and Beauty Salon.

LOCAL ATTRACTIONS

Even the non-golfing guests can find much to delight them in and around Breadsall. Only a short drive away is one of the world's most famous country seats, Chatsworth House, home to the Duke and Duchess of Devonshire and one of England's foremost 'treasure houses'. Alton Towers offers thrills and spills for the whole family. Especially appealing to lovers of nature are the simple pleasures of walking in the glorious Peak District National Park. Those seeking the products of some of the world's leading names in porcelain – Denby, Royal Crown Derby – will find many bargains in the factory shops.

Priory Course 6201 yards, par 72, 18-hole. Moorland Course 6028 yards par 70, 18-hole heathland/woodland course

Practice facilities: Practice ground with covered bays, practice holes and putting green.

Instructions: Tuition and video facilities.

Hire: Trolley, buggy and club hire.

CARD OF THE COURSE
Moorland Course

1	178	Par 3	10	307	Par 4
2	452	Par 4	11	360	Par 4
3	300	Par 4	12	406	Par 4
4	342	Par 4	13	436	Par 4
5	366	Par 4	14	145	Par 3
6	126	Par 3	15	417	Par 4
7	294	Par 4	16	475	Par 5
8	440	Par 4	17	160	Par 3
9	479	Par 5	18	345	Par 4
Out	2977	Par 35	In	3051	Par 35

Marriott Breadsall Priory Hotel & Country Club
Moor Road, Morely,
Derbyshire DE7 6DL
Tel: 01332 832235
Fax: 01332 833509
Rooms: 112.
Restaurants: Priory Restaurant; Long Weekend Bar & Restaurant; Cocktail bar, Golf Bar.
Hair and Beauty: Health & Beauty Salon, Solarium.
Other Fitness Facilities: Indoor heated swimming pool, spa bath, sauna, gyms, steam room, aerobics studio.
Other Sporting Facilities: Tennis courts.

DINNER, BED & BREAKFAST
(Mon-Sun)

Prices start from **£77** per person, per night, including a round of golf on either course. Based on two sharing.

Travelling north, leave the M1 at Junction 25 turning left onto the A52 towards Derby. At the first roundabout after approximately 7 miles take exit to Chesterfield. Straight over next 2 roundabouts, fourth roundabout turn right into Breadsall village. Turn left into Rectory Lane, signposted Breadsall Priory following the road sharp right past the Post Office. Turn left into Moor Road. Breadsall Priory is approximately 1½ miles on the left.

Carden Park Hotel , Golf Resort & Spa

C arden Park, a golf resort that ranks alongside the best in the world, is set in 750 acres of beautiful countryside. The golf facilities are unrivalled in Great Britain and include the magnificent new Nicklaus course - a resort style with 5 tee positions on each hole to provide challenging enjoyment for everyone, the 18 hole championship Cheshire course, the

LOCAL ATTRACTIONS

Being only 30 mins from junction 16 of M6 and 15 mins from the historic town of Chester, Carden Park is ideally located for exploring the many attractions and great days out that are available in the area. The Carden Estate nestles between contrasting and beautiful landscapes of the Cheshire Plain and Welsh Hills, from picturesque black and white buildings, delightful gardens, sweeping hills and historic towns there is something for everyone. And nearby you will find Chester Zoo, Chester Races and Oulton Park, Beeston, Peckforton and Chirk Castles, the Cheshire cheese experience, Cheshire military museum and Stretton Water Mill.

9 hole Par 3 Azalea course and Europe's first Jack Nicklaus residential golf school. The golf school with its team of Nicklaus/Flick accredited teaching pros caters for everyone from complete beginners to scratch players. Visitors have use of a unique range of facilities for learning, practising and improving golf including the all weather driving range with fully landscaped target area, an extensive short game practice area and putting greens. Inside is a theatre for group tuition, computerised video equipment for individual instruction, an indoor putting course and golf simulators where you can test your skills on the world's best courses. The luxurious AA/RAC 4 Star hotel with its 192 bedrooms and suites offers an interesting range of dining options to suit your mood. Carden also has an extensive Spa with 20 metre pool, wet and dry relaxation areas, gymnasium, dance studio and 15 individual treatment rooms for the ultimate in pampering. Other leisure activities on the estate include bowls, boules, croquet, tennis, mountain biking and horse riding. Carden Park offers a wide range of golf packages including playing and tuition, as well as interesting options for non golfers that include use of the superb spa.

45 hole, The Nicklaus course 7010 yard, The Cheshire course 6891 yard, all mature parkland with challenging water features.

Par Nicklaus 72 & Cheshire 72

Golf Professional: David Llewellyn
Tel: 01829 731600

Practice facilities: Covered driving range.

Instructions: Groups and individuals catered for, plus Jack Nicklaus residential golf school.

Hire: Clubs and buggies.

CHESHIRE

CARD OF THE COURSE

	The Nicklaus			The Cheshire	
1	428	Par 4	1	355	Par 4
2	319	Par 4	2	569	Par 5
3	172	Par 3	3	461	Par 5
4	522	Par 5	4	397	Par 4
5	426	Par 4	5	190	Par 3
6	353	Par 4	6	273	Par 4
7	398	Par 4	7	165	Par 3
8	153	Par 3	8	363	Par 4
9	549	Par 5	9	335	Par 4
Out	3320	Par 36	Out	3108	Par 36
10	406	Par 4	10	165	Par 3
11	430	Par 4	11	559	Par 5
12	219	Par 3	12	350	Par 4
13	547	Par 5	13	372	Par 4
14	338	Par 4	14	370	Par 4
15	393	Par 4	15	539	Par 5
16	136	Par 3	16	424	Par 4
17	352	Par 4	17	217	Par 3
18	487	Par 5	18	460	Par 4
In	3308	Par 36	In	3456	Par 36

Carden Park Hotel, Golf Resort & Spa
Chester, Cheshire
England CH3 9DQ
Tel: 01829 731000
Fax: 01829 731032
Rating: 4 Star AA & RAC, Relais Du Golf, Virgin Collection.
Rooms: 192.
Restaurants: The Seventeenth – Fine dining: The Garden Restaurant – A la Carte: Brasserie Renard – informal: The Clubhouse.
Hair and Beauty: Ladies hair dressing salon + extensive spa.
Fitness Facilities: 20 metre pool, saunas, steam rooms, wet & dry relaxation areas, 15 treatment rooms, dance studio and gym.
Other Sporting Facilities: Tennis, bowls, boules, mountain biking, extensive walks.

Ambassador Double:
£110.00 Sgl – £125.00 Dbl.
Ambassador Deluxe (with golf view): £145.00 Sgl – £145.00 Dbl.
Earl Suite: £175.00 Sgl – £175 Dbl.
Duke Suite: £250 Sgl – £250.00 Dbl.
(All inclusive of VAT)

Special Golf Packages:
Dinner, bed and breakfast + 18 holes, per person, based on 2 sharing;

	Nicklaus Course	Cheshire Course
April – September	£140.00	£110.00
November – March		£ 90.00

From the South: take the M6 to junction 10a joining the M54, Then take junction 3 off the M54 onto the A41. Stay on the A41 Chester for approx. 35 minutes. Turn left at the Broxton roundabout onto the A534 Wrexham. Continue along the A534 for approx. 1.5 miles, Carden park entrance is on the left.

From the North: take the M6 junction 20 signposted M56 North Wales/Runcorn, then take junction 15 off the M56 for M53 Chester. Take the A41 junction for Whitchurch, staying on the A41 for approx. 8 miles. At the Broxton roundabout turn right onto the A534 Wrexham continuing for approx. 1.5 miles, Carden Park entrance is on left.

ALVASTON HALL HOTEL

Middlewich Road, Nantwich, Cheshire CW5 6PD
Tel: 01270 624341 Fax: 01270 623395

HOLES: 9	YARDS: 1854	PAR: 32

MOTTRAM HALL HOTEL

Wilmslow Road, Mottram St Andrews, Prestbury,
Cheshire SK10 4QT. Tel: 01625 828135 Fax: 01625 829284

HOLES: 18	YARDS: 7006	PAR: 72

BANK HOUSE HOTEL GOLF & COUNTRY CLUB

Bransford, Worcester WR6 5JD. Tel: 01886 833551 (Golf 833545) Fax: 01886 832461

18 HOLES   PAR 72   6200 YARDS
TYPE OF GOLF COURSE: Florida style course with 14 lakes
RATING: Best Western – 4 Crowns English Tourist Board
GOLF PROFESSIONAL: Craig George
TEL: 01886 833621
B&B + 18 HOLES: £80.00 per player
OTHER SPECIAL GOLF PACKAGES: Society Golf from £30 per player

70 bedrooms, all en-suite, 2/3 bars, restaurant full a la carte & table d'hote. Fitness centre, sauna, jacuzzi, sunbed, outdoor swimming pool. Conference facilities for up to 350 delegates. Bowling green, golf course, driving range (20 bays) practice area.

BELLS HOTEL & THE FOREST OF DEAN GOLF CLUB

Lords Hill, Coleford, Glos GL16 8BD. Tel: 01594 832583 Fax: 01594 832584

18 HOLES   PAR 70   6033 YARDS
TYPE OF GOLF COURSE: Parkland
GOLF PROFESSIONAL: John Hansel
TEL: 01594 833689
B&B + 18 HOLES: From £44.75
OTHER SPECIAL GOLF PACKAGES:
Half board: £51 p.p.p.n.
Weekend Breaks: £119.00
Society Days: £29.50

Situated in the beautiful Forest of Dean in the heart of the M4, M5, M50 triangle, Bells Hotel is adjacent to the 1st Tee of it's own 18 hole course. Established in 1971 it has 32 en-suite bedrooms, conference and banqueting facilities for up to 160, bar and restaurant open all day, live music at weekends. Golf cars are for hire, practice and putting area, golf shop on site with extensive range of equipment and clothing.

BELMONT LODGE & GOLF COURSE

Belmont, Hereford HR2 9SA. Tel: 01432 352666 Fax: 01432 352717

Belmont Lodge and Golf Course offers a 30 bedroom lodge, bar and restaurant facilities as well as tennis court, bowling green and snooker room. Situated along the beautiful River Wye, yet conveniently located just a few minutes drive from the historic cathedral city of Hereford.

18 Holes	Par 72	6511 Yards
Type of Golf Course: Parkland		
Hotel Rating: AA+RAC 3 Star Heart of England 3 Crowns, commended.		
Golf Professional: Mike Welsh		
Tel: 01432 352717		
B&B + 18 Holes: From £31.50 to £51.50		
Other Special Golf Packages: DBB + 18 Holes from £42,50 to £64.50		

CADMORE LODGE HOTEL & COUNTRY CLUB

St. Michael's, Tenbury Wells, Worcestershire WR15 8TQ. Tel: 01584 810044 Fax: 01584 810044

Lakeside hotel and country club. 14 en-suite rooms (5 luxury suites). Swimming pool (indoor), gym, sauna, jacuzzi, bowling green, spike bar and Lakeside Restaurant. Idyllic location in rural Worcestershire. Aromatherapy and massage sessions also available.

9 Holes	Par 68	5132 Yards
Type of Golf Course: Valley & Woodland, with feature lake		
Hotel Rating: 2 Star AA		
Golf Professional: Mr Robin Farr		
Tel: 01584 810306		
B&B + 18 Holes: 2 Nights DB&B + Unlimited Golf from £89,00pp.		
Other Special Golf Packages: Luxury 2 night DB&B £125.00 pp Society Days from £15 pn.		

BRIGGATE LODGE COUNTRY HOTEL

Ermine Street, Broughton, Nr Brigg, North Lincolnshire DN20 0AQ.
Tel: 01652 650770 Fax: 01652 650495

The Briggate Lodge Country Hotel lies within the grounds of Forest Pines. All 86 en-suite bedrooms are equipped with colour satellite TV, trouser press, hairdryer and direct dial telephone. A 24 hour room service and a next day laundry service are also available.

27 Holes	Par 73/35	6882/3102 Yards
Type of Golf Course: Undulating Wooded and open heathland setting.		
Hotel Rating: AA 3 Star + RAC 5 Crowns		
Golf Professional: David Edwards		
Tel: 01652 650756		
B&B + 18 Holes: From £75.00 p.p.		
Other Special Golf Packages: Golf Societies welcome		

Golf facilities include the 27 hole championship golf course and floodlit all-weather driving range. Forest Pines was recently voted the best new course in England and offers challenging play across an undulating wooded and open heathland setting. Designed by PGA Seniors Tour player John Morgan, Forest Pines features a state of the art irrigation system, which combined with excellent drainage ensures all year round play.

Hawkstone Park Hotel

awkstone Park is known as the 'Jewel of Shropshire' and is able to provide the perfect location for all your golfing needs. The facility is set in 400 acres of idyllic parkland, which offers the peace and tranquillity of the Shropshire countryside within a few miles of the motorway networks.

The hotel is bounded on all sides by two 18 hole championship courses. Supporting these is a 6 hole par 3, academy course, a driving range, practice area and a purpose built golf centre incorporating a well stocked golf shop. We have high class changing rooms and Golf Professional Services offering teaching facilities for the beginner and improver. The top floor Terrace Room offers all day bar and restaurant facilities with wonderful, panoramic views over the courses. The hotel's 65 en-suite bedrooms, all newly refurbished have tea and coffee making facilities, radio and satellite T.V., trouser press, iron and hairdryer. The elegant restaurant which overlooks the landscaped gardens offers a high standard of traditional British and classical French cuisine. There is a large, comfortable snooker room with two tables and a card room and private bar and variety of comprehensively equipped meeting and conference rooms. Hawkstone Historic Park and Follies complements the hotel and golf courses where Sandy Lyle learned his game.

GOLF INFORMATION

36 (18 x2) holes, 6491/6253 yards Hawkstone - parkland course, Windmill - Links course.

Par 72/72

Golf Professional: Paul Wesselingh
Tel: 01939 200611

Practice facilities: Outdoor driving range.

Instructions: Groups and individuals catered for. Video swing analysis studio; Academy 6 hole par 3 course.

Hire: Clubs and buggies.

Green Fees: Mon-Fri from £25.00 – Sat-Sun from £32.00.

Preferential green fee rates are available for additional rounds of golf on all residential golf packages. Please enquire of details.

CARD OF THE COURSE
Hawkstone

1	374	Par 4	10	517	Par 5
2	402	Par 4	11	438	Par 4
3	216	Par 3	12	145	Par 3
4	332	Par 4	13	373	Par 4
5	371	Par 4	14	485	Par 5
6	364	Par 4	15	315	Par 4
7	434	Par 4	16	256	Par 4
8	481	Par 5	17	383	Par 4
9	188	Par 3	18	417	Par 4
Out	3162	Par 35	In	3329	Par 37

SHROPSHIRE

HOTEL INFORMATION

Weston-under-Redcastle,
Shrewsbury
Shropshire
SY4 5UY
Tel: 01939 200611

Fax: 01939 200311

Rating: HETB 4 Crown Highly commended.

Rooms: 65.

Restaurants: Hawkstone restaurant – formal, classic French with traditional British food. Terrace restaurant – All day.

TARIFF

B&B from £67.50 per room per night.

Special Golf Packages:
From £51.00 per person per night, dinner, B&B + one round of golf.

DIRECTIONS

Located in North Shropshire between Shrewsbury and Whitchurch off the A49, easily accessible from the M6 and M54. Follow the brown and white signs into the village of Weston-under-Redcastle.

Hellidon Lakes Hotel & Country Club

ituated in 240 acres of unspoilt countryside Hellidon Lakes offers 27 championship holes of golf, covered driving range, putting green and 20 buggies. Our AA 4-Star 49 en-suite bedroom hotel is complemented by The Lakes Restaurant, which has received an AA rosette award for its good food and wine.

LOCAL ATTRACTIONS

Hellidon Lakes Hotel is situated within easy reach of all the major motorway junctions, M1, M40, M6 and A14. We are approx. 45 minutes from Warwick Castle and Stratford-upon-Avon, Shakespeare country, The Cotswolds are also within 45 minutes of the hotel. Althrop House, the late Princess of Wales family home is situated in Northampton, a 20 minute drive away from the hotel. Situated 30 minutes from Althrop is the famous Silverstone Grand Prix race circuit. The historic city of Oxford is also well worth a visit with its great university buildings, scenic gardens and river walks.

Our health facilities include an indoor swimming pool steam room and spa bath. A 32 station gymnasium, solarium, one-to-one trainer and a beauty salon with 3 resident beauticians offering a wide range of the latest beauty treatments. An indoor Smartgolf simulator enables play over 20 different championship courses around the world. There are four lanes of Cosmic ten pin bowling and a 100 seater casual themed bar restaurant.

Hellidon Lakes is a haven for wildlife and for those seeking to experience the country side as it used to be. The mature 27-hole course winds between 16 lakes, ponds and woodlands in an area designated as a special landscape. The course has been carefully designed to provide challenges for the accomplished golfer while offering easier routes for the higher handicapper – making it an ideal venue for societies and corporate events, and a relaxing break for delegates at our well equipped conference centre.

GOLF INFORMATION

27 holes. 18 hole 6600 yard, 9 hole 2791 yard heathland/woodland course

Par 72 & 35

Golf Professional: Mr G. Wills
Tel: 01327 262551

Practice facilities: Covered driving range.

Instructions: Groups and individuals catered for.

Hire: Clubs and buggies.

CARD OF THE COURSES

18-hole			9-hole		
1	302	Par 4			
2	417	Par 4	1	157	Par 3
3	396	Par 4			
4	340	Par 4	2	190	Par 3
5	332	Par 4			
6	506	Par 5¼	3	270	Par 4
7	410	Par 4			
8	479	Par 5	4	268	Par 4
9	142	Par 3			
Out	3324	Par 37/₃₆	5	364	Par 4
10	233	Par 4			
11	535	Par 5	6	341	Par 4
12	427	Par 4			
13	150	Par 3	7	476	Par 5
14	400	Par 4			
15	415	Par 4	8	402	Par 4
16	419	Par 4			
17	242	Par 4	9	323	Par 4
18	456	Par 4			
In	3277	Par 36		2791	Par 35

HOTEL INFORMATION

Hellidon Lakes Hotel and Country Club,
Hellidon, Daventry,
Northamptonshire NN11 6LN
E-mail: stay@hellidon.demon.co.uk
www.demon.co.uk
Tel: 01327 262550
Fax: 01327 262559
Rating: AA 4 Star.
Rooms: 49.
Restaurants: Award winning restaurant and casual restaurant.
Hair and Beauty: 3 Full time beauticians offering full range of beauty treatments.
Fitness Facilities: 32 Station Gymnasium, sunbed and steamroom. One to one fitness trainer.
Other Sporting Facilities: Indoor swimming pool, tennis courts, ten pin bowling, spa bath, smartgolf simulator, fishing, country walks, horse riding.
Other Leisure Activities: Relaxing rock pool garden with 26' waterfall and ornate heather garden.

TARIFF

B&B – Single:
Deluxe £89.50; Deluxe Lake View £105.00; Executive Room/Suite £120.00.

BB – Double:
Deluxe £120.00; Deluxe Lake View £130.00; Executive Room Suite £140.00

Special Golf Packages:
B&B including 18 holes: Deluxe £79.50; Deluxe Lake View £84.50; Executive Room/Suite £89.50.
Single supplement of £20.00 per night available at weekends only. Book Sunday night as a third night of your stay excluding Bank Holidays from only £44.50. Extra golf is payable at £10.00 per 18 holes and £5.00 fro 9 holes weekdays and £20.00 for 18 holes and £10.00 for 9 holes at weekends and Bank Holidays. Prices are subject to change without prior notice.

DIRECTIONS

Travelling North or South on the M1
Leave M1 at junction 16 and take the A45 to Daventry. From Daventry take the A361 towards Banbury. Approx. 5 miles from Daventry (just before the village of Charwelton) turn right towards Hellidon and Priors Marston. Approx. 2.2 miles take the second turning on the right towards Hellidon Lakes Golf Course. Hellidon Lakes is on the left.

Travelling North or South on the M40
Leave the M40 at junction 11 (Banbury) and take the A361 towards Daventry. Approx. 11 miles from Banbury, just after passing through Charwelton, turn left towards Hellidon and Priors Marston. After approx. 2.2 miles take the second turning on the right towards Hellidon Lakes Golf Course. Hellidon Lakes is on the Left.

Hill Valley Hotel

Hill Valley is home to two magnificent Golf Courses. The Emerald Championship layout was designed nearly 30 years ago by the TV and golfing stars Peter Alliss and Dave Thomas. The shorter, but no less challenging, Sapphire course has matured into a stern test of the short game. Peter Alliss did oversee the construction of the Sapphire Course without actually laying down the fundamental designs.

The attractive and well shaped fairways, highlighting the very best of rural Shropshire, thread their challenging way through 300 exciting acres of trees, lakes and picturesque streams, to American style greens defended by sand and water.

Hill Valley's mature Championship Emerald Course has been home successively to world international stars, Ian Woosnam, Jonathan Lomas and Michael Welch. Additionally, Ryder Cup players such as John O'Leary and John Garner have been associated with the club in the past.

The hotel has 28 on-course bedrooms, all en-suite and can offer a 70 seat luxury à la carte restaurant and a conference suite with a capacity of 200 for business meetings and social functions. A separate bar and breakfast room is located in the conference suite area. Also situated in the complex is the Leisure Suite comprising a gym, jacuzzi, sunbed, sauna, steam room and snooker table.

LOCAL ATTRACTIONS

Just a short drive are the Welsh Mountains, the Vale of Llangollen, the Horshoe Pass and the Snowdown National Park. An absolutely perfect location from which to explore North Wales and the Border Country.

Whitchurch is only 1 hour from Manchester, Birmingham or Liverpool, or 30 minutes from Stoke, Shrewsbury or Chester, and is in the heart of Hunting, Fishing and Shooting country.

Emerald 18 hole and Sapphire 18 hole, 6628 and 4801 yards, parkland with American trapped and holding greens. Par 73 & 66.

Golf Professional: Tony Minshall
Tel: 01948 663032

Practice facilities: Driving range.

Instructions: Groups and individuals catered for.

Hire: Clubs and buggies

CARD OF THE COURSE

Sapphire Course			Emerald Course		
1	388	Par 4	1	471	Par 5
2	157	Par 3	2	405	Par 4
3	360	Par 4	3	411	Par 4
4	123	Par 3	4	196	Par 3
5	326	Par 4	5	524	Par 5
6	166	Par 3	6	187	Par 3
7	314	Par 4	7	501	Par 5
8	149	Par 3	8	434	Par 4
9	323	Par 4	9	370	Par 4
Out	2306	Par 32	Out	3499	Par 37
10	104	Par 3	1	392	Par 4
11	288	Par 4	2	390	Par 4
12	301	Par 4	3	355	Par 4
13	190	Par 3	4	477	Par 5
14	308	Par 4	5	357	Par 4
15	477	Par 5	6	178	Par 3
16	310	Par 4	7	490	Par 5
17	169	Par 3	8	175	Par 3
18	348	Par 4	9	315	Par 4
In	2495	Par 34	Out	3129	Par 36

Hill Valley Hotel
Terrick Road, Whitchurch
Shropshire SY13 4JZ
Tel: 01948 663584
Fax: 01948 665927
Rooms: 28.
Restaurants: A La Carte + Society Room
Childcare: By arrangement
Hair and Beauty: By arrangement – Mobile visitor.
Fitness Facilities: Gym, Sauna, Steam room, Jacuzzi, sun bed.
Other Sporting Facilities: Snooker, shooting, fishing and horse racing nearby.
Other Leisure Activities: Cabaret Nights, shopping trips to Chester, Chauffered Rolls Royce.

Dinner + B&B + Golf from £45 per person per day.

Society Day S/S Golf and Dinner, from £32.

Special Golf Packages:
B&B including 18 holes from **£40.00**
Residential Golf rates from **£45.00**pppn

Society Golf rates available to meet all requirements – prices on application.

With its excellent road, rail and airport links, Hill Valley is easily accessible from anywhere in the UK or aboard. Manchester International airport – 1 hour. Crewe (railway station) – 30 mins. Chester & Shrewsbury are just 30 mins down the road.

Directly off Whitchurch ring road A41/A49 well signposted 1 mile north of Whitchurch.

*T*his attractive, modern hotel is surrounded by two 18 hole golf courses, with the championship Arden Course being one of the most famous golf courses in England. In recent years it has regularly hosted The English Open and, in 1997, played host to The British Masters.

LOCAL ATTRACTIONS

One of the main reasons for staying at the Forest of Arden must lie in its convenience to the Heart of England with its many attractions. Stratford-upon-Avon, the world centre of Shakespearean culture is half an hour away. Nearby Birmingham can offer music and ballet and the NEC for trade fairs and exhibitions. Also near at hand is Warwick Castle, a magnificent medieval fortress towering above the river, beautifully preserved as a Civil War stronghold.

The Broadwater Restaurant has recently received awards which reflect the multi-national tastes and skills of the hotel's chef and his resourceful team. Alternatively, dine a little more informally in the Long Weekend Café Bar.

Both courses at the Forest of Arden appeal to keen golfers, with accomplished players enjoying the challenge of the Arden Course which winds around the trout lakes.

Your bedroom, one of 215 in total, either overlooks the celebrated fairways of the Arden and Aylesford courses or the ornamental courtyard.

The Leisure Club at the Forest of Arden offers a wide variety of leisure activities. The heated indoor pool is a wonderful escape, designed to resemble a tropical paradise. Beside the pool are the accompanying luxuries of steam room, sauna and spa bath.

Relaxation of the more active variety can be found in the fully equipped fitness gym and exercise studios. The Health and Beauty Salon offers body, nail and eye treatments as well as aromatherapy. There is even a Nature Trail for those wanting to experience the prolific wildlife.

GOLF INFORMATION

Arden Course, 7096 yards, par 72, 18-hole. Aylesford Course, 6525 yards, par 72, 18-hole.

Practice facilities: Driving range with covered bays, putting green and short game practise area.

Instructions: Tuition and video facilities.

Hire: Trolley, buggy, club and shoe hire.

CARD OF THE COURSE
Arden Course White Tees

1	345	Par 4	10	434	Par 4
2	361	Par 4	11	342	Par 4
3	527	Par 5	12	543	Par 5
4	380	Par 4	13	432	Par 4
5	180	Par 3	14	446	Par 4
6	417	Par 4	15	187	Par 3
7	482	Par 5	16	399	Par 4
8	138	Par 3	17	480	Par 5
9	423	Par 4	18	202	Par 3
Out	3253	Par 36	In	3465	Par 36

HOTEL INFORMATION

Marriott Forest of Arden Hotel & Country Club
Maxstroke Lane, Meriden,
Warwickshire CV7 7HR
Tel: 01676 522335
Fax: 01676 523711
Rooms: 215.
Restaurants: Broadwater Restaurant: Award winning, multinational food. Long Weekend Café Bar, Country Club Lounge, Spike & Fly Bar and Cocktail Bar.
Hair and Beauty: Health & Beauty Salon, Solarium.
Other Fitness Facilities: Indoor heated swimming pool, spa bath, sauna, gym, steam room, dance studio.
Other Sporting Facilities: Tennis Court, table tennis.

TARIFF

DINNER, BED & BREAKFAST
(Mon-Sun)

Prices start from **£107** per person, per night, including a round of golf on the Arden course. Based on two sharing.

DIRECTIONS

Take Junction 6 from the M42 and follow A45 to Coventry. After 1 mile turn left into Shepherds Lane by the Little Chef. The Marriott Forest of Arden Hotel is 1½ miles on the left. Birmingham International Airport 4 miles.

THE GRANGE & LINKS HOTEL

Sandilands, Sulton-on-Sea, Lincs LN12 2RA. Tel: 01507 441334

18 HOLES	PAR 70	6086 YARDS

TYPE OF GOLF COURSE: Links

B&B + 18 HOLES: (any 2 nights)
Sunday to Thursday £130.00 per person
Friday and Saturday £150.00 per person

OTHER SPECIAL GOLF PACKAGES:
2 night break (excluding golf) any two
nights £130.00 per person
Winter Breaks
19th Oct – 1 Mar 99 (excl. Xmas and
New Year 2 nights only £97.50 per person

Situated two minutes walk from the beach. The Grange & Links is a privately owned family run Hotel of great charm, our motto being service, courtesy and friendliness.

The Restaurant is renowned on the East Coast and enjoys a particularly attractive setting overlooking our own beautifully kept gardens.

The Sandilands Golf Club is an 18 hole links course, par 70 with a Standard Scratch of 69 (6086 yards). The course is noted for its outstanding greens and drainage allowing year round golf.

INGON MANOR HOTEL & GOLF CLUB

Ingon Lane, Snitterfield, Stratford on Avon, Warwickshire CV37 0QE.
Tel: 01789 731857 Fax: 01789 731657

18 HOLES	PAR 72	6554 YARDS

TYPE OF GOLF COURSE: Parkland

GOLF PROFESSIONAL: Craig Phillips
TEL: 01789 731938

B&B + 18 HOLES: £37.50 B&B (based on
2 persons sharing a twin/double room) –
£15.00 Golf

OTHER SPECIAL GOLF PACKAGES:
Two day golf break: Unlimited golf for two days
inc. B&B Weekdays £89.95p.p;
Weekends £99.95p.p
inc. evening meal Weekdays £119.95pp;
Weekends £129.95pp.

Highly acclaimed country house hotel and golf club, set within 171 glorious acres of the Welcombe Hills. At Ingon Manor you will find the finest teaching and practice facilities which include: driving range, practice bunker, putting green and PGA qualified professionals. Attached to the clubhouse are 9 bedrooms all with en-suite bathrooms, private functions and hospitality suites also available for business or pleasure including private parties, dinners and weddings, business meetings conference and corporate entertainment.

JARVIS GLOUCESTER HOTEL & COUNTRY CLUB

Robinswood Hill, Gloucester GL4 6EA. Tel: 01452 525653 Fax: 01452 307212

18 HOLES	PAR 70	6100 YARDS

TYPE OF GOLF COURSE: Parkland

HOTEL RATING: Tourist Information
4 Crown

GOLF PROFESSIONAL: Peter Darnell
TEL: 01452 411331

B&B + 18 HOLES: £65.00 (min 2nts stay)

OTHER SPECIAL GOLF PACKAGES:
£70 D.B.B + 18 holes (min 2nts stay)

The Jarvis Gloucester Hotel and Country Club is set in 240 acres of grounds. Situated within the boundaries of the city itself and a short drive from Cheltenham, the Gloucester boasts a choice of leisure facilities, including two golf courses, a Sebastian Coe Health Park and dry ski slopes.

NEW HALL COUNTRY HOUSE HOTEL

Walmley Road, Royal Sutton Coldfield B76 1QY. Tel: 0121 378 2442 Fax: 0121 378 4637

12th century New Hall is the oldest inhabited moated manor house in England. Personally run by Ian and Caroline Parkes, it is the holder of the RAC Blue Ribbon and AA Red Stars amongst many other accolades. Guests dine in the 16th century oak panelled, non-smoking restaurant where the award winning chef creates superb cuisine. New Hall features extensively wooded grounds with a croquet lawn, putting green, an all weather tennis court and a 9 hole par 3 golf course. Ideal for romantic weekends, small business meetings and as a touring base for Warwick Castle and the Cotswolds.

9 HOLES	PAR 27	773 YARDS

RATING: AA 4 Red Stars – RAC 4 Star blue ribbon, part of Small Luxury Hotels Consortium

B&B + 18 HOLES: From £136 per room for 2 persons

The Old Stocks, Stow, Glos.

Nailcote Hall Hotel

Nailcote Hall is a delightful 17th century country house set in 15 acres of parkland, ideally located just 10 minutes drive from Birmingham International Airport, the NEC and at the heart of the Midland's motorway network.

Small may be beautiful but in the case of the par 3 at Nailcote Hall, it can be very tough

LOCAL ATTRACTIONS

Being situated in the heart of England, local atttractions are Stratford-upon-Avon, Warwick and Kenilworth Castle, the Cotswolds and Coventry Cathedral.

too. Nailcote Hall was the host to the 'British Professional Short Championship' in June of this year, making this an annual event in the golf calendar when a number of European Tour players pit their wits against each other. The 9 hole Cromwell course has been specially designed to provide even experienced golfers with a tough test of their short game. All the hazards of a full scale course, ditches, water and 21 bunkers, not to mention the elevated greens, are here, with just that 1st big drive missing. Sid Mouland, 6 times Welsh Champion and World Cup player is the resident golf professional and is available to give either individual or group tuition and is the tournament director for all of Nailcote's golfing events. Famous golf courses within easy driving of Nailcote Hall include; The Belfry, The Forest of Arden and The Warwickshire. For dining, Nailcote offers the traditional style of the award winning Oak Room restaurant or the Mediterranean atmosphere of 'Rick's Bar' which provides a regular programme of live entertainment, combine all of this with 38 luxury bedrooms, superb leisure complex and tennis courts to make Nailcote a 'Venue for all Reasons'.

GOLF INFORMATION

9 hole Championship Short Course, 1023 yard parkland course

Par 27

Golf Professional: Sid Mouland

Tel: 01203 466174

www.nailcotehall.co.uk

Instructions: Groups and individuals catered for. Resident Professional

Hire: Clubs

CARD OF THE COURSE		
1	110	Par 3
2	114	Par 3
3	124	Par 3
4	87	Par 3
5	95	Par 3
6	108	Par 3
7	146	Par 3
8	106	Par 3
9	133	Par 3
Total	1023	Par 27

HOTEL INFORMATION

Nailcote Hall Hotel
Nailcote Lane
Berkswell
Warwickshire CV7 7DE

Tel: 01203 466174

Fax: 01203 470720

Rooms: 38.

Restaurants: Oak Room – Modern International cuisine – Rick's bar – Mediterranean Style Bistro.

Hair and Beauty: Kanebo Facial, body, hand nail and feet treatments, waxing and make-up.

Fitness Facilities: Roman style swimming pool, steam room, gym, jacuzzi, beauty salon championship 9 hole par 27 golf course, croquet, 2 all weather tennis courts.

Other Leisure Activities: Murder Mystery weekends, laser/clay shooting can be arranged (for groups).

TARIFF

Special Golf Packages:
2 nights DBB £189p.p. including green fees for Stoneleigh Deer Park Golf Club. Overnight golf break at Nailcote Hall £135 per room + £7.50 green fee per person.

Other Special Golf Packages:
Health & Beauty Breaks from £129.00 to £149.00 per night + "Away for a Day" breaks from £69.99 to £98.00.

DIRECTIONS

Nailcote Hall is situated on the B4101 Balsall Common/Coventry Road within 10 minutes of Birmingham International Airport/Station.

North Shore Hotel & Golf Course

*T*he North Shore Hotel, built in 1910, is a privately owned hotel and golf course situated within its own extensive grounds on the quiet fringes of Skegness, only a five minute walk from the centre, or a step away from the sea.

The golf course, one of the main attractions at the North Shore, was designed and built in 1910 by the legendary James Braid. He took advantage of the many undulations in the ground and constructed a fine three-tier, eighteen hole course, split into two distinct halves. A peaceful and calm drift from the Links, facing the sea, to a mature Parkland course. Although the course will test every area of your game, the expansive fairways are forgiving to the higher handicap player.

The hotel boasts 33 bedrooms, all with en-suite facilities, a fine oak panelled restaurant offers the finest in cuisine and hospitality. Overlooking the rolling fairways and sea and offering an extensive quality bar menu is the James Braid Bar with a full range of premium lagers and real ales, all of which are served throughout the day. The Pro Shop, public bars, restaurant and separate games room and function room are available to both members and residents alike.

The North Shore prides itself on offering excellent service with friendly staff and has been established as one of the top venues in Lincolnshire and the east coast for society days, corporate hospitality, society group bookings, golfing breaks and holidays.

LOCAL ATTRACTIONS

Less than a mile away is Skegness with beach walks, the Promenade, amusement rides, Skegness pier, with ten-pin bowling and Laserquest, horse rides along the beach as well as an abundant area of unspoilt East Lincolnshire countryside.

The historic city of Lincoln is within easy driving distance.

18 hole, 6257 yard half links, half parkland

Par 71

Golf Professional: John Cornelius

Tel: 01754 764822

Instructions: Groups and individuals catered for.

Hire: Clubs

CARD OF THE COURSE			
1	503 Par 5	10	410 Par 4
2	418 Par 4	11	157 Par 3
3	186 Par 3	12	309 Par 4
4	373 Par 4	13	358 Par 4
5	472 Par 4	14	141 Par 3
6	267 Par 4	15	429 Par 4
7	499 Par 5	16	417 Par 4
8	399 Par 4	17	349 Par 4
9	251 Par 4	18	319 Par 4
Out 3368 Par 37		In 2889 Par 34	

LINCOLNSHIRE

The North Shore Hotel and Golf Course
North Shore Road, Skegness, Lincolnshire PE25 1DN
Tel: 01754 763298
Fax: 01754 761902
Rating: RAC 3 Star, ETB Welcome Host.
Rooms: 33.
Restaurants: All day home cooked bar food, plus restaurant serving traditional English food.
Childcare Facilities: Baby listening through switch board.
Other Leisure Activities: Easter weekend, Valentines weekend, Christmas weekend, September open competition week.

B&B from £32.00 per person per night.
DB&B from £42.00 weekdays, £47.50 weekends.

Special Golf Packages:
B&B including 18 holes Midweek £49.00, Weekend £59.00.

Other Special Golf Packages:
Winter x 2 nights + 3 rounds golf £85.00
Summer x 2 nights + 4 rounds golf from £150.00

When approaching on the A158 turn left onto Roman Bank at the traffic lights (Ship Inn) and follow the road for ½ mile. Turn right just after the pelican crossing onto North Shore Road. The hotel is situated on the left, at the end of the road.

When approaching on the A52 from Boston, follow the one way system onto Roman Bank signed 'Mablethorpe' and Ingoldmelds and continue past the traffic lights (Ship Inn) and follow road for ½ mile. Turn right just after the pelican crossing onto North Shore Road, the hotel is situated on the left, at the end of the road.

Stakis Puckrup Hall

*T*his former Regency Manor House set in 160 acres of parkland has been sympathetically extended into a luxury 84 bedroomed hotel offering extensive conference and banqueting facilities, full health and leisure club comprising swimming pool, superb gymnasium, saunas, steam room and beauty treatment room.

LOCAL ATTRACTIONS

Set between the Cotswolds and The Malverns, the hotel is just 12 miles equidistant between Worcester with its famous cathedrals, Royal Worcester China Factory and cricket ground and Cheltenham with beautiful shops and famous racecourse. Stratford-on-Avon is less than an hour away, Eastnor Castle is within half an hour and the Malvern Hills, within sight of the hotel, are a 20 minute drive across country.

Balharries Restaurant offers a carvery style and à la carte menu in a continental atmosphere, whilst private dining is available in any of our 13 function rooms or 2 ballrooms for up to 180 people.

The golf course opened in 1992 and was recently re-designed to provide an excellent practice area. Tipped 'Out of the Top Drawer' in Golf Monthly May 1996, the 6189 yard par 70 course is set in mature parkland and provides a test of golf for both the novice and experienced golfer alike.

The Par 5 fifth hole measuring 531 yards requires two long and accurate shots to set up a birdie opportunity. There are three lakes and bunkers to manoeuvre the ball over and around, with superb views of the Malvern Hills.

Strategic bunkering and fairway sculpturing around dog-legs set up a fine back nine, culminating in the magnificent 18th hole. Measuring 200 yards over water with the Hotel as a backdrop, it's a finishing hole of top quality. The grounds also hold a dedicated area for clay pigeon shooting, archery and buggy driving.

GOLF INFORMATION

18 hole, 6189 yard parkland course

Par 70

Golf Professional: Kevin Pickett
Tel: 01684 271591

Instructions: Groups and individuals catered for.

Hire: Clubs and buggies.

CARD OF THE COURSE

1	337	Par 4	10	319	Par 4
2	126	Par 3	11	185	Par 3
3	486	Par 4	12	457	Par 4
4	338	Par 4	13	475	Par 5
5	531	Par 5	14	559	Par 5
6	332	Par 4	15	389	Par 4
7	160	Par 3	16	184	Par 3
8	320	Par 4	17	345	Par 4
9	446	Par 4	18	200	Par 3
Out	3076	Par 35	In	3113	Par 35

HOTEL INFORMATION

Stakis Puckrup Hall
Puckrup
Tewkesbury
Gloucestershire GL20 6GL
Tel: 01684 296200
Fax: 01684 850788
Rooms: 84.
Restaurants: 1–Balharries–Carvery & English a la Carte.
Childcare Facilities: None offered – Private arrangements can be made.
Hair and Beauty: Beauty facilities on sight, hair can be arranged.
Fitness Facilities: Gymnasium, swimming pool, saunas, steam room, fitness assessment room.
Other Sporting Facilities: Buggy driving, archery, clay pigeon shooting available by arrangement for parties over 20 people.
Other Leisure Activities: Murder mystery weekends, wine weekends.

TARIFF

£115 Single occupancy of Double room.
£130 Double room
£150 Suites and four posters.

Special Golf Packages:
Breaks from £82.50 B&B + Golf for 2 nights sharing double or twin room.

Other Special Golf Packages:
£92.50 DB&B + Golf, 2 nights, sharing double or twin.

DIRECTIONS

M50 junction 1 - take A38 towards Tewkesbury, hotel and golf club is 200 yards down road on the right hand side.

Tewkesbury Park Hotel Golf & Country Club

Set high on a hill overlooking the Abbey town, Tewkesbury Park is based around an 18th century manor house transformed into a comfortable 78 bedroomed hotel and country club.

Set in 176 acres of parkland, the Frank Pennick designed course provides a variety of challenges from wooded areas to water

LOCAL ATTRACTIONS

Visit the medieval town itself, the historic Abbey and the "Bloody Meadow" battlefield. The Cotswold villages, the Malvern hills, Cheltenham Spa, Gloucester Docks and Stratford-upon-Avon are all within easy reach.

hazards, with spacious fairways opening up as the round progresses.

The five par 5's, all over 500 yards do offer Birdie opportunities. The 431 yard fourth is a testing par 4 with a long up hill approach. The fifth is a very attractive par 3, over a lake to a raised green.

There are covered bays on the practice ground, which includes a driving range with targets and distance markers.

Additional facilities include professional tuition from our fully equipped golf shop, which also offers trolley, buggy, club hire and video facilities.

The hotel offers a selection of suites for private dining if your golf break is with friends or family. The Cocktail Lounge overlooks the course and opens onto the terrace – idyllic for pre-dinner drinks.

All rooms have panoramic views across the golf course and are en-suite, offering tea/coffee making facilities, colour TV, satellite TV, trouser press, hand-dryer and telephone. The hotel also offers a full Health & Leisure Club, complimentary to Golfing Break guests.

GOLF INFORMATION

**18 hole, 6533 yard parkland course
Par 73**

Golf Professional: Robert Taylor
Tel: 01684 294892

Practice facilities: Covered driving range.

Instructions: Groups and individuals catered for +
Swing Analysis.

Hire: Clubs and buggies

CARD OF THE COURSE			
1	519 Par 5	10	200 Par 3
2	321 Par 4	11	422 Par 4
3	503 Par 5	12	517 Par 5
4	431 Par 4	13	416 Par 4
5	146 Par 3	14	339 Par 4
6	575 Par 5	15	501 Par 5
7	128 Par 3	16	178 Par 3
8	349 Par 4	17	371 Par 4
9	352 Par 4	18	265 Par 4
Out 3324 Par 37		In 3209 Par 36	

HOTEL INFORMATION

Tewkesbury Park Hotel Golf & Country Club
Lincoln Green Lane
Tewkesbury
Gloucestershire GL20 7DN
Tel: 01684 295405
Fax: 01684 292386
Rating: 3 Star AA+RAC – 4 Crowns ETB.
Rooms: 78.
Restaurants: Garden Restaurant – Table d'hôte and à la carte. Pavilion Restaurant – Light lunches and snacks.
Childcare Facilities: Baby Listening – Free. Babysitters creche can be arranged.
Health and Beauty: Salon on site offering all facilities e.g. massages, facials, waxing etc.
Fitness Facilities: *Complimentary:* indoor heated swimming pool, fully equipped gymnasium, fitness centre, jacuzzi, sauna and solarium.
Other Sporting Facilities: *Complimentary:* 6 hole par 3 course, tennis courts, squash courts and 10 acre activity field.
Other Leisure Activities: All themed events can be organised for private parties – details on request.

TARIFF

Dinner Bed and Breakfast from £64 per person based on 2 people sharing a twin or double room for a minimum of 2 nights stay.

Other Special Golf Packages:
Dinner, Bed, Breakfast + 18 Holes of Golf £75.

Special offers may be available on certain dates.

DIRECTIONS

Leave the M5 at Junction 9 or the M50 at Junction 1. Follow the signs into Tewkesbury Town Centre, go over the roundabout and follow signs to Tewkesbury Abbey. The Abbey will appear on your left and Lincoln Green Lane is approximately 500 yards past the Abbey on your right, immediately before the Esso Garage. The Hotel is at the end of Lincoln Green Lane.

PATSHULL PARK HOTEL, GOLF & COUNTRY CLUB

Pattingham, Shropshire WV6 7HR. Tel: 01902 700100 Fax: 01902 700374

18 HOLES	PAR 72	6147 YARDS

TYPE OF GOLF COURSE: Parkland

RATING: 3 Star

GOLF PROFESSIONAL: Richard Bissell
TEL: 01902 700342

B&B + 18 HOLES: From £87.50

OTHER SPECIAL GOLF PACKAGES:
From: £49.59pp

Patshull Park Hotel is situated within 280 acres of spectacular parkland, midway between Wolverhampton & Telford and within a few miles of the M54 which provides excellent access to the major motorway networks. The 49 en-suite bedrooms are all attractively furnished and provide all expected facilities. The Lakeside Restaurant has a panoramic view of the Great Pool while Bunkers Coffee shop offers light refreshments. Designed by John Jacobs and constructed in 1979, Patshull's scenic course meanders through parkland and provides a testing challenge.

SHRIGLEY HALL

Shrigley Park, Pott Shrigley, Nr Macclesfield, Cheshire SK10 5SB.
Tel: 01625 575757 Fax: 01625 573323

18 HOLES	PAR 71	6281 YARDS

TYPE OF GOLF COURSE: Parkland

HOTEL RATING: 4 Star

GOLF PROFESSIONAL: Granville Ogden
TEL: 01625 575626

B&B + 18 HOLES: From £95.00 + dinner

Shrigley Hall Hotel, Golf & Country Club is a 4 star resort containing one of Cheshire's premier golf courses. The 6281 yards, par 71, 18 hole championship golf course offers breathtaking views across the Cheshire Plains. The back 9 holes at Shrigley are the tougher of the two nines – particularly from the 14th onwards. The 16th is a long and difficult Par 3 of 226 yards, 17 is the other of Shrigley's two "signature" holes, with a 'ravine' to carry from the tee to what is a small target fairway.

With a choice from morning's golf to a residential break, Shrigley Hall offers the usual range of excellent facilities expected from a hotel of this standard.

ST. DAVIDS PARK HOTEL

St Davids Park, Ewloe, Nr Chester CH5 3YB. Tel: 01244 520800 Fax: 01352 840440

18 HOLES	PAR 72	6750 YARDS

TYPE OF GOLF COURSE: Parkland
RATING: 4 Star
GOLF PROFESSIONAL: Matthew Pritchard
TEL: 01352 840440
B&B + 18 HOLES: £95.00 per person twin/double sharing. B&B + 3 course dinner
OTHER SPECIAL GOLF PACKAGES:
2 nights, dinner & B&B at St David's hotel, 1 round of golf at Northop Country Park. The Cheshire course at Carden, The Nicklaus course at Carden. £199 per person, twin or double sharing.

This 4 star hotel offers luxury surroundings, an ideal base close to Chester and the golfing challenge of Northop Country park's 18 hole championship course, designed by former Ryder Cup captain, John Jacobs. Alternatively, guests can arrange to play one of two 18 hole courses at sister hotel Carden Park, including the brand new Nicklaus course. The St. David's Park has 145 bedrooms and health club with swimming pool, gymnasium, wet and dry relaxation areas and a snooker room. The Fountains Restaurant has an excellent reputation or guests can choose to dine in the colonial inspired far Pavilions restaurant at Northop, with its 'international' menu.

TAVERTON PARK

Staverton, Daventry, Northants NN11 6JT. Tel: 01327 30200 Fax: 01327 311428

Hotel accommodation available weekends only, superb new clubhouse now open offering excellent facilities for society days, new 18th hole in operation from early 1999 with large water feature

18 HOLES	PAR 71	6661 YARDS

TYPE OF GOLF COURSE: Parkland

GOLF PROFESSIONAL: Richard Mudge
TEL: 01327 705506

B&B + 18 HOLES: From £65.00 pp.
(weekends only)

OTHER SPECIAL GOLF PACKAGES:
From £28.00 pp.

TELFORD GOLF & COUNTRY CLUB

Great Hay Drive, Surton Hill, Telford TF7 4DT. Tel: 01952 429977 Fax: 01952 586602

Located overlooking the splendour of the Ironbridge Gorge, the 18 hole parkland course is a popular venue, whether visiting on business or for a leisure break. Full leisure facilities are available to residents, together with extensive golf practice areas.

18 HOLES	PAR 72	6761 YARDS

TYPE OF GOLF COURSE: Parkland

B&B + 18 HOLES: From £45.00

OTHER SPECIAL GOLF PACKAGES:
Dinner, Bed & Breakfast + Golf.
£65.00

TOFT HOUSE HOTEL

Toft, Near Bourne, Lincolnshire PE10 0JT. Tel: 01778 590614 Fax: 01778 590264

A family run converted farmhouse, the hotel has 20 en-suite bedrooms. The course covers 107 acres of undulating land and affords picturesque views of the lake and countryside. Motorised golf buggies and electric trolleys for hire, practice area.

18 HOLES	PAR 72	6486 YARDS

TYPE OF GOLF COURSE: Parkland

GOLF PROFESSIONAL: Mark Jackson
TEL: 01778 590616

B&B + 18 HOLES: From £50.00 p.p.

OTHER SPECIAL GOLF PACKAGES:
Dinner, B&B + Golf from £65.00 p.p.

The Belfry

The Belfry is set in 500 acres of North Warwickshire countryside. It is in the centre of the country, close to the M42 motorway and only ten minutes drive from Birmingham International railway station and airport.

The Belfry's famous fairways and greens are known to golfers throughout the world. The Belfry is unique as the only venue to have staged the biggest golf event in the world – The Ryder Cup Matches – an unprecedented 3 times with a 4th returning in 2001. The Brabazon is regarded throughout the world as a great championship course with some of the most demanding holes in golf. A £2.4million redevelopment made it even more challenging and atttractive; holes, lakes and streams have been reshaped and several holes have been given a dramatic new look. Famous holes like the 10th (Ballesteros's hole), and the 18th, with its amphitheatre final green, will of course remain as they were.

For those who like their golf a little easier, the Derby course is ideal and can be played by golfers of any standard. Alternatively, the PGA National Course, designed by Dave Thomas is a challenge and has been used for professional competition.

The Belfry Resort is made up of a 324 bedroom 4-star hotel, 21 conference and meeting rooms, 5 restaurants and 8 bars. There is a Leisure Club and The Bel Air Nightclub in the hotel grounds.

LOCAL ATTRACTIONS

Warwick Castle, Cadbury World and the acclaimed Symphony Hall in Birmingham and the city's exciting shopping, are within easy reach. However, for extra excitement, residents receive complimentary entry to one of Britain's most popular amusement parks Drayton Manor Family Theme Park (excluding Bank Holiday Mondays). There are plenty of other local attractions and tickets for many local places of interest can be purchased from reception.

GOLF INFORMATION

3 x 18 holes, 7118 yard (The Brabazon at The Belfry), 6737 yard (PGA National Course) 6009 (Derby Course).

Par 72 (The Brabazon at The Belfry), 72 (PGA) and 69 (Derby).

Golf Professional: Peter McGovern

Tel: 01675 470301

Practice facilities: Covered driving range and putting green

Instructions: Groups and individuals catered for and full team of PGA Qualified golf professionals.

Hire: Clubs and buggies.

Green Fees to 31/10/99 The Brabazon at The Belfry £85 – PGA National £70 – Derby £40.

Winter Green Fees on request.

CARD OF THE COURSE

The Brabazon			PGA National		
1	411	Par 4	1	344	Par 4
2	379	Par 4	2	521	Par 5
3	538	Par 5	3	181	Par 3
4	442	Par 4	4	388	Par 4
5	408	Par 4	5	432	Par 4
6	395	Par 4	6	522	Par 5
7	177	Par 3	7	439	Par 4
8	428	Par 4	8	204	Par 3
9	433	Par 4	9	426	Par 4
Out	3611	Par 36	Out	3457	Par 36
10	311	Par 4	10	479	Par 5
11	419	Par 4	11	183	Par 3
12	208	Par 3	12	546	Par 5
13	384	Par 4	13	402	Par 4
14	190	Par 3	14	423	Par 4
15	545	Par 5	15	178	Par 3
16	413	Par 4	16	326	Par 4
17	564	Par 5	17	376	Par 4
18	473	Par 4	18	367	Par 4
In	3507	Par 36	In	3280	Par 36

HOTEL INFORMATION

The Belfry
Wishaw
North Warwickshire B76 9PR
Tel: 01675 470033
Fax: 01675 470256
Rating: 4 Star
Rooms: 324.

Restaurants: 5 Restaurants inc. Garden Room carvery style, Riley's Golf restaurant and bar, The French Restaurant holder of 2 AA rosettes, Leisure Club cafe etc.

Childcare: Baby Monitoring and Child Listening Service.

Hair and Beauty: Beauty Treatments available

Fitness Facilities: Fully equipped Leisure Club with swimming pool, fitness centre, squash, sauna and whirlpool.

Other Sporting Facilities: Squash, Snooker, Jogging Trail, Tennis, Putting green, Driving Range. Any on-site activity by arrangement.

TARIFF

Standard Leisure Break
Rate until 31st August 1999
£99.00 per person sharing. Includes 3 course dinner in Riley's or the Garden Room Restaurant, accommodation in a standard Belfry/Woodland Lodge room, full English breakfast and use of the Leisure Centre + VAT @17.5%

Special Golf Packages:
B&B including 18 holes 01/04/99 to 31/10/99 The Brabazon at The Belfry £175pp shared, PGA National £155pp shared, Derby course £130pp shared.

DIRECTIONS

Leave M42 at Junction 9 and follow signs for Lichfield along the A446. The Belfry is one mile on right.

Thornbury Golf Lodge

*T*he Old Farmhouse exterior of Thornbury Golf Lodge disguises a completely refurbished interior with 11 elegant and comfortable bedrooms, most of which afford stunning views over the Severn Estuary and our two courses.

The bedrooms are spacious and individually designed with traditional furniture and fittings, all with ensuite bath or shower. Tea and coffee making facilities, satellite TV and direct dial telephones are provided in every room.

Meals are available in the Clubhouse, where there is a snack bar, restaurant and well-stocked bar, all served in welcoming, informal surroundings.

There are two 18 hole courses, one of which is a Par 3. In addition there is a 25 bay floodlit range complete with video tuition bay. Golf lessons with the resident PGA qualified professional can be arranged in either group or individual format. The comprehensive golf shop carries a full range of equipment and clothing, together with club and trolley hire.

Conference facilities are also available, enabling you to combine business with pleasure. We will be delighted to provide a competitive personal quotation based upon a tailor-made programme designed specifically for your needs.

LOCAL ATTRACTIONS

The Lodge is perfect for visiting golfers or simply as a touring holiday base. Bristol is only 10 miles away and the City of Bath, the Cotswolds and the Wye Valley are within easy reach.

An ideal base for the duration of the Badminton or Gatcombe Park Horse Trials combined with a visit to view the exterior of Highgrove House.

The magnificent Slimbridge Wildfowl Trust is less that 20 minutes away.

Those who enjoy shopping will find something to cater for all their needs at "The Mall" the recently opened out of town Regional Shopping Centre.

GOLF INFORMATION

18 hole, 6154 yard parkland course
Par 71

Golf Professional: Simon Hubbard
Tel: 01454 281155

Practice facilities: Covered driving range.

Instructions: Groups and individuals catered for +
Video tuition.

Hire: Clubs

CARD OF THE COURSE

1	508	Par 5	10	394	Par 4
2	148	Par 3	11	303	Par 4
3	356	Par 4	12	135	Par 3
4	359	Par 4	13	444	Par 4
5	337	Par 4	14	158	Par 3
6	145	Par 3	15	480	Par 5
7	308	Par 4	16	327	Par 4
8	394	Par 4	17	386	Par 4
9	451	Par 4	18	521	Par 5
Out	3006	Par 35	In	3148	Par 36

HOTEL INFORMATION

Thornbury Golf Lodge
Thornbury Golf Centre
Bristol Road
Thornbury
South Gloustershire

Tel: 01454 281144
Fax: 01454 281177

Rooms: 11.

Restaurants: English Food

Other Sporting Facilities: Leisure Centre
half a mile from lodge.

TARIFF

B&B + two nights
dinner including 18 holes
of golf from £50 per
person per night. Based on
two sharing a twin room.

Special Golf Packages:
B&B including 18 holes £36 per
person per night (based on two
sharing).

Other Special Golf Packages:
Available on request.

DIRECTIONS

At Junction 16 of M5
head north on A38 for 5
miles - at traffic lights
adjacent to Rover main
dealer (Berkeley Vale
Motors) turn left towards
Thornbury. One mile downhill
opposite Leisure Centre the
entrance to the Golf Club is on
the left.

Welcombe Hotel and Golf Course

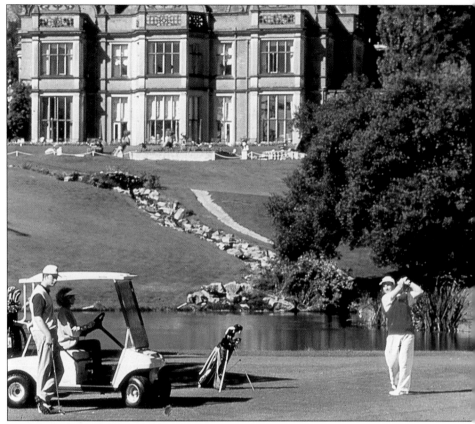

LOCAL ATTRACTIONS

- Royal Shakespeare Theatre

- Warwick Castle

- Blenheim Palace

- Cotswold Villages

- Shakespeare Tour

*E*njoying a reputation for its exceptional service and comfort, fine cuisine, traditional English country house ambience and an incomparable parkland setting, the Welcombe Hotel and Golf Course has long been the natural choice of those who appreciate the very best.

Set in 157 acres with a beautifully manicured championship golf course of undulating parkland with its wealth of mature trees and lakes, once owned by William Shakespeare, this Jacobean style mansion house hotel remains one of the jewels of the Heart of England. With a combination of luxurious accommodation in the form of 67 bedrooms, fine conference facilities, a health and beauty suite and award winning cuisine the Welcombe boasts every facility for business and pleasure.

GOLF INFORMATION

18 hole, 6288 yard parkland course

Par 70

Director of Golf: Carl Mason
Tel: 01789 295252

Golf Shop: 01789 299012

Practice facilities: Outdoor driving range.

Instructions: Groups and individuals catered for.

Hire: Clubs, buggies and trollies.

Green Fees: £40 – **Early morning/twilight:** £20

Company Golf Days welcome, prices upon application.

CARD OF THE COURSE

1	477	Par 5	10	380	Par 4
2	174	Par 3	11	201	Par 3
3	454	Par 4	12	373	Par 4
4	390	Par 4	13	390	Par 4
5	312	Par 4	14	173	Par 3
6	181	Par 3	15	402	Par 4
7	362	Par 4	16	521	Par 5
8	407	Par 4	17	400	Par 4
9	186	Par 3	18	505	Par 5
Out	2943	Par 34	In	3345	Par 36

HOTEL INFORMATION

Welcombe Hotel and
Golf Course
Warwick Road,
Stratford-upon-Avon
Warwickshire CV37 0NR
Tel: 01789 295252
Fax: 01789 414666

Rating: 4 Star & 2 AA Rosettes for cuisine.
Rooms: 67.
Restaurants: Trevelyan Restaurant (Award winning) French/English
Childcare Facilities: Babysitting available.
Hair and Beauty: Hair, Health & Beauty salon on site.
Fitness Facilities: Small multi-gym.
Other Sporting Facilities: 18 hole golf course, tennis courts (all weather + floodlit).

TARIFF

2 Day Golf Break including dinner, bed & breakfast + 2 rounds of golf **£250** per person. Accommodation from **£110** per room single occupancy. Corporate golf day rate **£105.00** inc B&B.

Special Golf Packages:
No packages – All arrangements tailored to suit.

DIRECTIONS

Situated on the main Warwick to Stratford-upon-Avon A439, 1 mile from Stratford Town Centre.

From M40, exit at Junction 15, Warwick, taking the A46 then A439 to Stratford-upon-Avon.

Whitefields Hotel, Golf & Country Club

Situated in the heart of the Warwickshire countryside, Whitefields Hotel, Golf and Country Club is an ideal base for visitors to the Heart of England. Close to the M1, M45, M6, The National Exhibition Centre, The National Agricultural Centre and both Birmingham and Coventry airports it is an ideal venue for business meetings, conferences and corporate hospitality days.

The 18-hole course overlooks the beautiful Draycote Water where water sports and country pursuits are available to visitors. A recently-opened 16-bay driving range offers state-of-the-art facilities.
Golf clubs and societies are particularly welcome.

Our deluxe rooms provide a high standard of comfort for our guests. A total of 33 rooms, 16 with bath and shower en-suite, 17 with shower en-suite, have colour TV, telephone and tea and coffee making facilities. One bedroom has been adapted for disabled guests. All rooms are non smoking.

You can enjoy fine dining and excellent wines in the Garden Restaurant or choose the more informal atmosphere of the Draycote Bar or Club Lounge.

LOCAL ATTRACTIONS

The National Exhibition Centre, National Agricultural Centre, Stratford-on-Avon, Warwick Castle, Coventry Cathedral and Rugby School are within easy driving distance. Car hire is available from the hotel.

Water sports, country pursuits, wind surfing and trout fishing are all within easy reach.

18 hole, 6223 yard course
Par 71
Golf Professional: Mark Chamberlain
Tel: 01788 817777
Practice facilities: Covered driving range.
Instructions: Groups and individuals
catered for. 18 hole putting green.
Hire: Clubs and buggies.
Green fees: April 1 to November 31.
Visitors: Monday to Friday **£18** a round **£25** per
day. Weekends and Bank Holidays **£22** a round
£30 per day.
Members Guest: Monday to Friday **£10,** Weekend &
Bank Holidays **£12** and 9 Holes **£8.**

CARD OF THE COURSE					
1	361	Par 4	10	188	Par 3
2	349	Par 4	11	351	Par 4
3	318	Par 4	12	329	Par 4
4	359	Par 4	13	435	Par 4
5	194	Par 3	14	483	Par 5
6	448	Par 4	15	251	Par 4
7	450	Par 4	16	174	Par 3
8	476	Par 5	17	314	Par 4
9	359	Par 4	18	384	Par 4
Out 3314 Par 36			In 2909 Par 35		

HOTEL INFORMATION

Whitefields Hotel Golf &
Country Club
Coventry Road,
Thurlaston, Rugby,
Warwickshire CV23 9JR
Tel: 01788 521800/815555
Fax: 01788 521695
Rating: AA 3 Star.
Rooms: 33.
Restaurants: Serves a la carte –
table de hote or bar snacks daily.

TARIFF

Special Golf Packages:
Summer Breaks –(April 1999
to November 1999):
SOCIETY DAY GOLD
(with accommodation);
Bed, Breakfast, Evening Three
Course Dinner and Golf £74.50, based
on two sharing a room. Minimum of ten
persons. £15 Single Room Supplement.
SOCIETY DAY SILVER: £39.50
SOCIETY DAY BRONZE: £34.50
Winter Breaks – Please telephone for
packages available.

DIRECTIONS

Whitefields can be
located on the A45
between Rugby and
Coventry. Birmingham
Airport is close by. M1 on
to the M45 will take you
straight onto the A45.

109

The Home Counties

The Home Counties

*I*f you were to draw a 50 mile radius around the centre of London, and just concentrate on playing golf in that area, then there's a safe bet you could do so for two or three months and never get bored.

The Berkshire, Sunningdale, Wentworth, Walton Heath, Swinley Forest, Stoke Poges, Ashridge, Woburn, Hankley Common, The Addington, Berkhamsted, Hanbury Manor, Moor Park, the list of great golf courses goes on and on. Small wonder that golfers who work in London prefer to commute into town. It's not the property prices – it's the fact they can be near some of these marvelous golf clubs.

Of course, Surrey is well known for it's golf. Wentworth, Sunningdale, Walton Heath, there are no shortage of great championship venues to play. And while everyone should try to play these courses at least once, even if it's getting more and more expensive to do so, there are a number of less well known courses where you can still get the flavour of Surrey golf.

Courses like Stoke Poges, Camberley Heath, Cuddington, Foxhills, Hindhead, Kingswood, Purley Downs, St George's Hill, the three Ws of Woking, Worplesdon, and West Hill. They're all good golf courses often lying just a good drive and mid iron from some of the famous Surrey fairways. Indeed, if you were to play the trio of Woking, Worplesdon, and West Hill over the course of a week, you would soon know what Surrey golf was all about – and you wouldn't have to travel too far either.

Or how about Foxhills near Chertsey? There are two good courses here with fantastic facilities on hand, including a new hotel extension. Perfect for a short break. Or what about the combination of Hankley Common, West Surrey and Hindhead, three good examples of heathland golf at its best, especially Hankley Common. It has shades of Walton Heath about it in places, is used as an Open Championship regional qualifying course and has one of the best finishing holes in inland golf.

Woburn has two lovely courses – the Dukes and the Duchess. Soon there will be a third – the Marquis – due to open in 1999. There's no hotel here, but there's plenty of accommodation roundabout. Everything from hotel to B & B accommodation. The two tree lined layouts put a premium on driving accuracy, especially the shorter Duchess layout, and they are always in good condition.

Nearby you will find Berkhamsted, a truly great, under-publicised course at is unique because it contains not one bunker. Anyone scared of the sand will ve this course, although there are other dangers lurking on this fine layout. Not r away is Ashridge, where the late Sir Henry Cotton lived and worked for many ars. Like Berkhamsted, this is a beautiful course in a beautiful setting that erhaps doesn't get as much press as it deserves.

Of course, being so close to the capital means that some of these layouts can e quite busy. Memberships are normally full, many with long waiting lists, owever with perseverance most can still be played.

At many, too, the lunch is an essential part of the day. To sample lunch at, y, Woburn, Ashridge, Sunningdale, Walton Heath, or any number of courses in e home counties, is to sample British food at it's best. Indeed, it's the main ason you play 36 holes – for the morning 18 you look forward to the lunch, hile the afternoon round is to work it off. How civilised.

King's Lynn

A47

A15

A47

Peterborough

Kettering

A1(M)

A141

Cambridgeshire
Moat House
Hotel

Newr

Northampton

Abbotsley
Golf Hotel

Bedford

Cambridge

Farthingstone

A5

A1

Beadlow
Manor
Hotel

Marriott
Hanbury Manor
Hotel

A43

Man
Gro

M1

A5

A41

Aylesbury

Luton

A10

M11

Stocks Hotel

St Albans

A40

M10

Oxford

Ch

A1

M2

A420

M40

Watford

A34

Maidenhead

Stoke Poges
Golf Club

Swindon

M4

Slough

LONDON

Dartforc

Reading

Windsor

B

Donnington
Grove

Newbury

Pennyhill
Park

M3

Foxhills

Croydon

Selsdon P

Wokefield Park

Coulsdon
Manor
Hotel

Woking

M25

A34

Guildford

Oatlands
Park

A22

A3

Home Counties

Page

Barnham Broom Hotel

Just a few miles west of the ancient historic city of Norwich in East Anglia, the River Yare runs through a tranquil valley surrounded by Norfolk farmland. Here lies the Barnham Broom Hotel, Golf, Conference and Leisure Centre. An extensive complex with two 18 hole golf courses: The Valley par 72 and The Hill par 71, a five acre practice ground with 3 academy holes and putting green, comprehensively stocked golf shop, and extensive leisure facilities including jet stream swimming pool.

The hotel offers 53 bedrooms all with private bathroom/showers, colour television, radio, direct dial telephone, trouser press, hairdryer and tea/coffee making facilities. The Flints Restaurant offers a full 'Good Morning' breakfast of hot and cold dishes, carvery at lunchtime and a choice of table d'hote and a la carte menu for dinner. The Bothways Buttery Bar offers a selection of light meals and snacks. The Valley Bar overlooks the terrace and golf courses.

Barnham Broom plays host to the Peter Ballinghall Golf Schools, three and four day residential instructional courses aimed at all levels of experience. Peter Ballinghall has earned the reputation as being one of the premier teachers in the game.

LOCAL ATTRACTIONS

There are many exciting and famous attractions all within easy driving distance of the hotel, including: the historic city of Norwich with its magnificent Cathedral and Castle, the Norfolk Broads, the Royal House of Sandringham, the Norfolk Lavender Fields and Blickling Hall - just a few of the many attractions surrounding the Hotel.

GOLF INFORMATION

36 hole, 6603 yard (Valley) and 6495 yard (Hill), river valley parkland course
Par 72 (Valley) & 71 (Hill)

Golf Director: Peter Ballingall

Golf Professional: Steve Beckham & Alison Sheard – Tel: 01603 759393 ext 278

Practice facilities: Outdoor driving range.

Instructions: Groups and individuals catered for. Short game facilities and 3 academy holes.

Hire: Clubs and buggies.

CARD OF THE COURSE

Hill Course			Valley Course		
1	371	Par 4	1	371	Par 4
2	212	Par 3	2	500	Par 5
3	394	Par 4	3	414	Par 4
4	432	Par 4	4	139	Par 3
5	537	Par 5	5	346	Par 4
6	135	Par 3	6	165	Par 3
7	369	Par 4	7	362	Par 4
8	402	Par 4	8	492	Par 5
9	473	Par 5	9	425	Par 4
Out	3325	Par 36	Out	3160	Par 36
10	411	Par 4	10	524	Par 5
11	173	Par 3	11	365	Par 4
12	463	Par 5	12	426	Par 4
13	409	Par 4	13	195	Par 3
14	396	Par 4	14	444	Par 4
15	403	Par 4	15	391	Par 4
16	381	Par 4	16	137	Par 3
17	152	Par 3	17	548	Par 5
18	382	Par 4	18	413	Par 4
In	3170	Par 35	In	3443	Par 36

HOTEL INFORMATION

Barnham Broom Hotel
Honingham Road
Barnham Broom
Norwich NR9 4DD
Tel: 01603 759393
Fax: 01603 758224
Rating: 3 Star AA & 3 Star RAC.
Rooms: 53.
Restaurants: Flints Restaurant – Table d'hote and à la Carte, Bothways snack bar.
Childcare Facilities: Morning Creche at Leisure Centre, Baby Listening.
Hair & Beauty: Hairdressers and Beauty Salon.
Fitness Facilities: Fitness studio, sauna, steam room, spa bath, swimming pool, tennis, squash.
Other Sporting Activities: Peter Ballingall Golf Schools, instructional courses run over 3 or 4 days, aimed at all levels of golfer.

TARIFF

2 night stay inc.
DBB & 3 rounds of golf.
July – August £167.00 pp
Nov – Feb   £125.00 pp
Additional nights available

Special Golf Packages:
B&B including 18 holes £67.00 per person sharing a twin room.

Other Special Golf Packages:
£179.00 per person 2 nights, dinner, bed and breakfast.

DIRECTIONS

From Kings Lynn heading towards Norwich on A47 bypass East Dereham go a further 9 miles and turn off to your right following brown tourist signs for Barnham Broom. From A11 travelling from Thetford to Norwich on approaching Wymondham follow brown tourist signs through local roads to Barnham Broom.

Coulsdon Manor

Set in 140 acres of Surrey parkland, a large part of it laid down as a challenging 18 hole golf course, Coulsdon Manor is just 15 miles from both central London and Gatwick and easily accessible from all parts of the South East.

Built for Thomas Byron in the 1850's and sympathetically restored, inside you will discover a country house flavour reflected in beautiful woodwork and chandeliers.

Dining is in the award winning Manor House restaurant or lighter meals are served in the very popular Terrace Bar.

The golf course is in a parkland setting with many rare and lovely trees and squirrel lovers will be enchanted by the large number who have made this their home.

Apart from the 18 hole course, Coulsdon Manor boasts all weather tennis courts, squash, sunbed, gymnasium, racketball, aerobics studio sauna, steam room and fitness assessment as well as children's climbing frame.

Only 25 minutes from London and all its major attractions and theatres, the village of Coulsdon in which you will find Coulsdon Manor provides an oasis on the edge of the bustling metropolis and is an ideal base from which to explore many places of interest.

If you want to get away from the hustle and bustle of city life, or are searching for the excitement of the big city but don't want to stay in the capital itself, then Coulsdon Manor provides the very best of both worlds.

LOCAL ATTRACTIONS

Close by there is riding, a dry ski slope, flying lessons, ice skating, ten pin bowling, indoor karting and a water park. Within easy reach there are many places of interest including Chartwell the house of Winston Churchill, Hever Castle, Thorpe Park, Chessington World of Adventure, Croydon Palace, Wisley Gardens, Brands Hatch, Wakehurst Place and Haxted Mill.

GOLF INFORMATION

18 hole, 6037 yard parkland course Par 70

Golf Professional: David Copsey
Tel: 0181 660 6083

Practice facilities: Outdoor driving range.

Instructions: Groups and individuals catered for.

Hire: Clubs and buggies.

CARD OF THE COURSE

1	318	Par 4	10	361	Par 4
2	447	Par 4	11	135	Par 3
3	170	Par 3	12	309	Par 4
4	393	Par 4	13	183	Par 3
5	537	Par 5	14	337	Par 4
6	161	Par 3	15	421	Par 4
7	326	Par 4	16	217	Par 3
8	366	Par 4	17	510	Par 5
9	476	Par 5	18	370	Par 4
Out	3194	Par 36	In	2843	Par 34

SURREY

HOTEL INFORMATION

Coulsdon Manor
Coulsdon Court Road
Coulsdon
Surrey CR5 2LL
Tel: 0181 668 0414
Fax: 0181 668 0342

Rating: AA 4 Star 77%, two AA Rosettes for high quality food. RAC 4 Stars merit awards for hospitality and service.
Rooms: 35.
Restaurants: Manor House Restaurant – Fine Dining.
Childcare: Baby Listening Service.
Fitness Facilities: Gymnasium, squash courts, tennis courts, solarium, sauna.

TARIFF

Double/Twin room only from £110.00 per night.
Marston Break – 2 nights dinner **B&B** from £65.00 per person per night sharing a double/twin room
Special Golf Packages:
B&B including 18 holes from £75.50 per person per night sharing a double/twin room.
Other Special Golf Packages:
Two nights dinner bed and breakfast including two rounds of golf per person – from £79.00 per person per night sharing a double/twin room.

DIRECTIONS

From M23/25 Junction 7 follow M23 going north towards Croydon until road becomes A23. Proceed on A23 for 2.5 miles passing Coulsdon South Railway Station on right. Just past station take right turning signposted 'Old Coulsdon, Caterham (B2030)'. Follow this road up-hill for 1 mile and turn left just past the pond, then turn left again on to Coulsdon Road (B2030 to Purley). After half a mile turn right into Coulsdon Court Road. At the end of this road you will find Coulsdon Manor.

Travelling south from London on A23 - after major intersection to Purley continue for approximately 1.1 miles then turn left into Stoats Nest Road (B2030) signposted Caterham. Follow the road for approximately 1 mile. Turn left into Coulsdon Court Road which leads to Coulsdon Manor.

THE CAMBRIDGESHIRE MOAT HOUSE HOTEL

Bar Hill, Cambridge CB3 8EU. Tel: 01954 249988 Fax: 01954 780010

18 HOLES	PAR 72	6734 YARDS

TYPE OF GOLF COURSE:
Undulating Parkland

RATING: AA 3 Star, English Tourist Board 4 Crowns.

GOLF PROFESSIONAL: David Vernon
TEL: 01954 780098

B&B + 18 HOLES: From £65.00 p.p

OTHER SPECIAL GOLF PACKAGES:
Societies welcome on application

The Cambridgeshire Moat House Hotel and Golf Club is situated in 134 acres of parkland just 6 miles from the splendid city of Cambridge and is easily accessible from major road routes. The hotel boasts excellent leisure facilities with tennis courts, swimming pool, gymnasium, steam room and jacuzzi. A well equipped sports shop stocks leading brand names in equipment and clothing. There are 99 en-suite bedrooms and Aubreys Restaurant has an extensive a-la-carte and table d'hote menu.

DONNINGTON GROVE COUNTRY CLUB

Grove Road, Donnington, Newbury Berks RG14 2CA. Tel: 01635 581000   Fax: 01635 552259

18 HOLES	PAR 72	7045 YARDS

TYPE OF GOLF COURSE: Parkland

GOLF PROFESSIONAL: Gareth Williams
TEL: 01635 551975

B&B + 18 HOLES: On application

OTHER SPECIAL GOLF PACKAGES:
On application

Donnington Grove is set in a secluded position on the outskirts of Newbury. The championship golf course designed by Dave Thomas (designer of The Belfry) is aesthetically pleasing and exciting to play. The clubhouse and hotel is located within a beautifully renovated 18th century Gothic house. Facilities available include buggies, tennis courts, conference rooms, bar and an excellent restaurant whose menu includes the finest Japanese cuisine and European dishes. A-la-carte and set meals available.

FARTHINGSTONE HOTEL & GOLF CLUB

Farthingstone, Nr Towcester, Northants NN12 8HA. Tel: 01327 361291 Fax: 01327 361645

18 HOLES	PAR 70	6299 YARDS

TYPE OF GOLF COURSE: Woodland

GOLF PROFESSIONAL: Gary Buckle
TEL: 01327 361533

B&B + 18 HOLES: £43.50

OTHER SPECIAL GOLF PACKAGES:
Golf Break Package – Dinner, B&B + 36 holes £59.50

Just ninety minutes from London and an hour from Birmingham you'll be playing golf in the tranquil seclusion of some of England's most beautiful countryside. The 16 bedroom, family run hotel is sited on the mature woodland golf course. Rooms have ensuite facilities and the hotel offers pool and snooker tables complemented by traditional country hospitality.

ABBOTSLEY GOLF HOTEL

Eynesbury Hardwicke, St Neots, Cambridgeshire PE19 4XN
Tel: 01480 474000 Fax: 01480 471018

HOLES: 18	YARDS: 5997	PAR: 72

BEADLOW MANOR HOTEL

Beadlow, Nr Shefford, Bedfordshire SG17 5PH
Tel: 01525 860800 Fax: 01525 861345

HOLES: 2 x 18	YARDS: 5763 6342	PAR: 71 73

PENNYHILL PARK HOTEL & COUNTRY CLUB

London Road, Bagshot, Surrey GU19 5ET
Tel: 01276 471774 Fax: 01276 475570

HOLES: 9	YARDS: 4110	PAR: 34

Ely, Cambridgeshire

The Links Country Park Hotel

Set in 40 acres of lightly wooded coastal parkland, designated an area of outstanding natural beauty, 'The Links' offers a warm welcome, a peaceful escape from everyday pressures and the opportunity to relax and unwind.

Proudly independent, 'The Links' has retained high standards of personal service. An imaginative menu is prepared from fresh, local produce, and extensive wine list caters for a wide variety of tastes.

All 40 bedrooms are comfortable, well appointed, with en-suite facilities. The Garden Rooms offer larger accommodation, ideal for families. For that really special occasion, luxuriously appointed executive rooms can make your break at 'The Links' a truly memorable event.

The hotel has its own 9-hole golf course, an all-weather tennis court, a nearby pony trekking centre and miles of beach and footpaths giving ample opportunity to enjoy the bracing sea air and unspoilt north Norfolk countryside. An indoor heated swimming pool, sauna and fast tanning sun bed offer year round activity whatever the weather. The hotel is also well-equipped to accommodate sales conferences and similar events.

LOCAL ATTRACTIONS

The cathedral city of Norwich with its rich variety of activity from cobbled streets of antique shops to theatres, cinemas and museum's, is only a short drive away. The hotel is also close to riding stables, a Shire horse centre, Sandringham Royal Estate, Blickling Hall and many others.

Sheringham and Cromer golf clubs are each 2 miles away and 25 other golf clubs are within a one hour drive.

GOLF INFORMATION

9 hole, 2421 yard seaside parkland course

Par 33

Golf Professional: Lee Patterson

Tel: 01263 838215

Hire: Clubs and buggies

CARD OF THE COURSE		
1	197	Par 3
2	502	Par 5
3	105	Par 3
4	426	Par 4
5	217	Par 3
6	320	Par 4
7	121	Par 3
8	265	Par 4
9	268	Par 4
Out	2421	Par 33

HOTEL INFORMATION

The Links Country Park Hotel & Golf Club
Sandy Lane
West Runton
Cromer
Norfolk NR27 9QH
Tel: 01263 838383
Fax: 01263 838264

Rating: 4 Crown, Highly Commended English Tourist Board.
Rooms: 40.
Restaurants: Edwardian Style – French, English and Seafood.
Hair and Beauty: In local village on visiting hairdresser
Fitness Activities: Planned to build gym 1999.
Other Sporting Facilities: Indoor heating pool, all weather tennis court, sauna & solarium.
Other Leisure Activities: Specialised weekends organised for winter months – Dates to be announced.

ALL LEISURE FACILITIES, INCLUDING GOLF, FREE TO HOTEL RESIDENTS.

TARIFF

Seasonal rates on application starting at **£45 B&B** per person (min 2 nights).

Special rates for golf societies – other special golf packages

DIRECTIONS

From Blakeney: turn right off A149 in the centre of West Runton following the Golf Couse sign.

From Holt: left off A148 at Aylmerton through Roman Camp to West Runton.

From Norwich: follow A140 until is joins A149 through Cromer and East Runton following Golf Couse sign.

Marriott Hanbury Manor Hotel & Country Club

Just 25 miles north of London and just 15 minutes from the M25, the Marriott Hanbury Manor Hotel & Country Club is set in 200 acres of parkland.

Each of the 96 bedrooms has its own distinctive style and surrounds you in traditional luxury yet with all the facilities of a modern hotel. The

LOCAL ATTRACTIONS

Visit the Verulanium Museum in St Albans, or the historic Houses of Hatfield and Knebworth. A little further afield is the Imperial War Museum at Duxford or take a trip into Cambridge or even London. Closer are the attractions of Hertford, Paradise Wildlife Park and Lee Valley Park.

Zodiac Restaurant was the Hanbury family's summer drawing room and serves as the main gourmet restaurant for traditional English and French cuisine. Alternatively, The Conservatory offers light and airy surroundings and enjoys beautiful views across the grounds. For a more relaxed dining experience Vardons Restaurant and Bar is ideal.

The 18 hole championship golf course, designed by Jack Nicklaus II, offers cleverly sited hazards, some of the best greens in Britain and has hosted the Women's European Tour in 1996, the Alamo English Open in 1997 and the National Car Rental English Open in 1998 - if you wish to play the course don't forget to pack your handicap certificate as you will be required to show it. A practice ground and putting green are also available.

Hanbury Manor can offer an extensive range of leisure facilities, and with echoes of ancient Rome, the large indoor heated pool and giant spa bath are star attractions, together with aroma baths, solaria, steam rooms and sauna. Tennis, croquet, dance, yoga, aerobics and a gymnasium are available plus beauty treatment rooms.

GOLF INFORMATION

18 hole, 6622 yard, Hanbury Course

Par 72

Practice facilities: Practice ground and putting green.

Instructions: Tuition and video facilites.

Hire: Trolley, buggy and club hire.
HANDICAP CERTIFICATES REQUIRED.

CARD OF THE COURSE White Tees				
1	314	Par 4	10 383	Par 4
2	529	Par 5	11 181	Par 3
3	425	Par 4	12 532	Par 5
4	167	Par 3	13 379	Par 4
5	456	Par 4	14 371	Par 4
6	164	Par 3	15 396	Par 4
7	341	Par 4	16 177	Par 3
8	425	Par 4	17 486	Par 5
9	528	Par 5	18 368	Par 4
Out 3349 Par 36			In 3273 Par 36	

HOTEL INFORMATION

Marriott Hanbury Manor Hotel & Country Club
Ware,
Hertfordshire SG12 9SD
Tel: 01920 487722
Fax: 01920 487692

Rooms: 96.
Restaurants: The Zodiac Restaurant, The Conservatory (open for dinner Friday and Saturday subject to availability) and Cocktail Bar.
Hair and Beauty: 5 beauty treatment rooms.
Other Fitness Facilities: Indoor heated swimming pool, steam rooms, sauna, dance studio with a variety of classes, cardiovascular gymnasium, resistance gymnasium, solaria.
Other Sporting Facilities: Tennis courts, croquet lawn, snooker lawn.

TARIFF

DINNER, BED & BREAKFAST
(Mon-Sun)

Prices start from **£154** per person per night, including a round of golf. Based on two sharing.

DIRECTIONS

Take Junction 25 from the M25 and the A10 northbound to Hertford. Remain on the A10 for 12 miles. The Hotel is situated on the left hand side just past the town sign of Thundridge. Stanstead Airport is 16 miles away and Heathrow 48 miles.

FIVE LAKES HOTEL GOLF & COUNTRY CLUB

Colchester Road, Tolleshunt Knight, Malden, Essex CM9 8HX.
Tel: 01621 868888 Fax: 01621 862326

18/18 HOLES PAR 72/71 6767/6188 YARDS	
TYPE OF GOLF COURSE: Lakes + Parkland & Links (sweeping fairways)	
HOTEL RATING: AA 4 Star/RAC 4 Star + ETB 5 Crowns	
GOLF PROFESSIONAL: Gary Carter TEL: 01621 862326	
B&B + 18 HOLES: £83.50 twin + £25 single	

A modern 114 bedroomed resort hotel, with extensive sporting facilities including tennis, squash, swimming, football etc. Golf facilities include practice bunkers, driving range, pitching area.

FOXHILLS

Foxhills, Ottershaw, Surrey KT16 0EL. Tel: 01932 87 20 50 Fax: 01932 87 47 62

45 HOLES PAR 73/72/27 6734/6429/1143 YARDS	
TYPE OF GOLF COURSE: Tree lined parkland courses.	
HOTEL RATING: 4 Star equivalent	
GOLF PROFESSIONAL: Alasdair Good TEL: 01932 87 39 61	
B&B + 18 HOLES: £125 pppn (2 sharing a room, 2 nights minimum on weekend)	

Just 5 minutes from the M25 in Surrey the 400 acre estate dates back to the Doomsday Book. The Manor house, the club's centrepiece, is over 150 years old. In addition to three very different golf courses, Foxhills has 12 tennis courts, a health club, spa, swimming pools, children's activities, a crèche and a driving range. For the less active there are conference rooms, luxurious bedrooms, three restaurants and private dining rooms supervised by one of the Master Chefs of Great Britain.

THE MANOR OF GROVES HOTEL, GOLF & COUNTRY CLUB

High Wych, Sawbridgeworth, Hertfordshire CM21 0LA. Tel: 01279 600777 Fax: 01279 600374
Golf Club Tel: 01279 722333 Fax: 01279 726972

18 HOLES PAR 71 6280 YARDS	
TYPE OF GOLF COURSE: Woodland and Parkland	
B&B: Single £90 Double £105 Delux Single £105 Delux Double £130	

A Georgian manor house set in 150 acres of rolling Hertfordshire countryside, which in itself has been developed into an 18 hole championship golf course. The 6280 yards, par 71 course is a mixture of woodland and parkland and provides a stern challenge to golfers of all standards.

There are 32 luxurious bedrooms all individually decorated with luxury marble bathrooms and furnished in the style of a private country house. The Colonnade Restaurant offers a wide range of international cuisine and an extensive wine list.

SELSDON PARK HOTEL & GOLF COURSE

Addington Road, Sanderstead, South Croydon CR2 8YA. Tel: 0181 657 8811 Fax: 0181 657 3401

The Hotel was purchased in March 1997 by Principal Hotels, who have added this distinctive property to its expanding portfolio of traditional hotels. Since then a £2.5 million refurbishment has transformed the extensive facilities, making the Hotel one of the highest graded in the area. The hotel now has 205 bedrooms and suites and a considerable range of conference and banqueting rooms.

The 18 hole championship course laid out by five times British Open Champion J.H. Taylor. The course is not perhaps for the novice, although it provides a stimulating challenge to low and high handicappers alike.

18 HOLES	PAR 73	6473 YARDS

TYPE OF GOLF COURSE: Parkland
HOTEL RATING: 4 Star delux
GOLF PROFESSIONAL: Mr Malcolm Churchill
TEL: 0181 657 4129
B&B + 18 HOLES: £99 DBB + 1 round golf
OTHER SPECIAL GOLF PACKAGES: Lots of packages, please call.

Thames at Cookham, Berkshire

Oatlands Park Hotel

*O*atlands Park Hotel is a four-star country house hotel set in the heart of the Surrey countryside, yet is only a 25-minute train journey from London's West End, with easy access to both Gatwick and Heathrow airports.

Oatlands Park boasts a wide range of accommodation – from the 'superior' rooms to the larger 'deluxe' rooms and suites. Many enjoy beautiful views over the extensive grounds and Broadwater Lake.

Our elegant Broadwater restaurant boasts a creative a la carte menu and an excellent table d'hôte menu. The resident pianist is here on Friday and Saturday evenings and Sunday lunchtimes.

Once surrounded by an 18-hole parkland golf course, the current owners of the hotel have long wished to return the remaining land to its former use and have done so by constructing a challenging Par 3 loop of 9 holes.

Using the profile of some of the existing holes the new course still retains the features of a parkland course. Three holes are located at the rear of the hotel along the shores of the Broadwater Lake, with the remaining six playing in front of the hotel along the tree lined drive.

An ideal course for the pure beginner, or a test of skill for the more advanced golfer trying to break par.

LOCAL ATTRACTIONS

The assets of the area are countless;

Places of historical interest include; Windsor Castle, Hampton Court, Guildford Cathedral and Brooklands Museum.

Places of natural beauty & gardens include; Wisley Gardens, Royal Botanical Gardens at Kew and Painshill Park.

Places of a sporting interest include; Twickenham, Wimbledon, Sandown Park, Kempton Park and Royal Ascot.

Places for the children include; Thorpe Park, Chessington World of Adventures, Gatwick Zoo and Legoland.

GOLF INFORMATION

9 hole, 1172 yard parkland course

Par 27

Instructions: Groups and individuals catered for.

Hire: Clubs

CARD OF THE COURSE		
1	137	Par 3
2	95	Par 3
3	100	Par 3
4	127	Par 3
5	198	Par 3
6	85	Par 3
7	106	Par 3
8	215	Par 3
9	109	Par 3
Total	1172	Par 27

HOTEL INFORMATION

Oatlands Park Hotel
Oatlands Drive,
Weybridge,
Surrey KT13 9HB
Tel: 01932 847242
Fax: 01932 842252
Rating: 4 Star

Rooms: 134.

Restaurants: Broadwater restaurant – English and International cuisine, also light meals in main lounge bar.

Other Fitness Facilities: Fully equipped 'Pulse' gymnasium.

Other Sporting Facilities: 1 all-weather hard tennis court.

Other Leisure Activities: 1 antiques fair per month on a Sunday. Various weekends throughout year – Bridge, Jazz + Golf tuition.

TARIFF

Monday – Thursday
Singles from   £111.00
Doubles from   £152.00

Friday – Sunday
Singles from £50.00
Doubles from £80.00

All prices inclusive of VAT @17.5% and Full English Breakfast

DIRECTIONS

Exit M25 at junction 11 following signs for Chertsey. Proceed along A317 following signs for Weybridge. Follow the road through Weybridge High Street. Follow through into Monument Hill to mini roundabout. Turn left into Oatlands Drive and the hotel is 500 yards on the left.

SURREY

STOCKS HOTEL GOLF & COUNTRY CLUB
Stocks Road, Alsbury, Nr Tring, Hertfordshire HP23 5RX. Tel: 01442 851341 Fax: 01442 851253

18 HOLES	PAR 72	7016 YARDS
TYPE OF GOLF COURSE: Parkland		
HOTEL RATING: 3 Crowns commended		
GOLF PROFESSIONAL: Peter Lane		
TEL: 01442 851491		
B&B + 18 HOLES: £85.00 per person – tiwn share D.B.B – 1 night		
OTHER SPECIAL GOLF PACKAGES: £77.50 p.p per night 2 nights £69.50 p.p per night 3 or more nights		

Superb location set in 200 acres of parkland, surrounded by 10,000 acres of National Trust land. Hotel and Clubhouse consist of 18 bedrooms, 2 restaurants, bar, swimming pool, jacuzzi, sauna, steam room, solarium, gym, snooker, table tennis, tennis, full practice facilities with complimentary range balls, putting green, chipping green, practice range.

STOKE POGES GOLF CLUB
Stoke Park, Park Road, Stoke Pogees, Buckinghamshire SL2 4PG.
Tel: 01753 717171 Fax: 01753 717181

27 HOLES	PAR 71	6600 YARDS
TYPE OF GOLF COURSE: Mature Parkland		
RATING: AA 4 Star + 2 Rosettes for restaurants		
GOLF PROFESSIONAL: David Woodward TEL: 01753 717172		
B&B + 18 HOLES: £361 per day (based on 2 people)		

A multi million pound refurbishment has been completed to Stoke Poges incorporating 21 bedrooms. Every room has a superb view of the magnificent golf course and gardens, designed by Capability Brown. Many rooms have open fires and private balconies and all offer exquisite bathrooms with heated marble floors,wrought iron baths and marble showers. The golf course was designed in 1908 by Harry Shapland Colt and is probably Colt's finest parkland creation. The 7th may be the celebrated hole, inspiring Alister MacKenzie to design the notorious 12th hole at Augusta. The club's facilities also include 4 outdoor tennis courts.

THORPENESS GOLF CLUB
Thorpeness, Aldeburgh, Suffolk IP16 4NH. 01728 452176 Fax: 01728 453868

18 HOLES	PAR 69	6271 YARDS
TYPE OF GOLF COURSE: Coastal Heathland		
RATING: 3 Crowns (commended)		
GOLF PROFESSIONAL: Frank Hill TEL: 01728 454926		
B&B + 18 HOLES: From £50.00		
OTHER SPECIAL GOLF PACKAGES: Over 55's ladies, gents, Xmas, New Year & Easter.		

30 en-suite rooms, bars, restaurant, snooker, tennis, further accommodation and dining at The Dolphin Inn, our sister hotel in Thorpeness village. We cater for individual golf breaks, societies and corporate days.

FFORD PARK HOTEL GOLF & LEISURE

rmouth Road, Ufford, Woodbridge, Suffolk IP12 1QW. Tel: 01394 383555 Fax: 01394 383582

t in over 120 acres of parkland. The hotel provides a rfect setting for the holiday and business visitor. For ose with time on their hands there are facilities, such the 18 hole golf course and extensive leisure club, aturing deck level swimming pool, sauna, steam om, spa bath, beauty and hair salon, dance studio, mes room and residents lounge. Golf academy now en for all categories of golfer.

18 HOLES	PAR 71	6325 YARDS

TYPE OF GOLF COURSE: Parkland

RATING: AA & RAC 3 Star/
E.T.B. commended 4 Crowns.

GOLF PROFESSIONAL: Stuart Robertson
TEL: 01394 382836

OTHER SPECIAL GOLF PACKAGES:
2 night Golf & Leisure Breaks

VOKEFIELD PARK GOLF CLUB

okefield Park, Mortimer, Reading, Berkshire RG7 3AG.
l: 0118 933 4000 Fax: 0118 933 4031

om the purpose built executive centre to the aditional Mansion House, Wokefield Park can cater r all your golfing requirements. Off course facilities clude indoor pool, sauna, jacuzzi, tennis urt,gymnasium, 250 bedrooms, 2 restaurants and rs.

18 HOLES	PAR 72	7000 YARDS

TYPE OF GOLF COURSE: Parkland

GOLF PROFESSIONAL: Gary Smith
TEL: 0118 933 4067

B&B + 18 HOLES: From £65.00

OTHER SPECIAL GOLF PACKAGES:
Corporate days from £39.00

ewmarket Races, Suffolk

The Essex Golf & Country Club

Set in over 250 acres of countryside, The Lodge is a modern hotel linked to Eddy Shah's Essex Golf & Country Club.

It has forty two bedrooms, all en-suite with remote control satellite TV, hairdryers and trouser presses. There are two suites, both with views over the 18 hole County Course.

LOCAL ATTRACTIONS

Within thirty minutes of the Club you could find yourself exploring Britain's oldest recorded town, Colchester, and its castle and zoo. Antique lovers are spoilt for choice with the local village of Coggeshall (made famous by the 'Lovejoy' TV series) just five minutes away. A little further afield is the Suffolk town of Long Melford, with reputedly the longest high street in England and a plethora of antique shops. Constable country is only 40 minutes away with the village of Dedham set in the magnificent Stour Valley. In the other direction is the town of Sudbury, home of the painter Gainsborough.

The Essex Golf & Country Club has comfortable club house facilities. The Sport Bar and Brasserie offering a full and varied menu in a relaxed and informal environment

Whether golf is your game or not, the combination of the friendly atmosphere and extensive range of things to do in the locality make The Essex an ideal choice for a short break and a good base to explore the Essex and Suffolk countryside.

Whilst residing at The Lodge, you receive complimentary use of the indoor heated swimming pool, spa bath, sauna and steam room. You will also benefit from privilege golf, tennis, aerobic and gymnasium rates. Golf and tennis coaching is available on either an individual or group basis, further details are available on request.

GOLF INFORMATION

**18 hole (County) 6982 yard,
9 hole (Garden) 2190 yard
parkland course
Par 73 & 34**

ESSEX

CARD OF THE COURSE					
1	566	Par 5	10	508	Par 5
2	394	Par 4	11	154	Par 3
3	470	Par 4	12	429	Par 4
4	351	Par 4	13	431	Par 4
5	143	Par 3	14	190	Par 3
6	395	Par 4	15	368	Par 4
7	189	Par 3	16	410	Par 4
8	523	Par 5	17	563	Par 5
9	399	Par 4	18	499	Par 5
Out	3430	Par 36	In	3552	Par 37

Golf Professional: Mark Spooner
Tel: 01787 224466

Practice facilities: Covered floodlit driving range.

Instruction: Groups and individuals catered for. Video Studio. Covered practice bunker.

Hire: Clubs and buggies

HOTEL INFORMATION

Essex Golf & Country Club
Earls Colne
Colchester CO6 2NS
Tel: 01787 224466
Fax: 01787 224410
Rating: Tourist Board – 3 Crowns commended
Rooms: 42.
Restaurants: Informal Sports Bar & Brasserie
Childcare: On site 6 day nursery. Baby sitting can be arranged, baby listening – free of charge.
Hair and Beauty: Independently run salons, bookings advisable, closed Sundays.

TARIFF

Room Only – £45 per room, per night single, £50 per room, per night twin/double, £65 per room, per night suite.
Weekend B+B – £50 per room (Single), £60 per room (twin/double), £70 per room (suite).

Special Golf Packages:
Phone for details.

Other Special Golf Packages –
Group packages available for 6 or more people.

DIRECTIONS

From A12 - take A120 sliproad off A12 signed for Stanstead and Braintree. Follow A120 for 4 miles, after signs for Coggeshall you will reach crossroads. Turn right onto B1024 signed for Earls Colne. Follow B1024 for 2 miles, past The Bird In Hand pub. The Essex is signed on the left hand side, taking you onto the airfield.

Yorkshire and
the Northeast

Swaledale

Yorkshire and the Northeast

We normally don't think of Yorkshire and England's Northeast coast as a top class area for golf. Usually our minds wander to the Kingdom of Fife, to Lancashire, Kent, Ayrshire. It takes a long time before we get round to Yorkshire and further "up coast, like".

That part of England is normally associated with cricket, good bitter and hearty lunches. Golf usually comes last on the agenda. It shouldn't, though, for it contains some of the best courses in these isles.

This is a very large area and one you won't want to whizz round. Ideally you would like two weeks to see all the top courses, so you may just have to come back another time. Shame.

If you're going to start anywhere in the Northeast, then it makes sense to start where Ryder Cup history was recorded in this part of the world. Lindrick is the historical spot in question, for it was here, in 1957, that Great Britain & Ireland, after seven straight defeats, defeated America.

It was heady stuff, back then, for the Ryder Cup had become a one sided affair. Little did Max Faulkner, Peter Alliss, Ken Bousfield and the rest of the team know that it would be another 14 matches before the Americans were overcome again.

Lindrick is classic English heathland golf. Situated on Lindrick Common, the layout is played over fairways bordered by gorse, with oak and silver birch trees thrown in. A must for anyone interested in the Ryder Cup and wishing to play one of the classics of English golf.

Not too far away from Lindrick you will find Ilkey. This also has connections with the Ryder Cup, even if the great match has not been staged there. Ilkley's fairways, you see, were once trod by a young Colin Montgomerie, the man who earned the winning half point for Europe at Valderrama in 1997.

Ilkley's professional Bill Ferguson was the man responsible for moulding the young Montgomerie's game, and the canny old pro is still there to take your green fees when you arrive to play this pretty course.

Set at the base of the escarpment that rises to Ilkley Moor, the course is wooded and the River Wharfe comes into play on the first six holes. With only two par-5s and five par-3s, par is 69. However, don't expect it to be a pushover. It isn't.

Neither is Moortown, another course with Ryder Cup connections. It was at Moortown in 1929 that the first official Ryder Cup was played. Great Britain and Ireland took the honours that year, with a 7-5 win over the Americans.

Typical of Yorkshire golf, Moortown is classic heath/moorland in character, with lots of heather and gorse to catch any wayward shot. After several changes to an original designed by

Dr Alister Mackenzie, the course now measures over 7,000 yards with a par of 72 and a SSS of 73.

Not far away you will find Yorkshire classics in the shape of Alwoodley, Pannal and Moor Allerton, all within a short drive of the city of Leeds. These are all good demanding courses, where you will have to work hard to match your handicap – just as a Yorkshireman would expect you to do.

For example, Pannal's scorecard reads to a par of 72, but the Standard Scratch Score is 73, and that's probably being just a wee bit stingy. Played over a moorland plateau, if you catch it on a windy day, as is often the case, then you will struggle to match your handicap. The same can be said of Alwoodley, especially from the back tees.

Further away from Leeds, just outside the city of York, you will find Fulford golf club. For years – 18 to be precise – this was the venue of the Benson & Hedges International Open, until the event was moved to St Mellion.

Lack of length was said to be the reason for moving the tournament, although handicap golfers will still find it long enough, and narrow, too. For the fairways aren't exactly generous. But the greens are receptive to a good shot and are usually in excellent condition. Perfect for a day out.

So, too, is Ganton, further up the road towards Scarborough.

This fine course also has Ryder Cup connections having hosted the 1949 match, when the Americans won 7-5.

Ganton is often mistakenly thought of as a links by people who have never visited the course. Situated some 10 miles from the sea, it is anything but – however, it does contain links characteristics. A sandy base and tight fairway lies will make you think you are playing by the sea when you play Ganton.

This is only a smattering of Yorkshire golf. There is more, much more. The fun is in exploring the area to find its hidden gems.

That's also part of the fun of venturing farther up the coastline and north of Yorkshire, to Northumbria. Here, too, you will find plenty of good golf to whet your appetite. From Seaton Carew in the south to Berwick-upon-Tweed at the end of the country, there are a number of challenging courses in between. Enough to make that county a separate holiday of its own. Brancepeth Castle, Eaglescliff, Morpeth, Hexham, Slaley Hall, try them all if you have the time. Particularly Slaley Hall, where the European Tour has held a tournament for the past two years. This course, too, could eventually have Ryder Cup ties for it's been hinted at by Ken Schofield, executive director of the European Tour, that this could be a possible venue for the 2009 match. Now there's a trip to think of – play the Ryder Cup venues of the Northeast. One thing's for sure, you wouldn't be bored.

Yorkshire & North East

Page

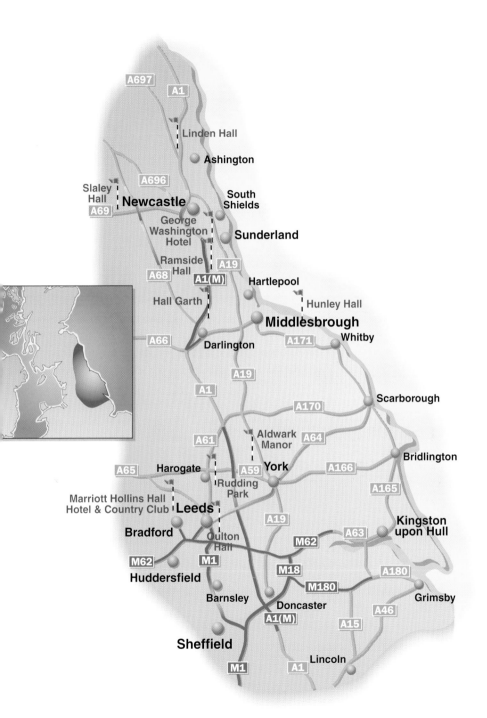

A697
A1
Linden Hall
Ashington
Slaley Hall
A696
A69
Newcastle
South Shields
George Washington Hotel
Sunderland
Ramside Hall
A19
A68
A1(M)
Hartlepool
Hall Garth
Hunley Hall
Middlesbrough
A66
Darlington
A171
Whitby
A19
A1
A170
Scarborough
A61
Aldwark Manor
A64
Harogate
A65
A59
York
A166
Bridlington
Rudding Park
A165
Marriott Hollins Hall Hotel & Country Club
Leeds
Bradford
A19
Kingston upon Hull
Oulton Hall
A63
M62
M62
M1
M18
A180
Huddersfield
M180
Grimsby
Barnsley
Doncaster
A46
Sheffield
A1(M)
A15
M1
A1
Lincoln

Marriott Hollins Hall Hotel & Country Club

Marriott Hollins Hall has a passion for golf. Our 6671 yard course is a masterpiece in tactical design. With very little land movement and a consideration for the local wildlife the course has been built in natural heathland amongst the beautiful Yorkshire moors and dales.

LOCAL ATTRACTIONS

For anyone on a leisure break this is an ideal base from which to explore local attractions such as Salt's Mill, Saltaire, Bronte Country, The Yorkshire Dales, Emmerdale Country and The Woolpack.

It is majestically challenging and classically designed in the spirit of the game.

Set in its own tranquil surroundings, the Marriott Hollins Hall Hotel & Country Club is perfectly located in the heart of Yorkshire. It is within easy reach of the M62 and a short drive away from the business and shopping centres of Leeds and Bradford. It is also only ten minutes from the airport.

Those on business will find a welcome retreat in the Hotel's 200-acre site, with its fully equipped leisure complex and extensive meeting facilities.

Hollins Hall was constructed bearing Elizabethan lines and styles in 1878. Today with the quiet tranquillity of the graceful surroundings combined with the very latest in health and fitness and golf activities, the hotel has become a relaxing and peaceful destination.

GOLF INFORMATION

18 hole, 6671 yard heathland/woodland course

Par 71

Practice facilities: Outdoor driving range (opening Summer 1999).

Instructions: Groups and individuals catered for (from Summer 1999).

Hire: Clubs and buggies.

CARD OF THE COURSE					
1	322	Par 4	10	512	Par 5
2	382	Par 4	11	455	Par 4
3	549	Par 5	12	365	Par 4
4	200	Par 3	13	199	Par 3
5	427	Par 4	14	363	Par 4
6	424	Par 4	15	161	Par 3
7	527	Par 5	16	396	Par 4
8	183	Par 3	17	344	Par 4
9	477	Par 4	18	385	Par 4
Out 3491 Par 36			In 3180 Par 35		

HOTEL INFORMATION

Hollins Hall Hotel & Country Club
Hollins Hill, Baildon, Shipley, West Yorkshire
BD17 7QW
Tel: 01274 53 00 53
Fax: 01274 53 01 87

Rooms: 122.
Restaurants: Heathcliff's restaurant (food from around the world). Long weekend Cafe Bar (informal setting).
Childcare Facilities: Creche available.
Fitness Facilities: Complimentary indoor heated swimming pool, four gyms, cardiovascular, aerobic, free weights, resistance, steam room, sauna, spa bath, activity classes, solarium, creche.
Other Sporting Facilities: 18 hole golf course – opening in Spring 1999.

TARIFF

DINNER, BED & BREAKFAST
(Mon-Sun)

Prices start from **£79** per person, per night, including a round of golf. Based on two sharing.

DIRECTIONS

Take junction 26 off the M62, join the M606 and take the A650 following signs to Salt's Mill. At the major traffic lights in Shipley follow the A6038 to Guiseley (straight across).
Continue straight ahead for three miles and the hotel is on the left hand side. From Leeds, join the A65 to Guiseley and then the A6038. The hotel is two miles on the right hand side. Bradford and Leeds railway stations are within 10 and 20 minutes drive. Leeds/Bradford airport is also close by.

Rudding Park House & Hotel

Rudding Park House & Hotel sits in the middle of its own 2000 acre estate, just two miles south of the historic spa town of Harrogate. Over the last 25 years the Mackaness family have carefully restored the estate until it has become one of Yorkshire's finest hotel, golf and conference resorts.

LOCAL ATTRACTIONS

Being situated on the outskirts of Harrogate, just off of the A658, Rudding Park is not far away from many of Yorkshire's most famous attractions.

Castle Howard, Harewood House, Ripley Castle, Fountains Abbey and the Bronte's Parsonage are but a few local places of interest. Equally the cities of York, with the Jorvic Viking Centre and the National Railway Museum, or Leeds with the Royal Armouries and fashionable shopping centres, are close at hand. Alternatively, if a more relaxing break is sought, the Yorkshire Dales are not far away.

Voted Yorkshire's Best Hotel in 1998 by the Yorkshire Tourist Board, Rudding Park Hotel provides quality accommodation as well as the contemporary Clocktower Bar & Brasserie. The large, open stone fireplace in the reception symbolises the warm welcome for which Rudding Park is renowned. The Hotel's fifty executive bedrooms, including two suites, each offer sweeping views over the surrounding gardens, open parkland or golf course.

The Hotel is adjacent to the Regency period House which overlooks Rudding Park's 18 hole, par 72 golf course. This 6871 yard course, designed by Martin Hawtree, has become known as "Yorkshire's premier parkland course". The course has won several national environmental awards, which shows Rudding Park's deep rooted commitment to preserving and enhancing the estate's natural flora and habitats.

For guests who wish to either practice their technique or take a lesson from a Professional, Rudding Park's 18 bay floodlit covered driving range and Golf Academy is open daily to all visitors.

GOLF INFORMATION

18 hole, 6871 yard parkland course Par 72

Golf Professional: Simon Hotham

Tel: 01423 873400

Practice facilities: Covered driving range.

Instructions: Groups and individuals catered for + Academy Holes (with bunkers) and Video studio.

Hire: Clubs and buggies.

CARD OF THE COURSE

1	393	Par 4	10	499	Par 5
2	384	Par 4	11	211	Par 3
3	463	Par 4	12	393	Par 4
4	442	Par 4	13	341	Par 4
5	164	Par 3	14	176	Par 3
6	533	Par 5	15	398	Par 4
7	456	Par 4	16	488	Par 5
8	202	Par 3	17	389	Par 4
9	525	Par 5	18	414	Par 4
Out	3562	Par 36	In	3309	Par 36

HOTEL INFORMATION

Rudding Park House & Hotel
Rudding Park
Follifoot, Harrogate
North Yorkshire HG3 1JH
Tel: 01423 871350
Fax: 01423 872286

Rating: AA/RAC 4 Star – ETB 5 Crown highly commended.
Rooms: 50.
Restaurants: Clocktower Bar & Brasserie – Contemporary cuisine in modern surroundings + Clubhouse.
Childcare Facilities: Babysitting on request.
Fitness Facilities: Academy Health Club – 3 miles away in Harrogate offering gym, sauna and swimming pool. Tennis and beauty treatments available as extra.

TARIFF

Leisure Breaks – Single Exec. £115 – Superior £135.
Double Exec. £150 – Superior £170 – Suite £250. Includes Dinner, Bed & Breakfast, complimentary newspaper, VAT + use of the Academy Club.
Special Golf Packages:
Golf breaks – include dinner, bed and breakfast, one round of golf per night stayed + basket of balls at the driving range, complimentary newspaper + VAT.
Single – Executive Room £135 – Superior Room £155.
Double – Executive Room £190 – Superior Room £210 – Suite £290.
Other Special Golf Packages:
Available on request.

DIRECTIONS

From the M1 or M62(M621) in Leeds follow the A61 Harrogate signs. At the roundabout with the A658 (Bradford/York road) take the exit for York, and follow the brown tourist signs to Rudding Park (3 miles).

143

ALDWARK MANOR HOTEL GOLF & COUNTRY CLUB

Aldwark, Near Alne, York YO6 2NF.
Tel (Hotel): 01347 838146 (Golf Club): 01347 838333 Fax: 01347 838867

18 HOLES	PAR 71	6171 YARDS
TYPE OF GOLF COURSE: Parkland		
B&B + 18 HOLES: From £45.00		
OTHER SPECIAL GOLF PACKAGES:		
Midweek: Sun-Thurs: £145.00 per person		
Fri-Sat: £165.00 per person		
OTHER SPECIAL GOLF PACKAGES:		
B+B Single: £55.00		
B+B Double/Twin: £90.00		

Aldwark Manor is a country house hotel situated within its own 18 hole golf course. The easy walking course is well developed with many attractive features, one being the river Ure, which meanders along the double dog leg 14th signature hole. The 6171 yard parkland course is suitable for all levels of golf. Mature Oaks, Beeches and Chestnut trees are a strong feature on the east side of the river.

The country house offers every comfort for its guests including four poster beds. The facilities include three bars, two lounges, a restaurant, Bistro Bar and a leisure complex opening in the spring of 1999.

GEORGE WASHINGTON COUNTY HOTEL

Stone Cellar Road, High Usworth, District 12, Washington, Tyne & Wear NE37 1PH
Tel: 0191 4029988 Fax: 0191 4151166

18 HOLES	PAR 73	6604 YARDS
TYPE OF GOLF COURSE: Parkland		
RATING: AA 3 Star – 4 Star RAC		
GOLF PROFESSIONAL: Warren Marshall TEL: 0191 4178346		
B&B + 18 HOLES: £50 (twin/double) £70 (single)		
OTHER SPECIAL GOLF PACKAGES:		
£60.00 (dinner, bed & breakfast + 1 rd golf – twin/double)		
£80.00 (dinner, bed & breakfast + 1 rd golf – single)		

At the George Washington we offer you a warm welcome to our comfortable hotel with its excellent facilities. The hotel is set within its own 18 hole golf course and also has leisure facilities including swimming, sauna, squash and spa baths.

HALL GARTH GOLF & COUNTRY CLUB

Coatham Mundeville, Darlington, County Durham DL1 3LU
Tel: 01325 300400 Fax: 01325 310083

HOLES: 9	YARDS: 6621	PAR: 72

rrogate, Yorkshire

UNLEY HALL GOLF CLUB

gs Lane, Brotton, Saltburn, North Yorkshire TS12 2QO. Tel: 01287 676216 Fax: 01287 678250

he club is set in over 265 acres of beautiful
untryside adjoining the Heritage Coast providing a
anquil setting for all standards of golfer. 29
terchangeable holes of golf give four varied courses
om a championship length 6918 yard, par 73 to a
ore gentle 5948 yard par 68.

he purpose built clubhouse and hotel provide a
iendly atmosphere in which to relax. Two
staurants and a lounge bar offer traditional
andards of service. Comfortable ensuite rooms,
ost with views of the course and coastline complete the facilities.

27 HOLES	PAR 73	6918 YARDS

TYPE OF GOLF COURSE: Parkland

HOTEL RATING: 3 Crown Commended
Tourist Board

GOLF PROFESSIONAL: Andy Brook
TEL: 01287 677444

B&B + 18 HOLES: From £40 per person

OTHER SPECIAL GOLF PACKAGES:
3 days unlimited golf, 2 nights DB&B
from £120.

Filey, Yorkshire

LINDEN HALL HOTEL

Longhorsley, Morpeth, Northumberland, NE65 8XF. Tel: 01670 516611 Fax: 01670 788544

18 HOLES	PAR 72	6486 YARDS

TYPE OF GOLF COURSE: Parkland
RATING: 4 Star, 5 Crown, Highly commended
GOLF PROFESSIONAL: David Curry
TEL: 01670 788050
OTHER SPECIAL GOLF PACKAGES:
Sunday Night: To include 18 holes of golf Sunday afternoon, dinner, overnight accommodation in one of our luxurious bedrooms, full English breakfast and 18 holes of golf Monday morning £85.00 per person.
Midweek One Night: As above £95.00
Two Night Package: As above £199.00

Linden Hall, a grade two listed country house set in 450 acres of private wood and parkland in Mid-Northumbria. This is one of the most splendid hotels in the North of England with a four-star, five crown highly recommended rating. The Linden Hall Golf Club and championship length 18 hole golf course is the latest addition to the extensive facilities available which also include fifty luxurious en-suite bedrooms, a fully equipped health & leisure spa, 6 conference and banqueting suites, grounds ideal for outdoor pursuits and a choice of dining in the Dobson Restaurant or Linden Tree Bar & Grill.

DE VERE OULTON HALL

Rothwell Lane, Oulton, Leeds, West Yorkshire LS26 8HN.
Tel: 0113 2821000   Fax: 0113 2828066

18 HOLES	PAR 71	6181 YARDS

TYPE OF GOLF COURSE: Parkland
RATING: 5 Star
GOLF PROFESSIONAL: Stephen Gromett
TEL: 0113 2821000
B&B + 18 HOLES: £81.00 per person, per night.
OTHER SPECIAL GOLF PACKAGES:
£100.00 DBB per person, per night.

The only 5 star hotel in the North of England, Oulton Hall Hotel is an elegant hotel surrounded by 19th century formal gardens. The hotel has a special agreement with the adjacent Oulton Park Golf Club, venue for the De Vere PGA City of Leeds Championship in July, to guarantee guest preferential tee times. The course is as varied and as dramatic as the Yorkshire countryside that shapes and influences its challenging character.

RAMSIDE HALL HOTEL & GOLF CLUB

Carrville, Durham DH1 1TD. Tel: 0191 3865282 Fax: 0191 3860399

0 Bedrooms including premier rooms and residential suites; 3 eating areas synonymous in the North East for over 30 years for good food at value for money prices; 2 busy 'local' bars, conference and banqueting facilities for over 700 in a variety of rooms, magnificent golf clubhouse adjoining a driving range and surrounded by 27 holes of golf, all just 500 yards from the A1/M.

27 HOLES	PAR 36/36/34
3235/3285/2892 YARDS	
TYPE OF GOLF COURSE: Parkland	
RATING: AA/RAC 4 Star – 4 Crowns Highly Commended	
GOLF PROFESSIONAL: Robert Lister TEL: 0191 3869514	

Hastingham, North Yorkshire

De Vere Slaley Hall

Situated in 1000 acres of prime Northumberland countryside yet only 30 minutes drive from the bustling provincial capital of Newcastle upon Tyne, De Vere Slaley Hall has in a short time established itself as one of the UK's finest golf resorts. The baronial style Edwardian stately home has been sympathetically integrated into a luxury 139 bedroom hotel with a wide range of facilities including a leisure club with 20 metre pool and gym, health and beauty spa and extensive function suites.

The Dave Thomas designed championship course is a regular venue on the prestigious PGA European Tour and has earned a reputation as one of Britain's most scenic and challenging tests. All 18 holes have a character of their own but the 452 yard, par 4 9th, played uphill through a towering avenue of pines and dense rhododendrons is Slaley's true signature hole. A second championship calibre course is due to open for full play in Spring 1999.

There are 17 highly individual bedroom suites and a variety of conference rooms. The Fairways Restaurant personifies culinary excellence while the conservatory clubhouse offers a variety of dishes at affordable prices.

Specialist health and beauty treatments are available in Slaley Spa while a well appointed leisure centre with 20 metre pool and gym provide opportunities for relaxation and exercise.

LOCAL ATTRACTIONS

The more adventurous can sample the many outdoor pursuits available on the estate. Gateshead's famous shoppers' paradise, the Metrocentre, is half an hour away as are the World Heritage sites of Hadrian's Wall and Durham cathedral. The Northumberland coast's superb beaches and historic castles are also within comfortable driving distance.

GOLF INFORMATION

18 hole, forest, park and moorland course, 7073 yards (championship), 6479 yards (mens) and 5862 yards (ladies)

Par 72 (men) and 75 (ladies)

Golf Professional: Mark Stancer
Tel: 01434 673154 (pro shop) Fax: 01434 673152

Practice facilities: Covered driving range.

Instructions: Groups and individuals catered for. Practice putting green and short game practice area.

Hire: Clubs and buggies.

CARD OF THE COURSE
Championship Tees

1	434	Par 4	10	363	Par 4
2	414	Par 4	11	565	Par 5
3	412	Par 4	12	533	Par 5
4	518	Par 5	13	390	Par 4
5	382	Par 4	14	179	Par 3
6	205	Par 3	15	331	Par 4
7	428	Par 4	16	396	Par 4
8	429	Par 4	17	182	Par 3
9	452	Par 4	18	460	Par 4
Out	3674	Par 36	In	3399	Par 36

HOTEL INFORMATION

De Vere Slaley Hall
Hexham,
Nr Newcastle Upon Tyne
Northumberland NE47 0BY
Tel: 01434 673350
Fax: 01434 673962
Rating: 4 Star.
Rooms: 139.

Restaurants: Fairways Restaurant – Modern international cuisine using only local produce. Informal meals in golf clubhouse.
Childcare Facilities: Creche available for young children most days of the week.
Hair and Beauty: Reflections hair salon, Slaley Spa specialist health & beauty treatments.
Fitness Facilities: Slaley health & leisure – 20 metre pool with whirlpool and jacuzzi, steam room and sauna with well equipped gym.
Other Sporting Facilities: 2nd championship 18 hole golf course opening 1999. Premier leisure outdoor pursuit centre based on site with full range of activities.

TARIFF

Special Golf Packages:
SUNDAY DRIVER break –
£109pp inc B&B + 2 rounds of golf.
FAIRWAYS BREAK –
£110pp inc B&B + 1 round of golf MIDWEEK. £120pp WEEKENDS. (rates based upon double/twin occupancy).

PACKAGES ARE SUBJECT TO AVAILABILITY

DIRECTIONS

Travelling north on the A1. As the A1 bypasses Newcastle upon Tyne take the A69 signed to Hexham. Continue on this road to the 'Styford' roundabout. Take the first exit left signed A68 to Darlington. Continue to the next roundabout from here Slaley hall is signed. Continue on to A68 to Kiln Pit Hill, follow the sign turn right. Continue on this road until the entrance to Slaley Hall is on the left.

Lancashire and Cumbria

Lancashire and Cumbria

*T*he Kingdom of Fife, courtesy of St Andrews, will always be the Home of Golf in the British Isles, but the capital of British golf arguably lies some 200 miles to the South.

We're talking Lancashire here, as in the Royal courses of Birkdale, Lytham & St Annes, Liverpool, as in Southport & Ainsdale, Hillside, Formby, Fairhaven, Wallasey, West Lancashire and St Annes Old Links, a truly formidable cast of great courses which you will struggle to find on any coastline anywhere in the world, let alone around the British Isles.

Twenty seven times the Open Championship has been played on this coast-line, starting at Hoylake (now Royal Liverpool) back in 1897, when amateur Harold Hilton won the championship. Hoylake staged the event 10 times before it was taken off the rota, while Royal Birkdale (8) and Royal Lytham & St Annes (9) has staged the grand old event 17 times between them.

In addition to the Open Championship, though, the Lancashire links have been host to six Ryder Cups as well as numerous amateur championships and other big events, professional and amateur.

This stretch of coastline has some of the best traditional links golf you are likely to find anywhere. Beautiful turf, towering sand dunes, pot bunkers, gorse and the most important element of all – wind.

Don't be too hung up on trying to play the big championship venues. Play them by all means, but don't miss the many hidden gems nearby. Courses like Formby, Hillside, West Lancashire and Wallasey don't quite get the same billing as their nearby neighbours, but what wonderful golf you will find there.

Don't think, though, that all of Lancashire is a series of giant sand dunes with fairways running in between. There are some good inland courses to be found in the capital of British golf. Take Pleasington, for example, or Clitheroe. The former is a delightful parkland course near Blackburn that many rate as one of the best inland courses in the north of England. Clitheroe is another good course that sits on the edge of the Forest of Bowland. While Heswall in the Wirral is another good parkland challenge beside the River Dee that offers fine views of the far Welsh Hills.

So don't just go to the seaside when you head for Lancashire. Take a look inland as well, you're sure to be surprised.

Similarly, if you travel further up the coast into Cumbria, head for the coast and you'll find Seascale and Silloth-on-Solway. The former is an underrated links that needs to be played, even if it lies near the nuclear installation of the same name. Silloth, on the other hand is one of the best courses in the north of England, a links that is not so well known because of its remote location some 25 miles to the West of Carlisle.

Inland in Cumbria you will find the golf courses of the Lake District. Windermere, Keswick, Kendal and Penrith all provide a most pleasant day out, with views that are almost unmatched anywhere.

Lancashire and Cumbria

Page

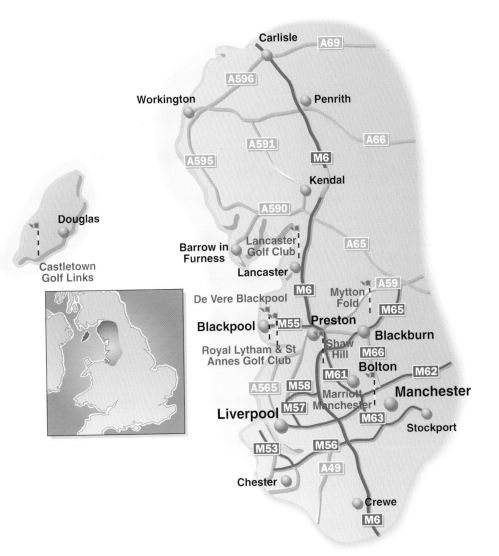

155

Marriott Manchester Hotel & Country Club

T he Marriott Manchester Hotel & Country Club is sited in the leafy suburb of Worsley in over 200 acres of parkland. Listed Victorian farm buildings form the basis of a £16 million development to suit all business and leisure needs.

LOCAL ATTRACTIONS

Granada Studios – television and themed visitor centre with "on set" tours.
Manchester Evening News Arena & NYNEX.
Trafford Centre – the ultimate in the indoor shopping experience with the only Selfridges outside London.
Manchester United & City FCs
Tatton Park – stately home, gardens and deer park.
Jodrell Bank – observatory and scientific centre
Close to Lake District and Yorkshire Dales.

The golf course offers a challenge to golfers of all abilities, requiring brains instead of brawn to make a successful score.

Try one of our stable block conversions or loft bedrooms overlooking the 1st tee and 18th green. All rooms offer minibars, trouser press, ironing centres, tea/coffee, fax/modem satellite and guestlink TV.

Dine in the relaxing atmosphere of the Club Cafe Bar overlooking the 18th from a selection of hot and cold snacks. Alternatively with views across to the Elizabethan Worsley Old Hall, Brindley's AA Rosette Award Winning Restaurant offers carvery buffet breakfast and lunch, turning to a la carte dining to suit all palates in the evening.

Drive out all those stress and tensions and have a work out in our 450sq metres of the latest cardio-vascular, resistance and free weights. Let our fitness instructors put you through a fitness programme designed to suit you and perhaps try one of our aerobic, yoga or step classes. Then relax in our spa bath, sauna or steam room or let our Beauty Therapists pamper you with a Decleor massage or treatment.

GOLF INFORMATION

PGA Championship 18 hole, 6689 yard heathland/woodland course Par 71

Practice facilities: Practice grounds.

Instructions: Tuition Available.

Hire: Trolley, Buggy, Clubs and Shoes.

CARD OF THE COURSE

1	433	Par 4	10	416	Par 4
2	372	Par 4	11	202	Par 3
3	461	Par 4	12	319	Par 4
4	186	Par 3	13	560	Par 5
5	560	Par 5	14	165	Par 3
6	545	Par 5	15	432	Par 4
7	179	Par 3	16	408	Par 4
8	421	Par 4	17	295	Par 4
9	208	Par 3	18	480	Par 5
Out	3365	Par 35	In	3324	Par 36

HOTEL INFORMATION

Marriott Manchester Hotel & Country Club
Worsley Park, Worsley,
Manchester M28 2QT
Tel: 0161 975 2000
Fax: 0161 799 6341

Rooms: 159.
Restaurants: Brindley's Restaurant and Club Cafe Bar.
Hair and Beauty: Health & Beauty Salon.
Other Fitness Facilities: 20 metre indoor heated pool, poolside mixed sauna, steam room and spa bath, solariums, 450sq metre cardiovascular, free weights and resistance gymnasium, fitness studio.
Other Sporting Facilities: Full size football pitch.

TARIFF

LEISURE BREAK
Mar – Nov '99 (Fri-Sun)
£54.00 B&B
£69.00 DB&B

Dec – Feb '00 (Fri-Sun)
£44.00 B&B
£59.00 DB&B

GOLF BREAK
May – Nov '99 (Fri-Sun) £99.00 DB&B.
Dec – Feb '00 (Fri-Sun) £89.00 DB&B.

Prices are per person per night. A single supplement of £30 per person per night applies.

DIRECTIONS

From the South: Take the M6 then M62 which become M60 heading towards Leeds. Exit at Junction 13 signposted Worsley. Go straight ahead at the first roundabout taking the A575 and the hotel is 400 yards on the left.
From the North: Take the M60 and exit at Junction 13. Take the fourth exit, the A572 towards Leigh. Take the third exit at the next roundabout. Follow the A575 and the hotel is 400 yards on the left.

CASTLETOWN GOLF LINKS HOTEL

Derby Haven, Isle of Man IM9 1VA. Tel: 01624 822201 Fax: 01624 824633

18 HOLES	PAR 72	6750 YARDS

TYPE OF GOLF COURSE: Links

RATING: 3 Star

GOLF PROFESSIONAL: Murray Crowe

TEL: 01634 822211

B&B + 18 HOLES: From £65.00 p.p.

Family run 3 star hotel, quiet location, surrounded by the sea with stunning views. No public transport – so car recommended.

THE DE VERE BLACKPOOL HOTEL

East Park Drive, Blackpool FY3 8LL. Tel: 01253 838866 Fax: 01253 798800

18 HOLES	PAR 72	6401 YARDS

TYPE OF GOLF COURSE: Parkland

GREENFEES:

£30.00 Monday – Friday

£35.00 Weekends and Bank Holiday

The De Vere Blackpool hotel is set in 236 acres of parkland and offers 164 bedrooms, 3 restaurants, 5 bars, swimming pool, tennis, snooker, squash, sauna, beauty room, gym and aerobics studio.

The Herons Reach Golf Course was designed by former Ryder Cup stars, Peter Allis and Clive Clark, and has staged five PGA events and a Schools International. The course is maturing into a true test of golf for players of all abilities, with eleven man-made lakes and thousands of trees it is a course with considerable aesthetic landscaping.

LANCASTER GOLF CLUB

Ashton Hall, Ashton with Stodday, Lancaster LA2 0AJ. Tel: 01524 751247 Fax: 01524 752742

18 HOLES	PAR 71	6500 YARDS

TYPE OF GOLF COURSE: Parkland

GOLF PROFESSIONAL: David Sutcliffe
TEL: 01524 751802

OTHER SPECIAL GOLF PACKAGES:
Minimum 2 night stay golf breaks
Visiting party groups taken Mon-Fri

Dormy, 10 Bedrooms and 18 beds.

House of Manannan, Peel, Isle of Man

MYTTON FOLD HOTEL & GOLF COMPLEX

Whalley Road, Langho, Blackburn BB6 84B. Tel: 01254 240662 Fax: 01254 248119

18 HOLES	PAR 72	6217 YARDS

TYPE OF GOLF COURSE: Parkland

RATING: RAC 3 Star, E.T.B. 4 Crowns

GOLF PROFESSIONAL: Gary P. Coope
TEL: 01254 245392

B&B + 18 HOLES: From – Single £50, Double £85.

OTHER SPECIAL GOLF PACKAGES:
Short Break: £90.00 pp, 2ngts stay, dinner each evening, bed and Farmhouse breakfast.

Mytton Fold is situated between the villages of Langho & Whalley, the gateway to the beautiful Ribble Valley. The hotel opened its 18 hole golf course in 1994 which is 6217 yards, par 72. Mytton Fold has won the best kept hotel trophy in the Lancashire Best Kept Village competition, it has also won the top hotel award in the North West area of the 'England for Excellence' awards. Mytton Fold is only 6 miles from Blackburn & Clitheroe, 8 miles from Burnley & 10 miles from Preston and the M6.

ROYAL LYTHAM & ST ANNES GOLF CLUB

Links Gate, Lytham St Annes, Lancashire FY8 3LQ
Tel: 01253 724206 Fax: 01253 780946

HOLES: 18	YARDS: 6685	PAR: 71

Shaw Hill Hotel, Golf & Country Club

*T*he golfing enthusiast will not be disappointed by the challenging 18 hole championship course at Shaw Hill, made all the more interesting by the fine landscaping and interesting design features. There are lakes on seven holes although the 18th is agreed to be the hardest, with a stream and lake strategically placed to catch any wayward drive.

LOCAL ATTRACTIONS

There are many local attractions within a short distance from Shaw Hill. Botany Bay hosts a feast of Craft Shops, Antique Amusement Arcade, a Museum, Restaurants and much more. Blackpool is 30 minutes away boasting its famous Tower Landmark and Pleasure Beach. Manchester is nearby for exquisite Restaurants and fabulous shopping opportunities at the newly opened Trafford Centre. Alternatively the surrounding countryside has many magnificent old houses such as Houghton Towers where Sirloin was knighted or Chingle Hall said to be the most haunted house in England.

A new wing has been added to the Georgian mansion, whilst still managing to convey the elegance of the original building.

The hotel has three classes of rooms. The best rooms overlook the golf course. The executive rooms are of somewhat smaller size, but still have some views of the course. All the rooms in this category have been recently refurbished to a high standard, no rooms are the same and each has its own individual style as can be expected of a country house of this high calibre. Whilst not having a view of the course, the standard rooms are very comfortable. All have en-suite bathrooms, direct dial telephone, television and radio.

The Vardons à la carte restaurant overlooking the golf course has attained an enviable reputation for its cuisine and extensive wine list. The beautifully decorated lounge with its warm and welcoming fire is filled with comfortable settees and chairs, a place in which to relax whilst having a drink or choosing from the menu.

GOLF INFORMATION

18 hole, 6239 yard wooded parkland course with water

Par 72

Golf Professional: David Clarke
Tel: 01257 279222

Instructions: Groups and individuals catered for.

Hire: Clubs, buggies and trollies.

CARD OF THE COURSE					
1	253	Par 4	10	206	Par 3
2	180	Par 3	11	360	Par 4
3	369	Par 4	12	405	Par 4
4	481	Par 5	13	379	Par 4
5	334	Par 4	14	517	Par 5
6	159	Par 3	15	468	Par 4
7	311	Par 4	16	143	Par 3
8	397	Par 4	17	498	Par 5
9	382	Par 4	18	397	Par 4
Out	2866	Par 35	In	3373	Par 36

HOTEL INFORMATION

Shaw Hill Hotel,
Golf & Country Club
Preston Road, Whittle-le-Woods,
Nr Chorley, Lancs PR6 7PP
Tel: 01257 269221
Fax: 01257 261223

Rating: 3 Star.

Rooms: 30.

Restaurants: Vardons Restaurant – Full à la Carte & Table d'Hote Menus available.

Hair and Beauty: Hairdressers & Beauty Salon.

Fitness Facilities: Indoor Heated Swimming Pool, Spa, Sauna, Steam Room, Hi-Tec Gym, Sun Beds, Toning Tables, Aerobics Studio and Sports Injury Clinic.

TARIFF

MINI BREAKS:
2-Nights – Dinner, Bed & Breakfast + 1 complimentary round of golf per day.

1 April – 31 May 1999
from £155.00 per person
(based on 2 people sharing).

1 June – 30 Sept 1999 from £170.00 per person
(based on 2 people sharing).

1 October – 31 March 2000 from £135.00 per person (based on 2 people sharing).

For single occupancy there will be a supplement from £45.00 for 2 nights. Extra nights are from £55.00 per person.

DIRECTIONS

2 miles from Junction 28 of M6 just off the A6 towards Chorley.

2 miles from Junction 8 of M61 just off the A6 towards Preston.

Wales

Cardiff City Hall

Wales

*I*t's taken the Welsh Tourist Board a little while, but finally they have woken up to one of their prime assets – golf.

Of course, a lot of golfers have known about the charms of Welsh golf for years. Aberdovey, Royal St David's, Royal Porthcawl, Southerdown, Tenby, Pennard, Porthmadog, Nefyn & District, Borth & Ynyslas, there are a host of good golf clubs in the province. Indeed, there are now over 170 and counting. For a long time there was just over 100, but a building boom has taken place that has seen golf become an ever increasing use of Welsh leisure time.

The Welsh Tourist Board has realised what has been under their nose for so long and is now pushing golf as part of its campaign to attract visitors to the country.

There are a number of attractions to travelling to Wales rather than some of the other more well known golf destinations in the British Isles. For a start it's still not a hugely popular place for golfers to visit, meaning you can usually get a game even in mid-summer. Secondly it is fairly easy to get to from most parts of the UK. Thirdly it has a host of hotels and B & Bs where the welcome is genuine and the prices won't break the bank.

Golfers travelling to Wales are advised to travel the entire coastline – from North to South or South to North, depending where you hail from – to get a true sample of the golf on offer. Okay, so you might not make it in one trip. Fine, it just means you'll have to go back. Pity.

Let's start in the South, if only because the jewel of Welsh golf lies there.

Royal Porthcawl is the gem on offer, a links course that has hosted numerous championships over the years. For example, it was venue for the 1995 Walker Cup, when Great Britain & Ireland defeated an American side that contained Tiger Woods. That Woods was not able to master the Porthcawl links should tell you that it isn't a course to be toyed with.

Porthcawl isn't blessed with the towering sand dunes typical of some links courses. Nor do the fairways seem to ripple and roll as they do on other traditional links. In fact, looking at it from the clubhouse, it looks fairly tame. It isn't. The absence of huge dunes means every hole at Porthcawl is exposed, so that when the wind blows it sweeps over the entire course. As the American Walker Cup team found to their horror, this is links to be treated with respect.

That's fairly typical of links golf in Wales. Aberdovey is another links course you must respect if you are to play, especially on a wild day. Wedged between the sea and the railway line, typical of Old Prestwick, Aberdovey nestles on perfect links terrain. So perfect that Bernard Darwin, the grandfather of golf writing, called it his favourite course in the world. Some claim, and one you may agree with after playing it. And if you discount old Darwin, then maybe this will spur you to pay this grand old course a visit: Ian Woosnam is an honorary member and regular visitor.

Further up the coast, in North Wales, you will find the third of the great trio of Welsh links golf – Royal St David's at Harlech. Lying in the shadow of Harlech Castle and within sight of Mount Snowdon are the Harlech links, where golf has been played since 1894.

While the card may only read par-69 on a course that measures less than 6,500 yards, by common consent St David's plays a lot longer. To give you a clue, the standard scratch score is 72. In other words don't be complacent when you take on St David's.

Aberdovey, Royal Porthcawl, Royal St David's these are the highlights of Welsh golf. Luckily there are no real lowlights, just plenty of hidden gems waiting to explored.

And if you're looking for golf of the inland variety, then the new Celtic Manor course at Newport is worth checking out. There's a hotel there and two Robert Trent Jones designed courses that have been built to impeccable standards. Or there's St Pierre, now owned by the Marriott hotel group, where a European Tour event used to be held. Or you might want to try the Rolls of Monmouth in the Wye Valley; just the name is tempting enough.

Or maybe you'll just want to explore, for Wales has numerous courses, some just delightful nine holers just waiting to be found.

Wales

Page

Henlly's Hall

Colwyn Bay

Bangor

Bryn Morfydd Golf Hotel

A55

Caernarfon

Wrexham

A487

A5

A494

A470

Oswestry

A5

Shrewsbury

Dogellau

Welshpool

M50

A49

Aberystwyth

A470

A487

Builth Wells

Hereford

Fishguard

M50

Carmarthen

A465

A40

Haverfordwest

A40

A48

Merthyr Tydfil

Ross-on-wye

A48

Milford Haven

Llanelli

Neath

St Mary's Hotel

Celtic Manor Hotel

Marriott St Pierre Hotel

Swansea

Pontypridd

Newport

M4

A48

Cardiff

167

Marriott St Pierre Hotel & Country Club

*T*he Marriott St. Pierre Hotel & Country Club is set in 400 acres of picturesque parkland in the beautiful Wye Valley. London is only a couple of hours away and Birmingham even less.

The hotel has over 140 bedrooms (including 16 suites), each one of them enjoying a most scenic view.

The Executive Chef has worked in the kitchens of the world's most famous hotels. Using the best local produce, such as freshly caught River Wye salmon and tender Welsh lamb, he has created a tempting variety of imaginative dishes for all tastes. The newly refurbished Long Weekend Café Bar offers a light hearted informal sports theme restaurant, and room service is available 24 hours a day.

You'll find plenty of ways either to wind yourself down or tone yourself up at the Marriott St. Pierre. The hotel has extensive health and beauty facilities, including a beauty suite with five treatment rooms, offering everything from a manicure to a full body massage.

If you're seeking more active relaxation, St. Pierre can offer a wealth of activities, including tennis, multi-gymnasium, aerobic suite, cycling and even hot air ballooning.

LOCAL ATTRACTIONS

St Pierre occupies a corner of the country with more than its fair share of attractions, such as the beauty of the Wye Valley, historic sights – from Tintern Abbey to the impressive Roman remains at Bath, as well as the famous Stuart Crystal works.

GOLF INFORMATION

Old Course, 6762 yards, Par 71, 18-hole. Mathern Course, 5732 yards, Par 68, 18-hole, heathland/woodland course.

Practice facilities: Practice ground, putting green and driving range.

Instructions: Groups and individuals catered for. Tuition and Video facilities.

Hire: Clubs & equipment, trollies and buggies.

CARD OF THE COURSE					
Old Course White Tees					
1	576	Par 5	10	362	Par 4
2	365	Par 4	11	393	Par 4
3	135	Par 3	12	545	Par 5
4	379	Par 4	13	219	Par 3
5	420	Par 4	14	521	Par 5
6	165	Par 3	15	375	Par 4
7	442	Par 4	16	426	Par 4
8	309	Par 4	17	449	Par 4
9	444	Par 4	18	237	Par 3
Out 3235 Par 35			In 3527 Par 36		

HOTEL INFORMATION

Marriott St. Pierre Hotel & Country Club
St. Pierre Park,
Chepstow NP6 6YA
Tel: 01291 625261
Fax: 01291 629975

Rooms: 148.
Restaurants: Orangery Restaurant, Long Weekend Café Bar, Panel Bar, Trophy Bar.
Hair and Beauty: Health spa including three treatment rooms.
Other Fitness Facilities: Indoor heated swimming pool, spa bath, sauna, gym, solarium.
Other Sporting Facilities: Tennis courts, crown green bowling, croquet lawn, snooker room, dance studio.

TARIFF

DINNER, BED & BREAKFAST
(Mon-Sun)

Prices start from **£84** per person, per night, including a round of golf on either course. Based on two sharing.

DIRECTIONS

Take Junction 21 off the M4 sign-posted M48 Chepstow. Then take Junction 2 off the M48 and follow the A466 sign-posted Chepstow. At the first roundabout turn left onto the A48 towards Caerwent. Marriott St. Pierre is approximately 2 miles on the left.

BRYN MORFYDD HOTEL
Llanrhaeadr, Nr. Denbigh, Benbighshire LL16 4NP. Tel: 01745 890280 Fax: 01745 890488

9/18 **HOLES** **PAR** 27/70 2000/5800 **YARDS**
TYPE OF GOLF COURSE: Parkland
HOTEL RATING: 3 Star RAC
GOLF PROFESSIONAL: Ivor Jones **TEL:** 01745 890488
B&B + 18 HOLES: £51 and £56 @ weekends

Set in over 100 acres of beautiful countryside, overlooking the magnificent Vale of Clwyd, the Hotel has 30 ensuite bedrooms with television, tea and coffee making facilities, telephone and trouser press. Meals are available in the restaurant or as bar snacks in the lounge.

The 2 parkland golf courses (27 holes) have been designed for accurate and intelligent golf.

THE CELTIC MANOR HOTEL & COUNTRY CLUB
Catsash Road, Newport, Gwent NP6 1JQ. Tel: 01633 413000 Fax: 01633 412910

36 (54 from Spring 1999) **HOLES**
PAR 70/60 7000/4000 **YARDS**
TYPE OF GOLF COURSE: Parkland
RATING: AA/RAC/4 Star
GOLF PROFESSIONAL: Steven Bowen **TEL:** 01633 410268
B&B + 18 HOLES: £87 (½ twin, incl dinner)
OTHER SPECIAL GOLF PACKAGES: Society rate: £30

There are at present two 18 hole courses at The Celtic Manor Hotel & Country Club, the Roman Road Championship course and Coldra Woods. The Roman road is a par 70 covering over 7000 yards. It runs along the ridge of Coldra Hill, straddling the ancient east/west Roman highway, via Julia. The Coldra woods offers a different kind of challenge. Par 60 and 4000 yards long it criss-crosses a lake-filled valley with magnificent natural ravines. In January 1999 the new 18 hole championship course, The Wentwood Hills will be ready for play. It is par 72 and 7200 yards.

HENLLY'S HALL HOTEL
Beaumaris, Isle of Anglesey, North Wales
Tel: 01248 810412 Fax: 01248 811511

HOLES: 18	**YARDS:** 6062	**PAR:** 72

ST. MARY'S HOTEL GOLF & COUNTRY CLUB (BEST WESTERN)

St. Mary's Hill, Pencoed, South Glamorgan CF35 5WA.
Tel: 01656 861100/860280 Fax: 01656 863400

24 bedrooms all with ensuite, trouser press, welcome tray, direct dial telephone.

27 hole golf complex set in 150 acres - clubhouse facilities include 3 bars, restaurant conservatory, conference facilities. Located 2 minutes from Junction 35 of M4 motorway.

9/18 HOLES PAR 35/69 2426/5291 YARDS
TYPE OF GOLF COURSE: Parkland
HOTEL RATING: Wales Tourist Board (4 Crowns)
GOLF PROFESSIONAL: John Peters
TEL: 01656 861599
B&B + 18 HOLES: £64.50 (single) plus golf £14 per person.
OTHER SPECIAL GOLF PACKAGES:
£109pp 2night stay w/end inc. 2 rounds golf + dinner basedon 10 players 2 people sharing.

Trearddur Bay, Isle of Anglesey

Western Scotland

Kilchurn Castle, Loch Awe

Western Scotland

*N*ot many people venture further down the Ayrshire coast beyond Turnberry. They come to play the famous Ailsa course, where the Open Championship has been staged three times, perhaps stay in the magnificent hotel, and then head for home. That's a pity.

Further down the coastline, down in Dumfries and Galloway, are to be found some surprisingly good golf courses. Portpatrick, Stranraer, Powfoot, Dumfries & County, there are plenty of hidden gems to keep you happy. Best of the bunch, though, is Southerness. This is a links golf par excellence that does not get the publicity it deserves because it is perceived to be off the beaten track, as if it was stuck out in the middle of the wild Atlantic Ocean or something. Any aficionado of links golf needs to put this 6,566-yard course on their must play list. It will not disappoint.

Nor will golf in the nearby Borders region disappoint. This area is too often bypassed by golfers hurrying towards Glasgow or Edinburgh, yet it contains a host of parkland gems well worth stopping for – Minto, Hawick, The newly opened Roxburghe, Selkirk, St. Boswells, all worthy of a round.

But it's to the giants of the Ayrshire coast that we are headed, and there is no bigger than Turnberry or Royal Troon.

Troon is the tougher of the two, especially over the closing nine, while Turnberry is more picturesque. To play them on consecutive days is to experience the twin peaks of Ayrshire golf.

Of course, with the boom in golf came more desire to play these courses, and both are hard to get on to. Troon especially does not accept too many visitors, so, like many Open venues, perseverance is required. Turnberry is more straightforward. By staying at the hotel you gain playing privileges on the course, although you do pay extra for the green fee. That's obviously a costly option as the hotel is five star throughout. However, in winter the hotel offers some good deals, and that may be your best option. It's a viable option, too, for this coastline is warmed by the Gulfstream and can be quite temperate in winter compared to the rest of Scotland.

If you can't beg, steal or borrow a round over these two famous links then don't despair too much – there are enough quality venues nearby to keep you happy. Glasgow Gailes, Kilmarnock Barassie, Irvine Bogside, Western Gailes, all Open Qualifying courses, are not too far away from Troon. All provide a great challenge and a good day's golf.

The same can be said of Old Prestwick, where the Open Championship began in 1860. Anyone remotely interested in the history of the game has to try to play here. Of course it's too short nowadays to challenge the top players, but not short enough for the top amateurs or your game either, especially if the wind blows.

As you would expect, there's good public golf to be found in this area. For example, the courses of Lochgreen, Darley and Fullarton are all good links layouts in their own rights. True, they may not be as manicured as some of the aforementioned layouts, but they offer good challenges and even better value for money. They do get quite busy in the summer so make sure you phone ahead. And don't worry about teaming up with a local; often you find yourself playing with someone who appears to be a few strokes better than his handicap. They take their golf quite seriously up here!

They take the "goff" quite seriously around Glasgow, too. No longer is Glasgow the grimy industrial city it once was. It's not too long ago that it was voted the European city of Culture, an honour it still lives up to admirably.

With close to 100 golf courses in and around the city, you're never short of a game.

South of the city try Lanark Golf Club, a moorland course that Old Tom Morris, Ben Sayers and James Braid have had a hand in creating – a trio to make most other clubs jealous. The R & A rate the Lanark layout so highly that it has been used as a regular course for Open Qualifying.

Closer to the city, you are not spoilt for choice. Haggs Castle should be at the top of your list. This fine parkland layout was venue for the now defunct Scottish Open in its inaugural year of 1986. Other courses in or near the city to consider include the James Braid designed Hilton Park, Glasgow Killermont, Renfrew and East Renfrew.

North of the city you might try Helensburgh, Cardross, the short but hilly Vale of Leven, a course offering tremendous views over Loch Lomond, and Buchanan Castle.

If you have lots of time on your hands, and you don't mind the three hour drive, then you should try and get to Machrihanish. How good is Machrihanish? Well, just prior to the 1994 Open Championship, American Ryder Cup player Brad Faxon drove round from Turnberry to play this testing links course. Faxon didn't seem to mind the long drive or the fact he had to have a catnap in his car.

The trip is worth it for Machrihanish, as Old Tom Morris said when asked to design it in 1879, was "specially designed by the Almighty for playing golf." That applies today. Just to play the opening hole is worth the effort. And if you can throw in a round at The Machrie over the water on Islay, then you will have played two of the most natural links in the world.

Western Scotland

Page

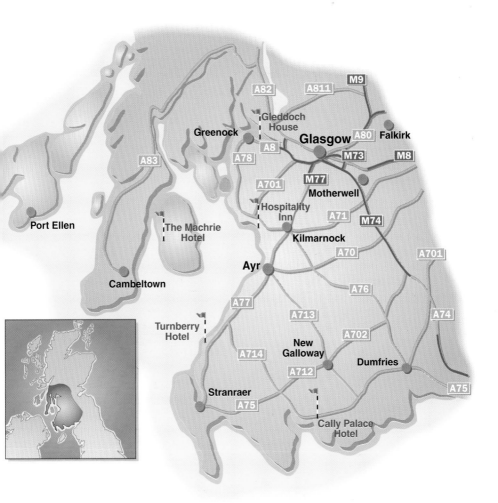

Port Ellen

Greenock

Gleddoch House

Glasgow

Falkirk

The Machrie Hotel

Hospitality Inn

Motherwell

Cambeltown

Kilmarnock

Ayr

Turnberry Hotel

New Galloway

Dumfries

Stranraer

Cally Palace Hotel

A82

A811

M9

A80

A83

A78

A8

A701

M77

M73

M8

A71

M74

A70

A701

A76

A74

A77

A713

A702

A714

A712

A75

A75

Cally Palace Hotel

*T*he Cally Palace Hotel in South West Scotland stands in its own grounds at the edge of the village of Gatehouse-of-Fleet. The house was built in 1763 and many original features remain. It is four star and deluxe in every respect, but with an ambience which is both elegant and formal yet warm and friendly.

LOCAL ATTRACTIONS

In the surrounding area there are lovely gardens and castles to visit and the hotel is just a few miles from the sea. Castles include Threave, Drumlanrig and gardens range from Castle Kennedy to the botanical Logan Gardens heading towards Stranraer.

The 18 hole golf course is 5800 yards with a par of 70 and is set in lovely rolling parkland and around Cally Lake. It is for the exclusive use of Hotel guests – no members, no day visitors and no competitions.

The 55 bedrooms are made up of standard, family, deluxe rooms and suites, most with delightful views of the grounds or across Cally Lake to the Galloway Hills. The food absolutely first class under the guidance of Head Chef David Alexander whose innovative style of cooking is very popular with regular guests and those visiting for the first time. In particular he makes best use of locally caught seafood and game, and of course Scottish Beef regularly appears on his menus.

Indoor leisure facilities include swimming pool, sauna, jacuzzi and games room and guests who enjoy the outdoor life will appreciate the 500 acres of grounds surrounding the hotel – for walking or boating on the lake. Salmon fishing, archery and pony trekking can all be arranged nearby

GOLF INFORMATION

18 hole, 5802 yard parkland course

Par 70

Hire: buggies

CARD OF THE COURSE					
1	287	Par 4	10	361	Par 4
2	165	Par 3	11	339	Par 4
3	381	Par 4	12	172	Par 3
4	335	Par 4	13	401	Par 4
5	378	Par 4	14	266	Par 4
6	128	Par 3	15	504	Par 5
7	332	Par 4	16	345	Par 4
8	579	Par 5	17	221	Par 3
9	337	Par 4	18	271	Par 4
Out	2922	Par 35	In	2880	Par 35

HOTEL INFORMATION

Cally Palace Hotel
Gatehouse-of-Fleet,
Castle Douglas,
Dumfries & Galloway
DG7 2DL
Tel: 01557 814341

Fax: 01557 814 522

Rating: AA + RAC 4 Star, AA Rosette for food, STB four Star.

Rooms: 56.

Restaurants: Scottish – using local produce.

Childcare Facilities: Baby listening service.

Other Fitness Facilities: 2 exercise bikes.

Other Sporting Facilites: Tennis court, croquet, putting and indoor swimming pool.

TARIFF

Weekend Breaks
from £166pp for 2 nights DBB & Golf.

**Mid-Week Breaks
(Min Stay 3 nights)**
from £83pppn DBB & Golf.
Over 60's deduction.

Weekly golf rates
from £76pppn DBB & Golf.

DIRECTIONS

Head north on the M6 and cross onto the A75 heading towards Dumfries/Stranraer. Alternatively head south on the A74 from Glasgow and then turn off on to the A75 following signs for Dumfries. Once at Dumfries follow A75 towards Stranraer. Approximately 15 miles west of Castle Douglas take the first right onto the B727 following signs for Gatehouse-of-Fleet – the Hotel is on the left before Gatehouse.

Ayr, South Ayrs

GLEDDOCH HOUSE HOTEL

Langbank, Renfrewshire PA14 6YE. Tel: 01475 540711 Fax: 01475 540201

Set amidst 365 acres Gleddoch Golf Club is a testing 6330 yards, par 72, parkland/moorland course with panoramic views of Glasgow to the East, Ben Lomond to the North and the Clyde estuary to the West. The golf course is part of Gleddoch complex which includes a 39 bedroom hotel with a restaurant awarded 2 rosettes from the AA. Gleddoch is situated 120 minutes drive from Glasgow airport and 20 minutes from Glasgow city centre.

18 HOLES	PAR 68	6335 YARDS

TYPE OF GOLF COURSE:
Parkland/Moorland

RATING: AA 4 Star, 2 AA Rosettes, RAC 4 Star, STB 4 Star.

GOLF PROFESSIONAL: Keith Campbell
TEL: 01475 540 711

B&B + 18 HOLES: From £90.00 pp

OTHER SPECIAL GOLF PACKAGES:
From £140.00 pp – weekend specials

HOSPITALITY INN, IRVINE

46 Awnick Road, Irvine KA11 4LD. Tel: 01294 274 272 Fax: 01294 277 287

The Moorish decor gives a taste of Tangier on the west coast of Scotland. Well situated within easy reach of Glasgow, yet in a holiday setting with Burns country, Culzean Castle, the Isle of Aran on the doorstep. A perfect location for experiencing the Ayrshire golf courses in a warm relaxed setting.

9 HOLES	PAR 27	1485 YARDS

TYPE OF GOLF COURSE: Parkland

RATING: 4 Star AA/RAC

GOLF PROFESSIONAL: Bill Lockie
(Associate) (contact through hotel)

B&B + 18 HOLES: £76.00 per night
(2 sharing)

TURNBERRY HOTEL

Turnberry, Ayrshire KA26 9LT. Tel: 01655 33100 Fax: 01655 331706

Turnberry Hotel is located on the West Coast of Scotland approximately one hour from Glasgow. The Hotel has 132 guest bedrooms including 21 suites and studio suites, three restaurants and four bars. The Ailsa course, host to three Open Championships in 1977, 1986 and 1994 is partnered by the equally challenging Arran course.

In addition to golf, the Hotel also has one of the country's finest health spa's with a range of up to 25 different treatments which include aromatherapy, hydrotherapy, mud and algae wraps. A beauty salon is also available together with gift shops and a golf professional shop in the Clubhouse.

18/18 HOLES	PAR 70/68	6976/6014 YARDS

TYPE OF GOLF COURSE: Links courses

HOTEL RATING: AA 5 Red Stars/RAC 5 Star Blue Ribbon/STB 5 Crowns Deluxe

GOLF PROFESSIONAL: Brian Gunson
TEL: 01655 331000

B&B + 18 HOLES: From £135.00

Machrie Hotel & Golf Links

The Machrie hotel was originally built about 250 years ago as a farmhouse. Nowadays it has 16 en-suite bedrooms, including a suite and a four poster. All rooms have colour TV, direct dial telephone and tea making facilities. There are also 15 two bedroom lodges sleeping between 4-6 which provide even more privacy and freedom and are fully equipped for self catering purposes. The lodges are also available for groups of golfers on a fully inclusive golf package. The island abounds in local beef and lamb, game, venison and shellfish and these feature widely on our menu. A Scottish base complemented by dishes with an international essence ensure a wide variety of choice of food cooked to perfection. We also have a private dining room seating up to 40 people should your group wish for a more intimate dinner. Settle down after dinner in front of a peat fire and savour one of the island's eight malts or if you are feeling more energetic why not try your hand at snooker, pool, table tennis or one of the other indoor sports on offer. The golf course laid out in 1891 by Willie Campbell has changed little since that time. Sand dunes provide natural hazards but will challenge most golfers and the blind shots make for an interesting first round. This is a course that takes you back in time to how golf used to be played. It is the golfer against nature and the challenge is to see who wins! Our aim is to ensure that everybody who comes to Machrie has the chance to play a challenging course, eat wonderful food and relax in the friendly atmosphere of the hotel and the island.

LOCAL ATTRACTIONS

The island is most famous for its malt whisky, which has a distinctive peaty flavour. There are 6 operational distilleries, four of which are very close to the hotel and we can arrange tours for you. Horse riding, stalking, fishing and birdwatching are some of the most popular sports on Islay, which is renowned for its extensive variety of bird life including geese, hen harriers and golden eagles. The Woollen Mill is a popular attraction with two spinning Jennies and the only Slubbing Billy in the country. The main attraction of the island is the peace and beauty and its numerous golden beaches, ideal for water sports or just relaxing.

GOLF INFORMATION

18 hole, 6226 yard links course

Par 71

Practice facilities: Outdoor driving range.

Hire: Clubs and Trollies.

CARD OF THE COURSE					
1	308	Par 4	10	156	Par 3
2	508	Par 5	11	357	Par 4
3	319	Par 4	12	174	Par 3
4	390	Par 4	13	488	Par 5
5	163	Par 3	14	423	Par 4
6	344	Par 4	15	335	Par 4
7	395	Par 4	16	411	Par 4
8	337	Par 4	17	352	Par 4
9	392	Par 4	18	374	Par 4
Out 3156 Par 36			In 3070 Par 35		

HOTEL INFORMATION

Machrie Hotel & Golf Links
Port Ellen, Isle of Islay
Argyll PA42 7AN
Tel: 01496 302310
Fax: 01496 302404
E-mail: machrie@machrie.com

Rating: 2 Star Scottish Tourist Board.

Rooms: 16 plus 15 two bedroomed lodges.

Restaurants: Scottish using local game and shellfish. Private dining room.

Childcare Facilities: Babysitting can be arranged. Childrens play area.

Hair and Beauty: Aromatherapy can be arranged.

Other Sporting Facilities: Croquet lawn, snooker, pool table, table tennis, darts, carpet bowls, bike hire, fishing, nature trail.

TARIFF

Golfing Breaks

March/Oct	–	£65.00
May/Sept	–	£80.00
Nov/Feb	–	£55.00
April	–	£75.00

All prices per person per night.

Golf Rates:

B&B from £36.00. Golf £18.50/rn.

DIRECTIONS

Ferry from Kennacraig to Port Ellen/Port Askaig. Take A846 from ferry. Scheduled air service twice daily from Glasgow. Free transfers to and from both ferry and airport can be arranged.

Eastern Scotland

Eastern Scotland

Y ou can't call yourself a true golfer if you haven't played golf in The Kingdom. We're talking Fife here, as in St Andrews, the home of golf. Every year thousands of visitors roll into St Andrews to play the Old Course, where the game began. It's a pilgrimage every golfer should make at least once, but many play St Andrews and then move on to other Open venues. Not that the likes of Turnberry and Royal Troon are to be sneezed at, but golf in Fife stretches farther than the Old Course – a lot farther.

Think of it. Where else will you find a better stretch of golf than the likes of Leven Links, Lundin Links, Elie, Crail, Scotscraig on the coast, and Ladybank in the heart of the Kingdom? Indeed, you could spend a week playing golf in Fife without going to St Andrews and still have a great experience, so good is the golf on offer. You could even have a good time if you play golf in the "auld grey toon" but don't happen to be lucky enough to get drawn from the ballot to play the Old Course. The New Course is not a bad stand-in for the old lady of golf. And the Eden and Jubilee courses are not to be snee zed at either. Neither is the new Duke's course at Craigtoun. A demanding layout which is the property of the Old Course hotel. This parkland course is built to excellent specifications and offers good views over the town and its most famous assets

Great golf is to be found if you head over the Tay Bridge to Tayside, or over the Forth Road Bridge south to the Lothians.

For example, in Tayside there is arguably the toughest of the current Open Championship courses – Carnoustie, to the north of Dundee. This demanding links will host the Open Championship in 1999, 24 years after Tom Watson won his first of five Old Claret Jugs in a playoff with Australia's Jack Newton in 1975.

Although you cannot view the sea from Carnoustie's fairways, this is a true links course in every sense of the word. It's a giant of a links too. The finish is arguably the toughest on the Open rota. Any player with the lead through 14 holes should not start preparing his victory speech, for the next four holes could send him hurtling back down through the field.

Good links golf in this area can also be found at Panmure, Monifieth and Montrose. Panmure is fairly short at just over 6,300 yards to a par of 70, but it's tight and tough and demands attention if you're to match your handicap. The legendary Ben Hogan was suitably impressed with this course when qualifying for the 1953 Open, which he won.

Both Monifieth and Montrose, further up the coast, are public links courses, so the green fee won't stretch your wallet, but the courses will, especially in a strong sea breeze.

Don't think golf in Tayside is just a collection of good links courses. There are also fine inland courses within striking distance of the city of Dundee. Downfield, Edzell, Letham Grange, all provide a welcome change from the seaside. Even further inland, towards the heart of Scotland, there is good golf to be found at Blairgowrie, at Pitlochry, at Crieff, at Murrayshall. Blairgowrie, for instance, is one of Scotland's true hidden gems, a club often missed on many itineraries for some strange reason. Yet the Rosemount course there is a joy to behold – heather, gorse, pine and silver birch trees and fine moorland fairways complete a fabulous picture.

All that's to the north of the Kingdom, to the south is yet another centre of great golf, where there are enough good links to keep you happy for a fortnight.

The centre is Gullane. Of course, the Open Championship rolls into this small town every five or so years. It comes to Muirfield, where the Honourable Company of Edinburgh golfers, the world's oldest golf club, are based.

Getting on to Muirfield is about as easy these days as getting an audience with the Prime Minister – in fact it's probably easier to see the PM! – so it might be a while before you sample its famous fairways. Fear not though, for almost literally within par-5 distance are a host of good courses.

Gullane has three courses and there are many who rate the Number 1 course as one of the best links in the country. Many also rate Luffness New which is also to be found in the town. Indeed, the R & A rate it highly enough to have held Open Qualifying over its links.

Not far from Gullane are to be found other fine links courses at Longniddry, Kilspindie, North Berwick and Dunbar. Indeed, the West Links at North Berwick is home to the famous Redan hole, the 15th, which has been copied on other courses all over the world.

Of course if you're in the Lothians then you will no doubt visit Edinburgh, the Athens of the North. The sights are what you will be going to see but don't forget your clubs. Around Edinburgh you will find good golf at Bruntsfield Links, Royal Burgess, Braid Hills, Dalmahoy and Royal Musselburgh, to name but a few. Some of these layouts are difficult to play and so a little advance planning is required. One thing's for sure – it will be worth the effort.

Eastern Scotland

Page

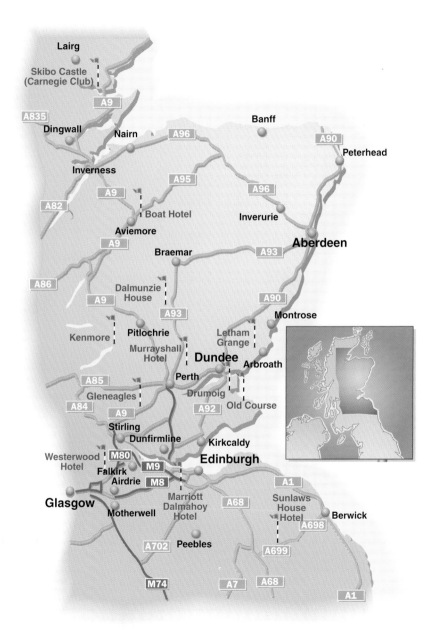

Lairg

Skibo Castle
(Carnegie Club)

A9

A835

Banff

Dingwall

Nairn

A96

A90

Peterhead

Inverness

A95

A96

Inverurie

A82

A9

Boat Hotel

Aviemore

Aberdeen

A9

Braemar

A93

A86

Dalmunzie
House

A90

Montrose

A9

A93

Pitlochrie

Kenmore

Letham
Grange

Murrayshall
Hotel

Dundee

Arbroath

A85

Perth

Gleneagles

Drumoig

A84

A9

A92

Old Course

Stirling

Dunfirmline

Kirkcaldy

Westerwood
Hotel

M80

Edinburgh

Falkirk

M9

A1

Airdrie

M8

Glasgow

Marriott
Dalmahoy
Hotel

Sunlaws
House
Hotel

Berwick

Motherwell

A68

A698

A702

Peebles

A699

M74

A7

A68

A1

189

Drumoig Golf Club & Hotel

*D*rumoig Golf Resort (near St Andrews) is Scotland's exciting new Golf location, with it's own 18 hole championship golf course and a unique lodge-hotel and clubhouse arrangement offering the golfer a relaxed environment. All rooms are en-suite with satellite TV, tea & coffee making facilities.

LOCAL ATTRACTIONS

There are many exciting attractions all within easy driving distance, including; Sea Life, Crieff, Secret Bunker, Edinburgh Zoo, The Great Houses of Scotland, British Golf Museum, Praytis Farm Park, The Glenturret, Rankeilout Park, as well as Whisky distilleries, The Mill Trail, The Whisky Trail all surround by spectacular landscapes.

Opening at Drumoig later in 1998 is the Scottish National Golf Centre planned to be UK's finest indoor and outdoor training and practice facility attracting golfers from throughout the world.

Drumoig's golf layout is wholly natural over sand based ground in rolling terrain. Links-like in parts with two greens nestling in the old whinstone quarries, water also plays an intrinsic part with three holes adjoining the somewhat intimidating lochs. The views are spectacular with St Andrews Bay and town seen to the south and Carnoustie to the north-east.

The superb new Clubhouse with it's restaurant and terrace provides outstanding views over the 9th and 18th greens and imposing water features beyond. A perfect setting to enjoy relaxing drinks or a meal in the bar or restaurant. During the day we offer a special prepared menu for the golfer or visitor on the move. In the evening the pace relaxes to allow the option of à la carte dining with an international Florentine flavour.

18 hole, 7006 yard Rolling links style – inland course
Par 72

Golf Professional: Jim Farmer
Tel: 01382 541800

Practice facilities: Covered driving range.

Instructions: Groups and individuals catered for. Drumoig is the Home of The Scottish National Golf Centre, due for completion Spring'99.

Hire: Clubs and buggies.

CARD OF THE COURSE					
1	432	Par 4	10	396	Par 4
2	218	Par 3	11	340	Par 4
3	563	Par 5	12	422	Par 4
4	214	Par 3	13	300	Par 4
5	565	Par 5	14	202	Par 3
6	430	Par 4	15	582	Par 5
7	379	Par 4	16	190	Par 3
8	358	Par 4	17	539	Par 5
9	434	Par 4	18	442	Par 4
Out	3593	Par 36	In	3413	Par 36

FIFE

Drumoig Golf Club & Hotel
Drumoig, Leuchars
St Andrews
Fife KY16 0BE
Tel: 01382 541800
Fax: 01382 542211

Rating: Scottish Tourist Board. 4 Crowns.
Rooms: 24 – 18 Twin and 6 Double.
Restaurants: Snacks, Bar Meals & à la Carte, Florentine/Italian Flavour.
Fitness Facilities: Scottish National Golf Centre will have Gym facilities.
Other Sporting Facilities: Rhynd Country Sports – Clay Shooting, Equestrian Centre, Fishing + Quad Biking.

Normal Tariff
Sharing twin/double*
B&B   £59.00
B&B+Dinner   £74.00
Single supplement £20.00
High Season Special
(April* to october incl.)
Sharing twin/double*
B&B   £39.00
B&B+Dinner   £53.00
*excluding Easter
Special Golf Packages:
B&B including 18 holes from £54.00.
Other Special Golf Packages:
2 nights DBB + 2 rounds £129 per person.

Drumoig is situated on the main Dundee to St Andrews road (A92/A914) four miles from Dundee and eight miles from St Andrews.

THE BOAT HOTEL
Boat of Garten, Inverness-shire PH24 3BH. Tel: 01479 831258 Fax: 01479 831414

18 HOLES	PAR 69	5866 YARDS

RATING: AA & RAC 3 star, STB 4 crowns commended

B&B + 18 HOLES: From £40 + £26 = £66

OTHER SPECIAL GOLF PACKAGES:
Dinner, B&B, full-day green fees on any of six local golf courses.
2 Days from £134 – 5 Days from £315.

A four crown, family run hotel in the magnificent scenery of Strathspey offering the highest standard of traditional highland hospitality. Boat of Garten lies in the heart of the picturesque Spey Valley, framed by the magnificent Cairngorm Mountains. In addition to our own Boat of Garten golf course, there are a further 5 local courses within 20 miles & 3 championship courses within 1.5 hours (transport can be arranged). Salmon & trout fishing on the Spey (in season), trout fishing at Inverdruie fish farm, 4 x 4 mountain safaris in the Monadliaths and estate safaris, clay pigeon shooting in the Rothiemurchus Pine Forest & pony trekking in the foothills at Alvie are just a few of the activities available.

Castle Fraser, Grampian Highlands

erth

DALMUNZIE HOUSE HOTEL

pittal, O'Glenshee, Blairgowrie, Perthshire BH10 7QG. Tel: 01250 885226

Dalmunzie House Hotel is a turreted baronial country house standing in its own 6,500 acre highland estate. It is family run by the Wintons, who have lived in the glen for decades and are experienced and genuine hosts. The house has a wonderfully friendly atmosphere, with log fire, comfy chairs and is hospitable and informal. Food is cooked fresh to order and we are in the Taste of Scotland scheme and have an AA rosette for dinner.

9 HOLES	PAR	2035 YARDS
TYPE OF GOLF COURSE: Parkland		
RATING: 3 Start Scottish Tourish Board		
B&B + 18 HOLES: From £58.00		
OTHER SPECIAL GOLF PACKAGES:		
Half board: £67.00 DB&B		

Outdoors we have our own 9 hole golf course, which a challenge to all standards and golfers and there are many very good courses within an ours drive, such as Blairgowrie, Alyth, Pitlochry, Kirriemuir, Braemar, Ballater and Aboyne.

Letham Grange Resort

Letham Grange Resort is situated amidst serene countryside in the County of Angus, which is an area of 842 square miles on the east coast of Scotland, between Dundee and Aberdeen. Attractive towns and villages are set amongst a diverse landscape that includes a wonderfully varied coastline, rich riverside pastures, breathtaking wooded hillslopes and high and silent open moorland.

A gracious and tastefully restored baronial mansion, Letham Grange offers a warm welcome to all who visit, reflecting the Victorian era, many of the original features of the house, designed by architect Archibold Simpson, remain. These are sympathetically enhanced by many, modern comforts on and around the estate.

The centrepiece of Letham Grange is undoubtedly the old course. Officially opened for play in April 1987, the course makes splendid and often dramatic use of the grandeur of the estate. The course incorporates water hazards, narrow fairways and undulating terrain. Water is a permanent feature of the course and can be found on 13 of the 18 holes. The par 3, 2nd is played over a picturesque lake onto a green surrounded by mature trees and rhododendrons.

LOCAL ATTRACTIONS

25 miles west of Letham Grange is Glamis Castle, the family home of the Earls of Strathmore and Kinghorne. The childhood home of H.M. Queen Elizabeth The Queen Mother and the legendary setting of Shakespeare's 'Macbeth', the castle and its magnificent gardens are open to visitors from March to October. The Angus Glens – where the Scottish Lowlands meet the Highlands – is less than a 40 minutes' drive from Letham Grange. Before exploring this haven for walkers, climbers, botanists and birdwatchers, be sure to stop off at the hill-edge town of Kirriemuir, the birthplace of Peter Pan's creator – J.M. Barrie.

GOLF INFORMATION

18 hole, 6968 yard parkland course

Par 73

Golf Professional: Steven Moir

Tel: 01241 890 373

Instructions: Groups and individuals catered for by arrangement with out Golf Professional.

Hire: Clubs and buggies.

Green Fees: £24.00 to £33.00.

CARD OF THE COURSE

1	402	Par 4	10	426	Par 4
2	176	Par 3	11	527	Par 5
3	553	Par 5	12	428	Par 4
4	391	Par 4	13	363	Par 4
5	440	Par 4	14	357	Par 4
6	204	Par 4	15	500	Par 5
7	359	Par 3	16	403	Par 4
8	541	Par 5	17	161	Par 3
9	218	Par 3	18	519	Par 5
Out	3284	Par 35	In	3684	Par 38

HOTEL INFORMATION

Letham Grange Resort
Colliston by Arbroath,
Angus DD11 4RL
Tel: 01241 890 373
Fax: 44 (0)1241 890 725
Rating: AA 4 Star, RAC 4 Star,
Scottish Tourist Board 4 Star.
Rooms: 42.
Restaurants: Rosehaugh formal restaurant + Golfer's retreat restaurant and conservatory.
Fitness Facilities: Nearby fitness facilities at the Saltire centre.
Other Sporting Facilites: Lawn tennis, croquet, fishing and numerous outdoor sports nearby.
Other Leisure Activities: See our website: www.lethamgrange.co.uk

TARIFF

B&B Summer (April-Sept '98)
Single (in Dbl.-Std. Room) £100
Twin/Double Standard £135
Executive Suites £210
Rapunzel Suite £310
B&B Winter (Oct 98 - Mar 99)
Single (in Dbl.-Std. Room) £80
Twin/Double Standard £110
Executive Suites £170
Rapunzel Suite £260

Special Golf Packages:
B&B including 18 holes from £85.00

Other Special Golf Packages:
Eagle Golf Breaks from £89.00 per person including golfers account + dinner + round of golf.

DIRECTIONS

Travelling by road from Glagow.
Take the A80/M80 to Stirling, then follow the A9/M9 to Perth and take the A90 to Dundee. Take the A92 to Arbroath and then the A933 towards Brechin. Take the 1st right after Colliston for Letham Grange.

Marriott Dalmahoy Hotel & Country Club

*D*almahoy House, a Georgian style mansion sheltering under the rolling Pentland Hills, looks out across a thousand acres of woodland estates towards Edinburgh Castle.

There are 215 bedrooms, many having fine views of the golf courses and the estate

grounds. The House's seven original bedrooms have been carefully restored and give a clear idea of how Dalmahoy was furnished in the 18th century.

The Pentland Restaurant, overlooking the lake with a sweeping view beyond to Edinburgh, offers a particularly friendly atmosphere for relaxed dining. A more informal setting is provided by the Long Weekend Café Bar beside the heated swimming pool.

The two courses at Dalmahoy offer enjoyable and taxing rounds where you play against a backdrop of wooded countryside with lakes and streams. The West Course has two quite spectacular crossings of the Gogar Burn, while the famous East Course will provide you with golf to a truly international standard – this course hosted the Solheim Cup in 1992 and regularly hosts the Scottish PGA Championship. Designed by James Braid in 1923 it has some exceedingly tricky holes, such as the par 3 15th, known as 'The Wee Wrecker'.

GOLF INFORMATION

West Course, 5185 yards, par 68, 18-hole. East Course, 6677 yards, par 72, 18-hole.

Practice facilities: Large putting greens, two short game practice greens, 12 bay all-weather floodlit driving range.

Instructions: Tuition available.

Hire: Trolley, buggy, club and shoe hire.

CARD OF THE COURSE
West Course

1	278	Par 4	10	170	Par 3
2	279	Par 4	11	365	Par 4
3	128	Par 3	12	344	Par 4
4	373	Par 4	13	540	Par 5
5	310	Par 4	14	311	Par 4
6	271	Par 4	15	339	Par 4
7	262	Par 4	16	117	Par 3
8	437	Par 4	17	172	Par 3
9	180	Par 3	18	309	Par 4
Out	2518	Par 34	In	2667	Par 34

HOTEL INFORMATION

Marriott Dalmahoy Hotel & Country Club
Kirknewton, Nr Edinburgh
Scotland EH27 8EB
Tel: 0131 333 1845
Fax: 0131 333 1433
Rooms: 215
Restaurants: Pentland Restaurant, Long Weekend Café Bar, Cocktail Bar and Club Bar.
Hair and Beauty: Health and Beauty salon, Solarium.
Other Fitness Facilities: Indoor heated swimming pool, spa bath, sauna, steam room, fully equipped gymnasium, dance studio.
Other Sporting Facilities: Riding, fishing, clay pigeon shooting, Tennis courts, Trim/jogging trail.

TARIFF

DINNER, BED & BREAKFAST
(Mon-Sun)

Prices start from **£79** per person, per night (low season), including a round of golf on the East Course. Based on two sharing.

DIRECTIONS

Dalmahoy can be found approximately 7 miles west of Edinburgh on the A71. Edinburgh Airport is 3 miles away.
The hotel is 45 minutes drive from Glasgow and just 5 minutes from the M8.

THE GLENEAGLES HOTEL

Auchterarder, Perthshire, Scotland PH3 1NF. Tel: +44(0) 1764 662231 Fax: +44(0) 1764 662134

18 HOLES PAR 73/69/72 6471/5965/7081 YARDS

TYPE OF GOLF COURSE: King's course, Queen's course, Monarch's course (all Parkland).

HOTEL RATING: AA 5 Red Star

GOLF PROFESSIONAL: Greg Scholfield
TEL: +44 (0) 1764 694343

B&B + 18 HOLES: Rooms from £140, Golf £55

Gleneagles is set in its own 830 acre estate, surrounded by breathtaking Perthshire scenery. The public rooms are elegant and spacious, the guest rooms luxurious. With its three 18-hole championship and one nine-hole golf courses, and a myriad of other sporting opportunities, it welcomes visitors throughout the year and is also a centre for top-level conferences.

Gleneagles, which holds the Automobile Association's supreme accolade of Five Red Stars, is one hour's drive north of Edinburgh and Glasgow airports and has its own railway station.

MURRAYSHALL HOUSE HOTEL & GOLF COURSE

Scone, Perth PH2 7PH. Tel: 01738 551171 Fax: 01738 552595

18 HOLES   PAR 73   6441 YARDS

TYPE OF GOLF COURSE: Parkland

RATING: 3 Star – S.T.B. Highly commended

GOLF PROFESSIONAL: Alan Reid
TEL: 01738 552784

B&B + 18 HOLES: From £57.50 p.p.

OTHER SPECIAL GOLF PACKAGES: Include tuition, all tailor made

A traditional Scottish country house hotel set amongst 300 acres of beautiful countryside. All 27 bedrooms are of a very high standard, many with spectacular views over the golf course. The immaculate 18 hole course is complemented by a floodlit, covered bay, driving range.

Putting green, chipping area and indoor golf school. Tuition can be tailor made to your individual needs. A choice of dining awaits the golfer at Marrayshall, our Old Masters Restaurant with a daily changing a-la-carte menu or the informal clubhouse serving good quality bar food all day.

OLD COURSE HOTEL GOLF RESORT & SPA

St. Andrews, Kingdom of Fife KY16 9SP. Tel: 01334 474371 Fax: 01334 477668

18 HOLES   PAR 72   7271 YARDS

TYPE OF GOLF COURSE: Parkland

RATING: 4 Star

GOLF PROFESSIONAL: Neil Paton; John Kelly
TEL: 01334 474 371

B&B + 18 HOLES: From £340.00

OTHER SPECIAL GOLF PACKAGES: from £148.00 p.p.

The Old Course Hotel, Golf Resort & Spa overlooks the Old Course. All 125 spacious bedrooms (including 17 luxury suites) have private bathrooms and outstanding views. A choice of relaxed and formal dining is available. The hotel's spa has a lap pool, whirlpool, steam and fitness rooms and solarium and a full range of massage and beauty treatments are available. The hotel's own golf course – The Dukes Course, in it's natural setting, complements St. Andrews' famous links courses, all of which are within walking distance.

THE CARNEGIE CLUB

Skibo Castle, Dornoch, Sutherland N25 3RQ. Tel: 01862 894600 Fax: 01862 894601

Originally the home of Andrew Carnegie, The Carnegie Club at Skibo Castle is now a private, residential golf and sporting club, set in its own 7500 acre estate. The club has 500 members from over 30 countries. The daily charges include all meals, beverages, house wines and spirits, unlimited golf on the championship Carnegie Links and/or Monks Walk Parkland Course and use of all the other club sporting facilities, which include archery, falconry, clay pigeon shooting, fishing, swimming, sauna and gymnasium. Guests may visit once, as non-members.

18 HOLES	PAR 71	6671 YARDS

TYPE OF GOLF COURSE: Links

GOLF PROFESSIONAL: Willie Milne

TEL: 01862 881260

Blair Castle, Perthshire

WESTERWOOD HOTEL GOLF & COUNTRY CLUB

St. Andrews Drive, Westerwood, Cumbernauld G68 0EW. Tel: 01236 457171 Fax: 01236 738478

Modern 49 bedroomed hotel nestling comfortably at the foot of the Campsie Hills, located between Glasgow and Edinburgh, Westerwood is ideally situated for relaxing and touring. Set in ideal golfing country the 18 hole par 72 course was designed by Seve Ballesteros and Dave Thomas.

18 HOLES	PAR 72	6616 YARDS

TYPE OF GOLF COURSE: Parkland

HOTEL RATING: 4 Star AA/RAC 5 Crown Highly commended STB

GOLF PROFESSIONAL: Steven Killin
TEL: 01236 457171 Ext 500

B&B + 18 HOLES: £82.50 + £17.50 golf
OTHER SPECIAL GOLF PACKAGES: Available on request

Sunlaws House Hotel

*S*unlaws is a leading country house hotel set amidst the stunning scenery of the Scottish borders. The hotel has 22 guest bedrooms and can offer meeting room facilities for up to 20 delegates as well as private dining for up to 150 people. Noted for excellent accommodation, cuisine and service, the hotel boasts 3 AA black stars, a 5 crown highly commended rating and 2 AA rosettes for food.

The Roxburghe Golf Course is set in over 200 acres, with a mix of parkland and woodland. Dave Thomas, the internationally renowned golf course architect was appointed in March 1995, and his brief was to create a golf course of the highest quality using the existing natural features of the site to maximum effect. The course bears all his unique hallmarks, numerous deep challenging bunkers, mature woodland to define fairways, dramatic water hazards and generous rolling greens.

Additional facilities at the golf course include a practice ground, putting green, a clubhouse with restaurant and bar together with a private dining room for up to 60 people.

In addition to the championship golf course and tennis courts, guests can enjoy fishing the hotel's private beats on the River Tweed or our stocked trout pond. Clay pigeon shooting is also available. The Elixir Health and Beauty Salon offers a wide range of treatments, ensuring that any stay here can offer the perfect blend of physical activity and restful relaxation.

LOCAL ATTRACTIONS

Guests at Sunlaws are able to tour the Duke of Roxburghe's ancestral home, Floors Castle, free of charge. Floors is set within beautiful gardens and is reputed to be the largest inhabited house in Scotland. A well-stocked garden centre, tea room and gift shop delight the visitor, while a relaxing restaurant serves dishes prepared in the Castle kitchens. In the area are the abbeys of Kelso, Jedburgh, Melrose or Dryburgh, and historic country houses such as Manderston, Mellerstain, Abbotsford (the home of Sir Walter Scott) and Thirlstane Castle. Nearby museums include Scotland's Teddy Bear Museum at Melrose, and there are gardens to visit at Kailzie, Peebles and Priorwood. Various other attractions in the area include woollen mills and shops, local arts and crafts, distilleries and golf courses.

GOLF INFORMATION

18 hole, 7111 yard parkland/woodland course Par 72

Golf Professional: Mr Gordon Niven
Tel: 01573 450333

Practice facilities: Outdoor driving range.

Instructions: Groups and individuals catered for + 2 PGA Golf professionals, lessons available on request. Putting Green.

Hire: Clubs, buggies and trollies.

CARD OF THE COURSE

1	421	Par 4	10	469	Par 4
2	396	Par 4	11	526	Par 5
3	364	Par 4	12	399	Par 4
4	188	Par 3	13	216	Par 3
5	581	Par 5	14	571	Par 5
6	382	Par 4	15	177	Par 3
7	520	Par 5	16	460	Par 4
8	203	Par 3	17	398	Par 4
9	403	Par 4	18	437	Par 4
Out	3458	Par 36	In	3653	Par 36

HOTEL INFORMATION

Sunlaws House Hotel &
The Roxburghe Golf Course
Kelso
Roxburghshire TD5 8JZ
Tel: 01573 450331
Fax: 01573 450611
Rating: 3 Black Star AA & RAC + 5 Crown highly commended by Scottish Borders Tourist Board. 2 Red AA Rosettes for food.
Rooms: 22.
Restaurants: Classical British Cuisine.
Childcare Facilities: Baby Listening, Cots, High Chairs.
Hair and Beauty: Elixir Health & Beauty salon, offers various therapeutic & Beauty treatment – No hairdressing facilities.
Other Sporting Facilities: Fishing on private beats or stocked trout pond. Clay pigeon shooting school. Falconry, all weather tennis croquet lawn.
Other Leisure Activities: New Year Package.

TARIFF

Single: £105
Twin/Double: £150
Four-Poster: £195
Suite: £245

Two Day Break:
Two nights dinner, bed and breakfast – per person.
Standard Room £220.
Executive Room £225.

Special Golf Packages:
B&B including 18 holes from £180 per person.

DIRECTIONS

Sunlaws House Hotel is situated at Heiton, 3 miles south west of Kelso on the A698, which intersects the A68 just outside Jedburgh, approximately 10 miles due east along this road.

Northern Ireland

Antrim,
Carrick-A-Rede Rope Bridge

Northern Ireland

*T*he continued efforts to find a lasting solution to the "Troubles" in Northern Ireland is good and bad news for golfers. Good news for those who have not sampled the glorious links of this province, but bad news for those who have been coming here for years, despite the threat imposed by militants on either side of the divide.

In all honesty the "Troubles" haven't really affected the pace of play that much. The golf course has been the one place to escape the sectarian extra-curricular activities. And what safe havens they are.

You'll struggle to find better links golf than that to be found in the province of Ulster. Just an hour's drive north of Belfast you'll find links courses to satisfy any dyed in the wool traditionalist. Royal Portrush, Portstewart, Castlerock, Ballycastle, they offer all the fun of seaside golf.

Of course Portrush is the jewel of this coastline. Still the only course outside mainland Britain to have staged the Open Championship – when Max Faulkner captured the Old Claret Jug in 1951 – Portrush is a true championship course in an age when that particular adjective has been devalued by modern golf course builders. Huge sand dunes, tight fairways, pot bunkers, undulating greens – in short everything you expect of seaside golf. It's a course that has been used for many important championships, amateur and professional alike. Look for it to return to the Open rota one day when the political scenario is much more favourable.

Anyone travelling to this coastline, to the Giant's Causeway – dubbed as such because of the strange geological rock formation where land meets sea, rocks which look like steps down into the cold waters of the Irish sea – needs to make a proper job of the visit. To do that you must play Portstewart, Castlerock and Ballycastle. Along with Portrush, these three courses provide the venue for the Blackbush, a huge amateur event held every June that attracts hundreds of golfers. All three are special in their own way. For example, Portstewart offers some of the best natural golf to be found anywhere. The new holes constructed in the dunes in the late 80s would not look out of place on Portrush, or any other great links course for that matter. Play them to your handicap and you'll be one happy golfer. Indeed, play this course to your handicap and you have either had a great day or you should be wearing a mask.

Castlerock and Ballycastle don't quite come up to the standard of Portrush and Portstewart, but they are very enjoyable. Castlerock is a wonderfully natural links with a good mix of testing and enjoyable holes. Ballycastle may be short but don't let that put you off. Play it first of the quartet – it's the perfect course to tone your game for the challenges of the other three.

If it's challenge your after, then you'll find it about two and a half hours south of Portrush, at Newcastle, home to Royal County Down.

Another magnificent links course, this one is even more natural than the ones to be found on the Causeway Coast. Here you'll find plenty of blind shots, especially from the tee, where you aim at a marker stone or post and fire away. It's long too, so don't play it off the back markers unless you've got your A game with you. If you haven't then fear not, the Mountains of Mourne provide a splendid backdrop for those content to look at the scenery.

Don't think golf in the province of Ulster is all played by the sea. It isn't. There's plenty of parkland challenges to satisfy those who don't like the wind to mess their hair. Malone, Belvoir Park, Clandeboye's two fine courses – the Ava and the Dufferin – are just a few of the courses for those who want a break from the sea.

Northern Ireland

Page

Situated in the picturesque Roe Valley countryside, Radisson Roe Park Hotel and Golf Resort is Northern Ireland's only Hotel with its own 18 hole golf course. This 4 Star Hotel is centred around the original building of Mullagh House, dating from the mid-18th century and combines the elegance and charm of a country parkland estate with

LOCAL ATTRACTIONS

Radisson Roe Park is the perfect base from which to discover some of the most enchanting countryside in Ireland. The legendary Giant's Causeway is a short journey away along the breathtaking North Coast, perhaps adding a visit to one of the world's oldest distilleries at Bushmills. If golf really is the object of your visit, other courses within a 30 mile radius include Royal Portrush, Portstewart, Castlerock, Ballyliffin and Rosapenna.

Radisson's renowned standards of service and hospitality.

The facilities at Radisson Roe Park offer the golfer a leisure break tailor made – as well as the challenging 6318 yards of the par 70 parkland course. Golfers enjoy on site a 10 bay floodlit driving range, putting green, pro-shop and the services of the resident PGA Professional.

The Resort caters also for the non-golfer. Residents enjoy complimentary use of The Fairways Leisure Club, featuring its own indoor heated pool, sauna, steam room, jacuzzi and two fitness suites. Located within the leisure club is Eden Health and Beauty Salon, providing a range of luxurious treatments for both men and women, including a golfer's tonic to relieve aching muscles after a round of golf!

Guests can relax in the spacious and inviting lounges of this country mansion, also enjoying bedrooms equipped with today's essentials. All rooms are either double or twin bedded and the hotel offers a large selection of rooms to sleep up to five guests.

GOLF INFORMATION

18 hole, 6318 yard parkland course
Par 70

Golf Professional: Seamus Duffy
Tel: 015047 60105

Practice facilities: Covered driving range.

Instructions: Groups and individuals catered for + video analysis.

Hire: Clubs, buggies and trollies.

CARD OF THE COURSE				
1	408	Par 4	10 421	Par 4
2	564	Par 5	11 338	Par 4
3	212	Par 3	12 171	Par 3
4	521	Par 5	13 386	Par 4
5	394	Par 4	14 326	Par 4
6	144	Par 3	15 272	Par 4
7	401	Par 4	16 504	Par 5
8	395	Par 4	17 237	Par 3
9	201	Par 3	18 423	Par 4
Out 3240 Par 35			In 3078 Par 35	

HOTEL INFORMATION

Radisson Roe Park Hotel and Golf Resort
Roe Park, Limavady,
County Londonderry, BT49 9LB
Tel: 015047 22222
Fax: 015047 22313
Rating: 4 Star

Rooms: 64
Restaurants: Courtyard Restaurant (Fine Dining) and Coach House Brasserie.
Childcare Facilities: Baby listening and babysitters available by arrangement.
Beauty Salon: Eden Health and Beauty Salon – treatments for men & women.
Fitness Facilities: The Fairways Leisure Club; indoor heated pool, sauna, steam room, jacuzzi, two fitness suites, children's pool, hydro-seat, dance studio, children's soft toy room & teenage games room.
Other Sporting Facilities: Croquet on site & Archery by arrangement. Within 15 mile radius; tennis, fishing.

TARIFF

Special Golf Packages:
B&B including 18 holes from £78.00 per person.
Other Special Group Golf Packages:
From £100.00 per person – 2 nights B&B – 2 rounds of golf – 1 Dinner.

DIRECTIONS

Radisson Roe Park Hotel & Golf Resort is situated on the A2 Londonderry-Limavady Road, 16 miles from Londonderry and 1 mile from Limavady. The Resort is 10 miles from the City of Derry Airport and 45 miles from Belfast International Airport.

Silverwood Golf Hotel & Country Club

*T*he Silverwood Golf Hotel and Country Club, situated in pleasant rural surroundings is only 2 minutes from the M1 motorway which links the hotel to Belfast and within 20 minutes of the air/seaports.

Over the years the hotel has built up a reputation for excellent food combined with friendly and efficient service in a relaxed and charming setting together with a 24-hour check-in service. Each of the 29 large bedrooms is luxuriously furnished with a bathroom en-suite and telephone, radio, CD and tape deck, satellite television, trouser press, iron and ironing board, hairdryer and tea/coffee making facilities. A number of executive rooms are also available. The dining room, in light sunny colours with pine and wicker furniture is extremely popular with both residents and locals. The lounge provides a carvery lunch and an extensive snack menu daily. The Topaz night club features live bands at the weekend as well as music in the lounge bar.

The Silverwood Golf/Ski Centre consists of an 18 hole parkland course, a 9 hole par 3 course, a pitch and putt course, putting greens and a floodlit driving range. The course has sand based well irrigated greens and has lakes incorporated into the 3rd and 10th holes.

LOCAL ATTRACTIONS

Northern Ireland's premier ski slope is situated to the front of the hotel. Jet skiing, water skiing, canoeing and windsurfing are available nearby.

In addition sailing, angling and bird watching all take place locally. Two National Trust properties, Ardress House and The Argory are much visited by tourists and have many fine woodland and garden walks.

GOLF INFORMATION

18 hole, 6188 yard parkland course

Par 72

Golf Professional: Des Paul
Tel: 01762 326606

Practice facilities: Covered driving range.

Instructions: Groups and individuals catered for.

Hire: Clubs and trollies.

CARD OF THE COURSE Yellow Tees					
1	396	Par 4	10	487	Par 5
2	539	Par 5	11	157	Par 3
3	314	Par 4	12	335	Par 4
4	310	Par 4	13	303	Par 4
5	141	Par 3	14	430	Par 4
6	417	Par 4	15	203	Par 3
7	422	Par 4	16	303	Par 4
8	376	Par 4	17	311	Par 4
9	455	Par 5	18	289	Par 4
Out	3370	Par 37	In	2818	Par 35

HOTEL INFORMATION

Silverwood Golf Hotel and Country Club
40 Kiln Road, Lurgan
Co. Armagh BT66 6NF.
Tel: 01762 327722
Fax: 01762 325290
Rating: Best Western 3 Star.
Rooms: 29.
Restaurants: Restaurant – English food, wide and varied menu. Lounge Bar – Carvery and extensive bar snack menu.
Childcare Facilities: Baby sitting facilities available.
Hair and Beauty: Available locally
Other Sporting Facilities: Dry ski slope on site, watersports centre – waterskiing, jetsking, canoeing, windsurfing (2 miles from hotel), sailing and boat trips on Lough Neagh. Angling – Lough Neagh and river Bann – both coarse and game fishing, bird watching – Oxford island on Lough Neagh – National Nature Reserve.
Other Leisure Activities: Music in bar at weekends and traditional music midweek, night club attached to hotel with live bands and disco. (Free to Residents). Lurgan public park 200 acres of woodland, lake and recretation areas, Lough Neagh Discovery Centre, Oxford Island – National Nature Reserve with 270 acres and 8km of walks, Discovery Centre tells the story of the history, culture and wildlife around Lough Neagh.

TARIFF

Std. rm: **£55** sgl; **£70** dbl;
Ex. rm: **£65** sgl; **£90** dbl, inc breafast.
Weekend Break:
(Fri/Sat or Sat/Sun) 1 day **£35**pps,
2 days **£65**pps; 3 days **£90**pps –
all weekend rates include B&B + dinners.

Golf Package: (Thurs to Sunday inclusive) 1 day b&b, 1 dinner + 1 day golf **£40;** 2 days b&b, 2 dinners, 2 days golf **£75** pps; 3 days b&b, 3 dinners, 3 days golf **£110**pps. Other packages available on request.

Special Golf Packages:
B&B including 18 holes **£27.50**pps.

DIRECTIONS

From Belfast Seaport & Belfast City Airport - Take the motorway M1 West towards Craigavon and exit at junction 10 on the Craigavon (Lurgan) exit road A76. Continue for about half a mile and take the first right hand turn marked Silverwood Golf/Ski Centre (Kiln Road) continue for about ¼ mile and the hotel lies on the right hand side.

From Belfast International Airport – Take the A26 South to the motorway M1 and enter on the motorway at junction 9. Head west and exit at next junction 10 as above

From Larne Seaport – Take the A8 South to Belfast and follow road to the motorway M1 exit from the M1 at junction 10 and continue as above.

Western Ireland

Dungaire Castle, Kinvara

Western Ireland

*T*here's something haunting about the west coast of Ireland. Maybe it's the wind, perhaps it's the emptiness of the place. Whatever it is it's often an eerie place to be. Just driving through this wild, rugged landscape gives one a feeling of helplessness against the elements. Of course this feeling is truly experienced by walking the coastline, and what better way to do that than with a golf bag on your shoulders?

So many of the courses of the West Coast seem to battle for existence with the Atlantic Ocean. This is where links golf truly lives up to its definition, for one thing you can always count on in the west of Ireland is the wind. Get a calm day on this coastline and you had better take advantage of it, for there aren't many days when the wind doesn't blow.

True there are inland courses to be found here, but you will always be drawn to the coast. From the hidden gems of Donegal – Murvagh, Ballyliffin, Rosapenna, Narin & Portnoo, Northwest – to the great links courses of County Kerry in the South – Ballybunion, Caenn Sibeal, Dooks, Tralee, Waterville – this is links golf par excellence. In between you'll find such classics links as County Sligo, Enniscrone, Lahinch and Connemara.

This is golf as it was meant to be played. Along the ground as opposed to through the air. Bump and run shots, putters from 10 yards off the green, punched iron shots and low flying drivers, you'll need a full repertoire of seaside stroke savers to help you match your handicap.

Some courses, like Ballybunion, Waterville, Tralee, Lahinch are magnets for golfers seeking links golf at its best. In summer you will find plenty of foreigners vying for tee times – Americans, Japanese, Swedes, Germans, golfers of just about every nationality visit these courses through the warmer months. However, there are plenty that have yet to be truly discovered by golfers around the world. The courses of Donegal are still relatively "undiscovered" by foreigners, although their attractions are starting to be broadcast far and wide, particularly the two excellent courses at Ballyliffin. The same goes for the likes of Caenn Sibeal, Enniscrone and the wild landscape of Connemara.

So perseverance is required in the summer months, but if you're willing to take a chance with the elements, then the spring and autumn are often the best times to visit this area.

If it's inland golf your after then fear not. There's plenty of good parkland golf to be found on the west coast of the Emerald Isle. Adare Manor, Beaufort, Galway Bay, and of course Killarney Golf and Fishing Club, venue for the Irish Open on a number of occasions. The two courses here are as pretty and as challenging as you are ever likely to find. Of course the beauty of the place is enhanced by the magnificent Macgillicuddy Reeks, Ireland's tallest mountain range, which tower over the two excellent parkland layouts.

However, the inland venues are just a pleasant distraction. If you want to play traditional Irish golf at its best, then head for the sea.

Western Ireland

Page

Adare Manor Hotel & Country Club

Set in the South West of Ireland, Adare Manor is a 5 star luxury resort nestling in 840 acres of rolling countryside complete with it's own championship golf course. As rich in beauty as it is in history, the Manor is an architectural jewel presiding over breathtaking formal gardens, majestic parkland and fascinating ruins dating back

over eight hundred years. This 5 star Manor House Hotel has 63 deluxe rooms in the Manor House and a further 63 being built with the new clubhouse for 1999. The magnificent public rooms include the Long Gallery, a warm and cosy library and the exquisitely appointed Cocktail Lounge. The hotels' restaurant overlooks the River Maigue and specialises in the best of modern Irish cuisine with all of the ingredients being sourced in the region.

The par 72, Robert Trent Jones senior designed course is rated as one of the finest this great man has completed and Adare has joined the list of top courses designed by Mr Jones which include Spy Glass Hills and Peachtree in the U.S., Las Brisas and Valderrama in Spain.

The course is gentle parkland making it a pleasure to walk but testing with water at 10 holes including the last which is particularly challenging.

GOLF INFORMATION

18 hole, 7138 yard Heathland/Woodland course Par 72

Tel: 61 395 044

Practice facilities: Outdoor driving range.

Instructions: Groups and individuals catered for.

Hire: Clubs and buggies.

CARD OF THE COURSE

1	433	Par 4	10	441	Par 4
2	413	Par 4	11	187	Par 3
3	403	Par 4	12	550	Par 5
4	180	Par 3	13	442	Par 4
5	419	Par 4	14	425	Par 4
6	205	Par 3	15	370	Par 4
7	537	Par 5	16	170	Par 3
8	427	Par 4	17	415	Par 4
9	577	Par 5	18	544	Par 5
Out	3594	Par 36	In	3544	Par 36

HOTEL INFORMATION

Adare Manor Hotel & Golf Club
Adare, Co Limerick
Ireland
Tel: 61 396566
Fax: 61 396124
Rating: 5 Star RAC, Small Luxury Hotels
Rooms: 63.
Restaurants: Formal dining in Restaurant – Bistro/Golfers buffet in Tack Room Bar.
Childcare Facilities: 24hr childcare service available on request.
Hair and Beauty: Available on request
Fitness Facilities: Indoor swimming pool, Fitness centre, Massage Therapy.
Other Sporting Facilities: Golf on our Championship courses, Clay Pigeon Shooting, Fishing (Gillies available), Hunting and Horse Riding.

TARIFF

B&B from **£215** room only – May to Sept
£165 room only – April to Oct
£120 room only – Jan to Mar and Nov/December

Special Golf Packages:
B&B including 18 holes from £110 per person sharing.

Other Special Golf Packages:
3 and 5 day Packages available on request.

DIRECTIONS

Only 24 miles from Shannon Airport, Adare Manor is 9 miles from Limerick city. From Limerick City, follow the N20 through the village of Patrickswell; then take the N21 to the village of Adare. The entrance to the estate of Adare Manor is right at the start of the village street.

Lakes of Killarney, Co Kerry

CLONLARA GOLF & LEISURE
Clonlara, Co. Clare. Tel: 061 354141 Fax: 0161 354143

12 HOLES	PAR 47	3377 METRES

TYPE OF GOLF COURSE: Parkland

RATING: 2/3 Star

B&B + 18 HOLES:
Self-catering Apartments

Clonlara Golf & Leisure is ideally situated, being in the heart of the West of Ireland and only a 20 minute drive from the centre of Limerick City.

It is located on the grounds of Landscape House, which was built in the 17th Century, and is now the private residence of Mr and Mrs O'Connell. The 12-hole (Par 47) golf course stands on 63 acres of mature parkland.

Whether you are on holiday in the area and would enjoy the pleasure of a leisurely game, or a golf society planning an outing, we will be more than please to welcome you. Accommodation is in self-catering apartments. Tennis, sauna, pool & table tennis are also available and a children's play area.

DROMOLAND CASTLE GOLF & COUNTRY CLUB

Newmarket on Fergus, Co. Clare. Tel: 061-368144 Fax: 061-363355

Built in the late 16th century, Dromoland Castle forms a majestic backdrop to the challenging course that bears its name. 18 holes since 1985 with a par of 71, Dromoland Golf & Country has earned an enviable reputation both for the quality of golf and the amenities of the new clubhouse, which include a fully equipped health & leisure centre and the brasserie style Fig Tree restaurant.

18 HOLES	PAR 71	6098 YARDS
TYPE OF GOLF COURSE: Parkland		
RATING: Relais & Chateau, AA		
GOLF PROFESSIONAL: Philip Murphy		
TEL: 061-351874		
B&B + 18 HOLES: High Season from £220 per room – Breakfast £13.50pp + 15% SC – Golf £19 – Resident.		

The Harbour at Rosses Point

GALWAY BAY GOLF & COUNTRY CLUB HOTEL

Oranmore, Co. Galway, Ireland. Tel: +353 91 790500 Fax: +353 91 792510

Luxury golf and accommodation base situated 8 miles from Galway City in an idyllic setting on the west coast of Ireland. Located overlooking Galway Bay and the Atlantic Ocean 18 hole championship golf course designed by Christy O'Connor Jnr.

Meeting room/conference facilities also available. AA rosettes awarded Grainne Uaile Restaurant.

18 HOLES	PAR 72	6533 YARDS
TYPE OF GOLF COURSE: Parkland/Coastal		
GOLF PROFESSIONAL: Eugene O'Connor TEL: +353 91 790503		
B&B + 18 HOLES: Oct '98–Apr '99 Mon-Fri £59 p.p.s Sat-Sun £63 p.p.s Until End Sept '98 Mon-Fri £84 p.p.s Sat-Sun £88 p.p.s.		
OTHER SPECIAL GOLF PACKAGES: Mid-week Breaks from £119 p.p.s. (2 B&B, 1 dinner + 1 golf).		

Great Southern Hotel, Parknasilla

*G*reat Southern Hotels has been on of Ireland's premier hotel groups since 1845.

Parknasilla is a 19th Century mansion set in 300 acres of magnificent gardens with a charming, luxurious, country house atmosphere. It is well-situated to benefit from the Gulf Stream which warms the Kerry coastline and results in sub-tropical climate and vegetation.

Guests can enjoy specially designed walks within the grounds of the estate; more experienced walkers can undertake 5-day programmes with expert guides.

The 9 hole golf course has seen the benefit of a major redevelopment over the past 3 years with the addition of 4 new holes and all the others improved and extended. Renowned for its scenic view, this course presents a challenge to both high and low handicappers alike.

The golf course is exclusively for the use of hotel guests and is supported by a driving range and golf academy.

Other facilities available are indoor swimming pool, steam room, sauna & jacuzzi Outdoors there is windsurfing, horse riding, inshore and deep-sea fishing, clay pigeon shooting, archery and cruises on the Parknasilla Princess.

LOCAL ATTRACTIONS

The legendary 'Ring of Kerry' is one of Ireland's most spectacular scenic attractions. You can follow the winding road along the dramatic coastline or stroll inland among the McGillicuddy Reeks – the highest mountains in Ireland.

Muckross House and Abbey, Ross Castle, the Franciscan Friary and Knockreer house are just a few of the places worth a visit.

Game and sea fishing, riding, wind-surfing, orienteering and mountaineering are near for the adventurous.

GOLF INFORMATION

9 hole, 5520 yard heathland/woodland course

Par 70

Instructions: Groups and individuals catered for.

Hire: Clubs and buggies

CARD OF THE COURSE					
1	314	Par 4	10	314	Par 4
2	122	Par 3	11	122	Par 3
3	454	Par 5	12	454	Par 5
4	156	Par 3	13	156	Par 3
5	290	Par 4	14	290	Par 4
6	341	Par 4	15	341	Par 4
7	346	Par 4	16	346	Par 4
8	407	Par 4	17	407	Par 4
9	330	Par 4	18	330	Par 4
Out	2760	Par 35	In	2760	Par 35

HOTEL INFORMATION

Great Southern Hotel,
Parknasilla,
Sneem, Co. Kerry.
Tel: 353 64 45122
Fax: 353 64 45323
Rating: 4 Star.
Rooms: 84.
Restaurants: Pygmalion.
Childcare: Baby-sitting on request.
Hair and Beauty: Massage & aromatherapy.
Fitness Facilities: Indoor heated swimming pool, steam room, sauna & jacuzzi.
Other Sporting Facilities: Tennis courts, golf academy & croquet.
Other Leisure Activities: Windsurfing, horse-riding, inshore & deep-sea fishing, pleasure cruises on the Parknasilla Princess, clay pigeon shooting and archery.

TARIFF

FEB 13-APR 30. OCT 24-DEC
Weekends: £115.00; Daily: £79.00; 4 Day Stay: £289.00

MAY 1-JULY 11. AUG 30-OCT 23
Weekends: £130.00; Daily: £89.00; 4 Day Stay: £330.00

JULY 12-AUG 29
Weekends: £145.00; Daily: £105.00 4 Day Stay: £390.00

DIRECTIONS

From Cork take the N22 to Killarney, turn left onto the A71 to Kenmare. Turn right along the A70. The hotel can be found after 15 miles along the Sneem Road.

GLENLO ABBEY HOTEL

Bushypark, Galway, Ireland. Tel: 091 526666 Fax: 091 527800

9 HOLES	PAR 71	6538 YARDS

TYPE OF GOLF COURSE: Lake-Side Parkland

RATING: 5 Star Bord Failte Rating, RAC Blue Ribbon (96-98), AA Red Star (97-98) AA resettes for cuisine AA romantic hotel of GB+IRL, Member of small luxury hotels.

GOLF PROFESSIONAL: Garry Todd

B&B + 18 HOLES: £160.00 High Season – £120.00 off season p.p.s 1st Oct 98 – 31/3/98 – Golf £10.00

Glenlo Abbey, an 18th century residence recently restored to its former splendour, was once home to the French and Blake families, two of the famous fourteen tribes that ruled Galway for centuries. The Hotel is set on a 138 acre golf estate overlooking the magnificent Lough Corrib. A variety of on-site activities are available which include golf, a 12 bay driving range, fishing, clay pigeon shooting and lake boating.

ROSAPENNA HOTEL & GOLF LINKS

Downings, County Donegal, Ireland
Tel: 00353 74 55301 Fax: 00353 74 55128

HOLES: 18	YARDS: 6271	PAR: 70

WATERVILLE HOUSE & GOLF LINKS

Waterville, County Kerry, Ireland
Tel: 00353 66 74102 Fax: 00353 66 74482

HOLES: 18	YARDS: 7184	PAR: 72

Sybil Head on the Dingle Peninsul

Cliffs of Moher

Limerick County Golf & Country Club

imerick County Golf & Country Club is located 5 miles south of Limerick City, along route R512 direction of Kilmallock/Lough Gur, 25 miles from Shannon Airport in Ireland's South West. The complex is easily accessible from all major Irish Cities, Airports and Ports.

LOCAL ATTRACTIONS

Numerous local attractions include the Aughinish Wildlife Sanctuary, Askeaton Mediaeval Town, Celtic Theme Park & Gardens at Kilcornan, Foynes Flying Boat Museum, Boyce Gardens at Loughill, Glin Castle & Gardens and the Glin Heritage, Genealogy & Graft Centre, in addition to the St. John's Art Centre in Listowel and Irish Offshore Adventures in Foynes.

The 6772 yards (6191 metres) Par 72 18 hole Parkland course opened in June 1994 was designed by Des Smyth and Associates. It is already established as one of the foremost inland courses in Ireland with beautiful rolling fairways and well matured greens, built to championship standards with spectacular views of the Limerick countryside. With its undulating greens and well positioned bunkers and lakes, the golf course represents a tough, but enjoyable challenge for golfers of all standards.

We are proud of our comprehensive range of facilities including an ultra modern clubhouse, driving range, par 3 practise holes and visitor holiday Cottages. There are twelve self-catering cottages in total, each built to 4 star standard, sleeping five people and comprising three bedrooms.

The Clubhouse caters for groups and functions of all sizes. In the award-winning Restaurant you can enjoy the very best of food and wine whilst the Ballyneety Bar overlooking the back nine holes offers a relaxing atmosphere in which to enjoy a drink or two.

GOLF INFORMATION

18 hole, 6772 yard parkland, championship course

Par 72

Golf Professional: Philip Murphy

Tel: 061-351874

Practice facilities: Covered driving range.

Instructions: Groups and individuals catered for.

Hire: Clubs and buggies.

CARD OF THE COURSE (Metres)					
1	373	Par 4	10	330	Par 4
2	158	Par 3	11	444	Par 5
3	367	Par 4	12	304	Par 4
4	489	Par 5	13	448	Par 5
5	408	Par 4	14	350	Par 4
6	169	Par 3	15	178	Par 3
7	283	Par 4	16	370	Par 4
8	386	Par 4	17	346	Par 4
9	379	Par 4	18	409	Par 4
Out	3012	Par 35	In	3179	Par 37

HOTEL INFORMATION

Limerick County Golf & Country Club
Ballyneety
Co. Limerick
Tel: 061-351881
Fax: 061-351384
E-mail: lcgolf@ioi.ie
Website: www.limerickcounty.com

Rating: 4 Star.

Rooms: 12 Cottages sleeping 5 people.

Restaurants: Full restaurant facilities, à la carte menu.

Childcare: Babysitters available on request.

Fitness Facilities: Jacuzzi, Steamroom & Showers.

TARIFF

Packages available on request.

DIRECTIONS

Located 5 miles south of Limerick City, route R512, 25 miles from Shannon Airport in south west.

Dublin &
Southern Ireland

Powerscourt Gardens, Co. Wicklow

Dublin & Southern Ireland

With flights to Ireland as cheap and as numerous as they've ever been, there's no reason for anyone not to pay a visit to Dublin and the Emerald isle. Of course if you already live there, then that's the least of your worries. With the road system in Ireland improving all the time, Dublin isn't the trek from other parts of Ireland that it once was.

As a golfer you cannot not go to Ireland to play golf. And if you haven't been to Dublin then what are you waiting for? It's the ideal city break if you enjoy this madly frustrating game. For what could be finer than a round on one of the city's truly great links and a night on the town trying to find the best pint of black stuff in the capital?

Portmarnock, Portmarnock Hotel & Golf Links, The European Club, Druid's Glen, Royal Dublin, Woodbrook, the Seapoint, County Louth, The Island, they, and many more, are within easy striking range of the Irish capital.

First and foremost on your list must be the two links courses at Portmarnock. The Old is hard to get access to but persevere, for it is arguably the best course in all of Ireland. The younger brother, the new links course at Portmarnock Hotel, is no weak relation either. Designed by Bernhard Langer, this is a truly great addition to Irish golf.

So are the newer inland courses such as Druid's Glen, The K Club, St Margaret's and Mount Juliet, a couple of hours to the South. Indeed, the last 10 or 15 years has seen a great explosion in Irish golf courses.

However, as usual it will be the classics of Irish golf that you'll want to play - and their are some outstanding ones. Besides the already mentioned Portmarnock Old, you must try County Louth at Baltray, one of the classic hidden gems in Irish golf, a traditional links course you'll want to take home with you. And if you have the chance then play Seapoint next door. Veteran European Tour pro Des Smyth is responsible for a good course that is a mixture of links and parkland. You may just want to sneak that course into your suitcase as well.

The same can be said about The European Club south of Dublin at Brittas Bay. Although it was only opened in 1989, play it for the first time and you'll swear it's been there for 100 years at least. It is arguably architect Pat Ruddy's finest creation, and he's been responsible for a fair few in Ireland.

In the south of the country, try the Jack Nicklaus creation of Mount Juliet, North of Waterford, a course favoured by Nick Faldo and one that has hosted the Irish Open. This is a beautiful parkland course that plays long and tough. Be advised: play it off forward markers.

No matter what markers you play off at the Old Head of Kinsale, you'll probably forget about golf and simply enjoy the view. This course is built in perhaps the most scenic location in all of Ireland – and that's saying something, for there a lot of courses with stunning scenery in the Emerald Isle.

However, the Old Head Links is set on a rocky promontory a few miles south of the town of Kinsale. You drive through a narrow isthmus high above the sea onto an outcrop just big enough for 18 holes. No less than nine holes are played along the edge of the cliffs. Often if you hook or slice then the ball ends up in the sea. It is truly spectacular stuff, but then you know that once you get to the clubhouse, for the views on a fine day are worth the green fee. A must for anyone travelling to this part of Ireland.

So too are the courses at West Waterford, Waterford Castle, Faithlegg, Tramore and St Helen's Bay. Good golf is to be found at all, but then it's hard not to find good golf in this part of Ireland.

Dublin & Southern Ireland

Slieve Russell
N3
Carrickmacross
N53
Dundalk
Nuremore
N52
Ballymascanlon House
Ardee
N52
Dunleer
N2
Kells
Slane
Drogheda
N51
Navan
Athboy
N3
N2
N1
Balbriggan
Luttrellstown Castle
Portmarnock Links Hotel
N4
M4
Finnstown Country House Hotel
M1
Deerpark Hotel
Maynooth
N41
Clane
Kildare Hotel & Country Club
Citywest Country House
N7
Dublin
Dun Laoghaire
Naas
Kilternan
Kildare
N9
M7
N81
M11
Charlesland
Powerscourt
Ballymore Eustace
N11
N78
Rathsallagh House
Glendalough
Wicklow
Kilkea Castle
Baltinglass
Rathdrum
Mount Wolseley
Arklow
Kilkenny
N80
N9
N8
Cashel
Mount Juliet
N76
N10
Enniscorthy
ary
New Ross
N9
N79
N11
ir
Clonmel
N24
Carrick-on-Suir
N25
N25
Waterford
Wexford
Cappoquin
N25
Waterford Castle
Bridgetown
St Helen's Bay
2
Tramore
Fethard
Rosslare Harbour
Dungarvan
Youghal
N25

The Kildare Hotel & Country Club

*T*he 330 acre grounds of The Kildare Hotel & Country Club are nestled amid lush green woodlands, just 40 minutes from Dublin, Ireland's Capital city and 30 minutes driving time from Dublin International Airport. This magnificent hotel, Ireland's only 5 Red Star Hotel graded by the Automobile Association, offers you the highest standards of comfort and service combined with the elegance and charm of an Irish Country House.

Each bedroom has been decorated in its own unique style and individually appointed to the highest standard, each with private bathroom.

The K Club course was designed by Arnold Palmer and has a par of 72. Covering 220 acres of prime Kildare woodland and featuring 11 lakes and the River Liffey, the course gives players of all standards a demanding test. The K Club has already hosted many major golf tournaments including The Irish PGA Championships and the Bi-annual mini Ryder Cup in September 1992 between Club professionals of America and Europe. The Club is now home to The Smurfit European Open which was first played here in 1995.

The Resort offers a superb range of recreational and leisure facilities allowing you to be as energetic as you like or just let time drift by and unwind at your leisure.

LOCAL ATTRACTIONS

Guided tours of Dublin and the local area can be arranged. The Curragh, Punchestown, Naas, Fairyhouse – some of Ireland's major racecourses are located thirty minutes driving time from the hotel. The National Stud Farm and Japanese Gardens are also nearby. Castletown House, Ireland's largest palladian house is close by to the hotel along with the steam museum and butterfly farm. Dublin City is seventeen miles for shopping and sightseeing and Wicklow, which is known as the garden of Ireland, offers a day to sample the Irish Countryside.

GOLF INFORMATION

18 hole, 7159 yard parkland course
Par 72

Golf Professional: Ernie Jones

Tel: 353-1-6017321

Practice facilities: Outdoor driving range.

Instructions: Groups and individuals catered for.

Hire: Clubs and buggies.

CARD OF THE COURSE					
1	584	Par 5	10	418	Par 4
2	408	Par 4	11	413	Par 4
3	173	Par 3	12	170	Par 3
4	402	Par 4	13	568	Par 5
5	213	Par 3	14	416	Par 4
6	446	Par 4	15	447	Par 4
7	606	Par 5	16	395	Par 4
8	375	Par 4	17	173	Par 3
9	434	Par 4	18	518	Par 5
Out	3641	Par 36	In	3518	Par 36

HOTEL INFORMATION

The Kildare Hotel & Country Club (The K Club)
Straffan, County Kildare
Ireland
Tel: 353-1-6017200
Fax: 353-1-6017299
Rating: 5 Red Stars AA + 5 Star Blue Ribbons RAC.

Rooms: 45 including additional garden courtyard suites.
Restaurants: The Byerley Turk (Hotel) The Legends (Golf Club).
Childcare: Baby sitting service available
Hair and Beauty: Hairdressing, 4 treatment rooms for professional health & beauty treatments.
Fitness Facilities: Full international gymnasium – equipment nautilus.
Other Sporting Facilities: Clay target shooting, ground course fishing – 5 stocked lakes – river fishing – salmon + trout, horseriding, archery.
Other Leisure Activities: Arranged on request.

TARIFF

Superior Room
IR£280.00 per night
Deluxe Room
IR£350.00 per night
Garden Courtyard Suites (2 Bedroomed) IR£320.00 per night
Fountain Courtyard Suites
IR£450.00 per night
1 Bedroomed Suite IR£550.00 per night
2 Bedroomed Suite IR£700.00 per night
Viceroy Suite IR£1,000.00 per night
Rates quoted are per room per night.

DIRECTIONS

From Dublin City (17 miles/27km – 40 minutes approximately) take the N7 (Naas Road) to traffic lights at Kill (village on left). Turn right at lights.
Approximately 3 miles/5km – T junction – turn right. Approximately ½ mile/800m – turn left (signpost for Kildare Hotel & Country Club). Approximately 1 mile/1.6km over Liffey Bridge – Hotel gates on left.

BALLYMASCANLON HOUSE HOTEL
Dundalk, Co. Loath, Ireland. Tel: 042 71124 Fax: 042 71598

18 HOLES	**PAR** 68	**5548 YARDS**

TYPE OF GOLF COURSE: Parkland

RATING: 3 Star

B&B + 18 HOLES: £55.00pp sharing

OTHER SPECIAL GOLF PACKAGES:
On request

Ballymascanlon Hotel situated on the picturesque Cooley peninsula is an old country house, recently refurbished and set in its own grounds. All rooms are en-suite with direct dial telephone, colour TV and tea/coffee making facilities. Our leisure centre incorporates a 20m deck level swimming pool, sauna, steam room, plunge pool, jacuzzi and gymnasium. Our 18 hole parkland golf course is proving to be a challenging though enjoyable to both the amateur and the experienced golfer alike. Superior rooms available at a supplement.

3 miles north of Dundalk on main Dublin-Belfast road, take 3rd exit from roundabout, drive along Carlingford Road - Ballymascanlon Hotel is on the left.

CHARLESLAND GOLF & COUNTRY CLUB
Greystone, Co. Wicklow. Tel: +353-1-2874350 Fax: +353-1-2874360

18 HOLES	**PAR** 72	**6162 YARDS**

TYPE OF GOLF COURSE: Parkland
RATING: Bord Failte approved – 3 Star
GOLF PROFESSIONAL: Paul Heeny
TEL: +353-1-2873225
B&B + 18 HOLES: £80 single; £130 double
OTHER SPECIAL GOLF PACKAGES:
Golf £25pp for groups of 12 or more

Situated in the Garden of Ireland, just 20 minutes drive from Dun Laoghaire car ferry port and within easy access from Dublin Airport, Charlesland was designed by one of Ireland's foremost golf architects, Eddie Hackett and opened in 1992. The 6162 metres par 72 course presents a testing but eminently fair challenge. The clubhouse at Charlesland incorporates a hotel and is the ideal place for visitors to Ireland's garden county. As well as playing golf here, one can play at such courses as Druids Glen, Powerscourt, Portmarnock and several other top Irish courses, all within easy reach of Charlesland.

CITYWEST HOTEL, CONFERENCE CENTRE & GOLF RESORT
Saggart, Co. Dublin. Tel: 00353-1-4588566 Fax: 00353-1-4588565

18 HOLES	**PAR** 70	**6314 YARDS**

TYPE OF GOLF COURSE: Parkland
RATING: Waiting for Grading
GOLF PROFESSIONALS: Gary McNeill, George Howey, Martin Lung
TEL: 003531-4587011
B&B + 18 HOLES: £70 per person sharing per night. £90 per person in a single per night.
OTHER SPECIAL GOLF PACKAGES:
Available throughout the year

City West Hotel is set in over 200 acres of majestic woodland only 20 minutes from Dublin's city centre. This deluxe hotel has 200 spacious bedrooms, each equipped with satellite TV, executive desk, ISDN lines fax modem, guestline system and trouser press. The restaurants serve Irish and continental cuisine. The golf course was designed by Christy O'Connor Jr and has a 20 bay driving range close by.

DEER PARK HOTEL & GOLF COURSES

Howth Co. Dublin, Ireland. Tel: INT + 353-1-8322624 Fax: INT + 353-1-8392405

This is Ireland's largest golf complex set in 600 acres, just 9 miles from Dublin City and the Airport. All rooms are en-suite with telephone satellite TV and tea/coffee facilities. There is an a-la-carte restaurant, bar and indoor swimming pool.

The golf facilities comprise two 18-hole full courses, a 12-hole short course and an 18-hole pitch and putt.

36 HOLES PAR 72/72 6830/6503 YARDS
TYPE OF GOLF COURSE: Parkland
RATING: Bord Failte (I.T.B) and RAC 3 Star
B&B + 18 HOLES: £60.00 per person
OTHER SPECIAL GOLF PACKAGES: £126 – 2 nights B&B, 1 dinner and 2 days golf.

Lismore Castle, Co. Waterford

The Kilternan Hotel

Situated on the Dublin-Wicklow border, Kilternan is a short drive from the famous spots of County Wicklow and just 25 minutes from the attractions of down town Dublin.

This Inn style Hotel has much to offer the visitor to Ireland including one of Ireland's most scenic 18 hole golf courses. Although relatively small (48 bedrooms) the Hotel offers a surprising variety of leisure facilities including a heated swimming pool, jacuzzi, sauna, 2 steam rooms, 4 indoor and 4 outdoor tennis courts, aerobics and cardiovascular workout studios and a junior club.

The Paddocks Stable in Sandord offers horse riding and trekking. Dry ski slope is available from September – March with lessons and ski hire.

Relax in the Library or have a game of snooker, visit the beauty salon or the Therapy Clinic, with the creche taking care of the children. Enjoy excellent Bistro food, or relax in the Bunker Bar.

LOCAL ATTRACTIONS

Located in a beautiful setting on the outskirts of Dublin. Kilternan Golf Hotel has every amenity on its doorstep. Many local golf courses, European, Druids Glen, Powerscourt, Edmonstown, Oldconna, a new 30 bay driving range, pubs, restaurants, theatres and state of the art shopping centres.

The Hotel has its own Night Club, Fitness and Tennis centres and from September – March access to dry ski slope in the hotel grounds.

For full details of these and many other attractions at Kilternan ask for our free brochure '101 things to do at Kilternan'

GOLF INFORMATION

18 hole, 4952 yard parkland course

Par 68

Golf Professional: Gary Hendley

Tel: 01 295 2986

Instructions: Groups and individuals catered for.

Hire: Clubs and buggies.

CARD OF THE COURSE					
1	324	Par 4	10	295	Par 4
2	271	Par 4	11	93	Par 3
3	189	Par 3	12	268	Par 4
4	302	Par 4	13	368	Par 4
5	350	Par 4	14	367	Par 4
6	288	Par 4	15	172	Par 3
7	257	Par 4	16	431	Par 5
8	352	Par 4	17	353	Par 4
9	105	Par 3	18	167	Par 3
Out	2438	Par 34	In	2514	Par 34

HOTEL INFORMATION

The Kilternan Hotel
Kilternan
Co. Dublin
Tel: 01 295 5559
Fax: 01 295 5670 IRL
Rating: 3 Star.

Rooms: 48.

Restaurants: Bistro.

Childcare: Creche & Junior Club, Junior Camp.

Hair and Beauty: Facials, Manicures, Massage and plenty of pampering.

Fitness Facilities: Indoor heated swimming pool, sauna, 2 steam rooms, jacuzzi, aerobics studios, gym & tennis centre.

TARIFF

Single – 2 day special £99.00 2 x B&B free golf.

Double – 2 day special £69.00 per person sharing 2 x B&B free golf.

Special Golf Packages:
B&B including 18 holes £40.00 per person sharing.

DIRECTIONS

Take the N11 south for 25 minutes (through Donnybrook and Stillorgan) until you reach Loughlinstown roundabout (first roundabout on the dual carriageway). Go right around the roundabout as though heading back towards Dublin. Take the first left, at the Silver Tassie Pub (Cherrywood Road), keep to the right. Continue along this winding road for about 3 miles – at T-junction (Statoil Garage on right) turn left. The Hotel is half mile along on the right hand side.

FERNHILL GOLF & COUNTRY CLUB
Carrigdive, Co. Cork, Ireland Tel: 021 372226 Fax: 021 371011

18 HOLES   PAR 69   6241 YARDS
TYPE OF GOLF COURSE: Parkland
B&B + 18 HOLES: From £40 per person

Fernhill Golf & Country Club Carrigdive, Co. Cork, is an 18 bedroomed hotel situated on the golf course. The hotel facilities include; an indoor heated swimming pool, sauna and tennis court. The clubhouse serves food & drink 7 days a week and has live music every weekend.

O'Connell Street, Dublin

FINNSTOWN COUNTRY HOUSE HOTEL
Newcastle ROad, Lucan, Co. Dublin. Tel: 01-6280644 Fax: 01-6281088

9 HOLES   PAR 66   2586 YARDS
TYPE OF GOLF COURSE: Parkland
RATING: AA, RAC, 3 Star Grade 4
GOLF PROFESSIONAL: Barry Power
TEL: 01-6280086
B&B + 18 HOLES: From £60 per person sharing.
OTHER SPECIAL GOLF PACKAGES: Golfing in conjunction with Luttnell down Castle available

While Finnstown Country House is only 15 minutes drive by motorway from the city centre, it appears to lie in the very depths of the countryside, being surrounded as it is by imposing grounds and an immaculately maintained 9 hole golf course. A host of facilities include tennis, gym, indoor swimming pool and Turkish bath. There are 51 beautifully appointed bedrooms and an AA rosette award winning restaurant.

KILKEA CASTLE HOTEL & GOLF CLUB

Castledermot, Co. Kildare. Tel: 0503 45555 Fax: 0503 45505.

Another of Ireland's country estates turned into a golf course and hotel, Kilkea Castle is one of the oldest inhabited castles in Ireland. It sits on River Greese, and the river serves as a hazard for many of the holes on the accompanying golf course.

Being one of Ireland's oldest, the castle has a lot of history attached to it. It is a 45 bedroom hotel where the service and accommodation is top notch. Throw in the excellent leisure facilities and you have a very good golf complex in the heart of County Kildare.

18 HOLES	PAR 70	6700 YARDS

TYPE OF GOLF COURSE: Parkland

GREEN FEES:
Weekdays: IR£25.
Weekend: IR£25
Weekdays (day): IR£40
Weekends (day): IR£40

FITZPATRICKS HOTEL

Silver Springs, Tivoli, Cork, Ireland
Tel: 00353 21 507533 Fax: 00353 21 505128

HOLES: 9	YARDS: 2000m	PAR: 32

LEE VALLEY GOLF & COUNTRY CLUB

Clashanure, Ovens, County Cork, Ireland
Tel: 00353 21 331721 Fax: 00353 21 331695

HOLES: 18	YARDS: 6434	PAR: 72

LUTTRELLSTOWN CASTLE GOLF & COUNTRY CLUB

Castleknock, Dublin 15. Tel: (01) 8089903 Fax: (01) 8089901 E-mail: aclarke@luttrellstown.ie

Luttrellstown Castle Golf & Country Club is situated within a 560 acre walled estate just twenty minutes from Dublin International Airport and city centre. Host to the Guardian Irish Open in 1997, the exceptionally well manicured 18 hole championship course offers an excellent test of golf for all handicaps.

The unique club house, framing wonderful views on all sides, has a bright airy restaurant, bar and pro-shop. The courtyard apartments within the Castle grounds provide quality self-catering accommodation and safe car parking.

18 HOLES	PAR 72	5000 YARDS

TYPE OF GOLF COURSE: Parkland

RATING: 4 Star

B&B + 18 HOLES: From £45.00

OTHER SPECIAL GOLF PACKAGES:
Half board: £51 p.p.p.n.
Weekend Breaks: £119.00
Society Days: £29.50

Portmarnock Hotel & Golf Links

*P*ortmarnock Hotel and Golf Links is set in splendid surroundings. The house was originally owned by the Jameson family, famous for their Irish Whiskey. Their home has been tastefully converted to an international hotel with the grounds now hosting a magnificent 18 hole Bernhard Langer designed golf links where Darren Clarke is attached as the Touring Professional.

The 103 bedrooms are cleverly designed to ensure that you are either looking over the sea or the golf course. A choice of elegantly appointed accommodation is yours, ranging from the historic four-posters, to executive suites and deluxe rooms.

In the Osborne Restaurant, a wonderful choice of international cuisine is served with style and friendliness ... along with a superb selection of wines. In the less formal Links Restaurant, golfers and locals alike can enjoy excellent dining in a relaxed setting.

Like most good new links courses, the new course at Portmarnock looks as if it's been there for a 100 years. Langer has ensured that the course looks as natural as it should given the land it sits on. Great care has been taken to make the course look and feel as traditional as possible. There are no long walks between green and tee and the bunkering is equal to that of the very best seaside layout. Each of the 100 or so bunkers have been carefully revetted, so that you feel as though you're at Muirfield or Carnoustie.

A selection of other interesting pastimes can be arranged for you to enjoy or maybe attempt for the first time. Try your hand at archery, clay pigeon shooting or even quad bikes over our specially designed obstacle course.

LOCAL ATTRACTIONS

Portmarnock Hotel & Golf Links is located just 11 miles from the bustling shops and traditional pubs of Ireland's capital city, Dublin. Set in a quiet position overlooking the sea between the villages of Portmarnock and Malahide it is the perfect base for so many activities, from golf to clay pigeon shooting, sailing to horse riding. Miles of beautiful beaches provide the enthusiastic walker with ample opportunities to stretch the legs.

18 hole, 6260 metres links course

Par 71

Practice facilities: Outdoor practice ground.

Instructions: Groups and individuals catered for.

Hire: Clubs

CARD OF THE COURSE					
1	354	Par 4	10	484	Par 5
2	360	Par 4	11	419	Par 4
3	178	Par 3	12	329	Par 4
4	527	Par 5	13	137	Par 3
5	431	Par 4	14	317	Par 4
6	486	Par 5	15	364	Par 4
7	412	Par 4	16	371	Par 4
8	342	Par 4	17	185	Par 3
9	156	Par 3	18	408	Par 4
Out	3246	Par 36	In	3014	Par 35

DUBLIN

HOTEL INFORMATION

Portmarnock Hotel & Golf Links
Portmarnock
Co. Dublin
Tel: 01 8460611
Fax: 01 8462442

Rating: 4 Star AA & RAC.

Rooms: 103.

Restaurants: Osbourne – International, Links – Brasserie.

Childcare Facilities: Babysitting available.

Hair and Beauty: on request

Other Sporting Facilities: 18 hole links golf course – designed by B. Langer.

TARIFF

Standard Daily Rates:
Standard: IR£125 Sgl.
IR£195 Twin/Dbl
IR£225 Triple
Executive: IR£155 Sgl.
IR£225 Twin/Dbl
IR£255 Triple
Jameson House: IR£160 Sgl.
IR£235 Twin/Dbl

Special Golf Packages:
B&B including 18 holes £145.00

Other Special Golf Packages:
2 B&B, 1 golf, 1 dinner from £179.00 per person

DIRECTIONS

Portmarnock hotel and golf links is situated only 15 minutes by road from Dublin International Airport and under 30 minutes from the city centre itself.

MOUNT JULIET

Thomastown, Co. Kilkenny. Ireland. Tel: 353 56 73000 Fax: 353 56 73019

18 HOLES **PAR** 72 **7142 YARDS**	

TYPE OF GOLF COURSE: Parkland
HOTEL RATING: 4 Star AA/RAC Blue Ribbon 4 Stars/Irish Tourist Board 4 Stars
GOLF PROFESSIONAL: David Leadbetter
TEL: 353 56 73061
B&B + 18 HOLES: From £137.50 (high season weekend)
OTHER SPECIAL GOLF PACKAGES: Early Bird – Sunsetter – Group rates on request

Deep amid the rolling green hills of Ireland's beautiful south east, lies Mount Juliet. Twelfth century origins, a leisurely pace of life and traditionally generous hospitality combine with world-class sporting and conference facilities. Enjoy golf, horse riding, fishing, shooting, tennis, the spa and leisure centre, or simply relax in the idyllic surroundings.

MOUNT WOLSELEY GOLF & COUNTRY CLUB

Tullow, Co. Carlow, Ireland. Tel: 0503 51674 Fax: 0503 52123

18 HOLES	**PAR** 72	**7106 YARDS**

TYPE OF GOLF COURSE: Parkland
GOLF PROFESSIONAL: Jimmy Bolger
TEL: 0503 51674
B&B + 18 HOLES + EVENING MEAL: £75 Midweek — £85 Weekends
OTHER SPECIAL GOLF PACKAGES: Groups over 20 – 10% discount.

20 ensuite bedrooms with telephone and multichannel television. Health centre and conference rooms available.

Christy O'Connor Jnr designed 18 hole par 72 golf course with 3 academy holes and putting green. Caddy car, Buggy and Club hire. PGA professional tuition available.

Full bar menu available from 12.30pm to 9pm and Restaurant open for à la carte meals from 6pm.

NUREMORE HOTEL

Carrickmacross, Co. Monaghan, Ireland. Tel: 00 358 42 61438 Fax: 00 353 42 61853

18 HOLES	**PAR** 71	**5870 YARDS**

TYPE OF GOLF COURSE: Parkland
HOTEL RATING: AA Bord Failte
GOLF PROFESSIONAL: Maurice Cassidy
TEL: 00 358 42 61438
B&B + 18 HOLES: £140 + £25

Country house hotel comprising 72 bedrooms and many leisure and conference facilities including 18 hole golf course, 18m swimming pool, whirlpool, steam room and sauna, squash court, snooker, conference facilities for 2-500 people.

POWERSCOURT GOLF CLUB

Powerscourt Golf Club, Enniskerry, Co. Wicklow. Tel: 00 353 2046033 Fax: 00 353 2761303

studio apartments have been imaginatively
onverted from outbuildings near the main
Powerscourt House. Each apartment is furnished in
keeping with the character of the building, and has
ully equipped kitchen, satellite TV and heating, all
have ensuite bathrooms. The Championship Golf
Course and Clubhouse are located within strolling
distance. Free access into the gardens, waterfall and
exhibition.

18 HOLES	PAR 72	6100 YARDS

TYPE OF GOLF COURSE: Parkland

GOLF PROFESSIONAL: Paul Thompson
TEL: 00 3531 2046033

B&B + 18 HOLES: From £75.00 p.p.s.

OTHER SPECIAL GOLF PACKAGES:
3 night weekend + Golf (36) for
2 people £150.00

ST. HELENS BAY GOLF & COUNTRY CLUB

St. Helens Bay, Rosslare Harbour, Co. Wexford. Tel: 053 33669/33234 Fax: 053 33803

Irish cottages overlooking beach beside the golf course.
Designed by Philip Walton and containing all the usual
facilities including bar, dining room and tennis courts
etc. Specialists in society golf groups.

18 HOLES	PAR 72	6800 YARDS

TYPE OF GOLF COURSE: Links & Parkland

RATING: 3 Star

B&B + 18 HOLES: £40.00/£45.00

OTHER SPECIAL GOLF PACKAGES:
Available on request

WATERFORD CASTLE

The Island, Ballinakill, Waterford, Ireland
Tel: 00353 51 871633 Fax: 00353 51 871634

HOLES: 18	YARDS: 6209m	PAR: 72

Rathsallagh House & Golf Club

*C*onverted from Queen Anne stables in 1978, Rathsallagh is a large comfortable house situated in 530 acres of peaceful parkland with a walled garden and its own 18 hole championship golf course. Situated in West Co. Wicklow, one hour South of Dublin off the main Dublin Carlow road, Rathsallagh is central to some of the most beautiful countryside in eastern Ireland. Rathsallagh House has 17 bedrooms all en-suite bathrooms, restaurant, bar conference centre, 18 hole championship golf course, heated indoor swimming pool, sauna, billiard room, tennis, croquet, award winning walled garden.

Peter McEvoy and Christy O'Connor Jnr have created one of the best conditioned courses you will play anywhere. Built to USGA specifications, Rathsallagh is one of the more demanding parkland courses you are likely to play. Measuring close to 7,000 yards, Rathsallagh is not a course the high handicapper should play from the back tees. Anyone brave enough to play the course at its full length had better be a good player, a very good player.

The food is Country House cooking at its best and is organically produced by local growers and in Rathsallagh's gardens. Rathsallagh's restaurant has been recommended by international good food and hotel guides. Game in season and fresh fish from Ireland's coast line are specialities. Breakfast in Rathsallagh is an experience and has won the national Breakfast Award three times.

LOCAL ATTRACTIONS

One of the great things about Rathsallagh is that it is so close to Dublin. At 32 miles from the city centre, it's an easy hours drive, even in the worst traffic. Rathsallagh is convenient to The K Club, Druids Glen, Mount Juliet and Carlow for golf and also to the Curragh, Punchestown and Naas, for racing enthusiasts.

Horse riding, clay pigeon shooting, archery and hunting are available by prior arrangement.

GOLF INFORMATION

18 hole, 6916 yard parkland course

Par 72

Practice facilities: Outdoor driving range.

Instructions: Groups and individuals catered for.

Hire: Clubs and buggies

CARD OF THE COURSE				
1	571	Par 5	10 465 Par 4
2	454	Par 4	11 519 Par 5
3	400	Par 4	12 390 Par 4
4	173	Par 3	13 153 Par 3
5	396	Par 4	14 351 Par 4
6	502	Par 5	15 382 Par 4
7	176	Par 3	16 536 Par 5
8	382	Par 4	17 169 Par 3
9	447	Par 4	18 450 Par 4
Out 3501 Par 36			In 3415 Par 36

HOTEL INFORMATION

Rathsallagh House & Golf Club
Dunlavin, West Wicklow
Tel: 00 353 (0)45-403112
Fax: 00 353 (0)45-403343
Rating: 4 Star Guesthouse.
Rooms: 17.
Restaurants: Country house cooking, game fish and beef specialities.
Hair and Beauty: By arrangement
Fitness Facilities: Swimming pool, sauna, billard table, tennis & croquet, claypigeon shooting by arrangement.
Other Sporting Facilities: By prior arrangement: Clay pigeon shooting, archery, fishing, deer stalking, fox hunting.
Other Leisure Activities: To be scheduled at a later date.

TARIFF

B&B from IR£55 to IR£95 per person sharing.

Special Golf Packages:
B&B including 18 holes from IR£75 to IR£120 per person sharing

Other Special Golf Packages:
2 Nights, dinner B&B + 2 rounds golf from IR£249 to IR£289 per person sharing.

DIRECTIONS

From Dublin, take the N7 South to Naas via M50 from airport) Take the M7 Naas bypass South. Exit M7 for M9 Southbound. (The Kilcullen bypass) head South, signs direct to Carlow. After approx. 6 miles pass the Priory Inn on left. 2 miles on turn left at signpost for Rathsallagh. Rathsallagh sign posted from this junction.

Slieve Russell Hotel Golf & Country Club

Set in 300 acres, including 50 acres of lakes, the Slieve Russell Hotel, Golf & Country Club offers unique experience in relaxation and leisure to our guests.

The one hundred and fifty guest rooms are designed to incorporate every comfort. Impeccably furnished, each of our bedrooms has a spacious ensuite bathroom, the majority of which are fitted with an airbath for your extra enjoyment. Choose from our range of specially designed executive and bridal suites, studios and family rooms.

We pride ourselves on the superb cuisine and the relaxed yet sophisticated atmosphere of the Conall Cearnach Restaurant, with its many interesting and varied courses. The Kells Bar has been specially designed to incorporate some of the magnificent illustrations of the internationally famous Book of Kells – a reproduction of which is on display at the entrance.

Our five star range of leisure and sporting facilities are second to none. The cleverly designed swimming pool incorporates a therapeutic whirlpool and massage seats, while providing a 20m length for the serious swimmer. Relax in the jacuzzi, steamroom or saunas, or try and energetic workout in the fitness suite. A snooker room, games room, two squash courts and four all-weather tennis courts complement this extensive range of facilities.

LOCAL ATTRACTIONS

Cavan's long established reputation as one of Europe's premier fishing locations is a great attraction, while a canal cruise on the Shannon-Erne Waterway cannot be missed. Killykeen Forest Park with its forest clad islands, interwoven with lakes, is a natural reserve of staggering beauty.

On your list of places to see in County Fermanagh should be the magnificent Marble Arch Caves, Enniskillen Castle which houses the county museum, and the stately Florence Court mansion house.

Alternatively, you can simply enjoy the rugged and beautiful scenery in this unspoilt part of Ireland.

GOLF INFORMATION

18 hole, 7053 yard parkland course

Par 72

Golf Professional: Liam McCool
Tel: 049 26444

Practice facilities: Covered driving range.

Instructions: Groups and individuals catered for. Lessons and clinics may be booked on request.

Hire: Clubs and buggies.

Par 3 course also available

CARD OF THE COURSE					
1	428	Par 4	10	411	Par 4
2	434	Par 4	11	193	Par 3
3	398	Par 4	12	442	Par 4
4	167	Par 3	13	529	Par 5
5	436	Par 4	14	374	Par 4
6	512	Par 5	15	453	Par 4
7	220	Par 3	16	176	Par 3
8	389	Par 4	17	399	Par 4
9	552	Par 5	18	540	Par 5
Out	3536	Par 36	In	3517	Par 36

HOTEL INFORMATION

Slieve Russell Hotel,
Golf & Country Club
Ballyconnell, Co. Cavan
Tel: 049 26444
Fax: 049 26046
Rating: 4 Star Hotel.
Rooms: 151.
Restaurants: Conall Cearnach Restaurant – sophisticated atmosphere/Brackley Restaurant – less formal.
Childcare Facilities: Younger guests are well taken care of in the creche and the ever popular 'Kiddies Klub' which is run during holiday times.
Hair and Beauty: Hair & Beauty Salon in Hotel.
Fitness Facilities: Five star range of leisure and sporting facilities with 20m swimming pool, jacuzzi, steamroom, sauna and fitness suite.
Other Sporting Facilities: Snooker room, games room, 2 squash courts and 4 all weather tennis courts.

TARIFF

Weekend
from £160.00 per person sharing – **2 B&B** and 1 Evening meal.

Special Golf Packages:
B&B including 18 holes available on request.

Other Special Golf Packages:
Available on request.

DIRECTIONS

From Dublin, follow the N3 through Navan and Cavan town to Belturbet and then follow the signs to Ballyconnell village. From Belfast, follow the M1 leading to the A4, through Five Mile Town, Lisnaskea, Derrylin and Ballconnell. The hotel is situated 1 mile past Ballyconnell.

Index

Index

The complete
finest courses
and

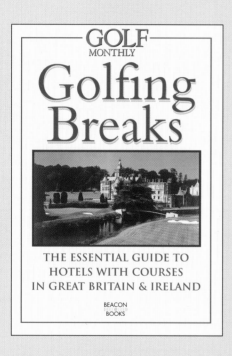

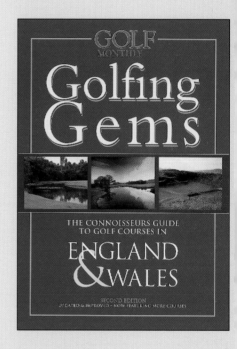

guides to the
of Great Britain
Ireland

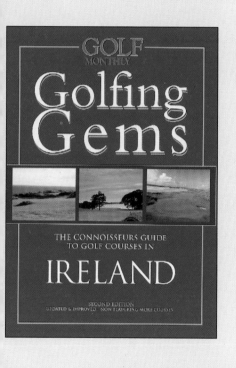

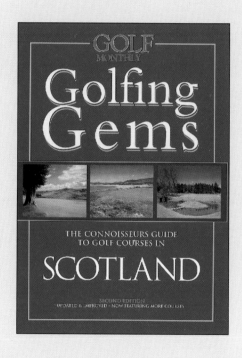

On Sale at all
good Bookshops